Sculpting the Art in Music
Observations of a Flutist

*To Bob,
Fellow curator
Ann Stockpittenller*

SCULPTING THE ART IN MUSIC

ANNE STACKPOLE-CUELLAR

LUMINARE PRESS
WWW.LUMINAREPRESS.COM

Sculpting the Art in Music
Observations of a Flutist
Copyright © 2020 Anne Stackpole-Cuellar

All rights reserved. This book or any portion thereof may not be reproduced or used in any manner whatsoever without the express written permission of the publisher, except for the use of brief quotations in a book review.

Printed in the United States of America

www.KeenEarArts.com

Cover design and interior layout by Claire Flint Last
Cover imagery by Anne Stackpole-Cuellar
Copy editing by Lori Stephens

Luminare Press
442 Charnelton St.
Eugene, OR 97401

www.LuminarePress.com

LCCN: 2019905210
ISBN: 978-1-64388-040-2

To Ralph,

MY ECLECTIC LISTENER

Contents

Introduction 1

   1. Why Musicians Work to Play 3

Flute Practice

   2. Body and Sound 13
   3. Breathe to Sing 34
   4. Brilliant Practice 55
   5. Avoiding Practice Pitfalls 72
   6. Aware Care 85

Musicianship

   7. Approach and Perspective 93
   8. Experimentation and Discovery 119
   9. Character and Emotion 132
  10. Creativity—Nakedness 148
  11. Performance Delight 162
  12. Performance Anxiety 183
  13. Plays Well with Others 207
  14. Speaking Clearly in Music 217

Art Outlook

  15. Don't Let Them Tell You 240
  16. Capable and Legitimate 265
  17. One Half of Humanity 282
  18. Art, Life, and the Dark Side 308
  19. Looking Back, Looking Forward 321

Epilogue	338
Acknowledgments	343
Notes	346
Selected Bibliography	369
About the Author	377

INTRODUCTION

As a performer or listener, the shape of a note as it is played, the shape of a musical phrase, can also shape our life. Music informs our life—our life informs our music. The journey is evolving and infinite. By revisiting our efforts to perceive and create, we build a larger process that allows us to become a musician, an artist in any art, and indeed to become a person. By nature, each individual approaches his or her art and life in a unique way. Individuality is the essential primary source in providing the diversity that is the underpinning in art, learning, and life.

This book grew from my collection of personal notes made over decades—notes about tackling problems, making discoveries, and finding new experiences and perspectives. Detailed as well as broader observations are presented in an informal style, the intention being to touch on topics that others may also be contemplating and to offer inspiration for further personal discoveries. In a nonacademic short-essay style, divided into titled sections, random topics are discussed—sometimes related to each other, sometimes overlapping, sometimes newly contrasting—to maintain a liveliness. They are not answers but explorations.

The arts inform each other. Although we tend to think of them as separate, their glories, their problems, their processes, are related. Highlighting interrelatedness to other arts, the specifics of flute practice are touched upon and include issues of artistry in music. The book speaks of a variety of social and cultural issues with the realization that they all pour into our personal experience of life where they influence our art, our music.

The words used here to describe music are often poetic—the meaning to be gleaned by association. A musical work may be referred to as a painting of a tree or the design of a cathedral. This way of thinking regards relationships of diverse arts broadly and specifically to inform one's own art of music. The book points to how we can learn from each other through the arts. It is valuable to consider the art of music through the lens of art in general and to consider art through the lens of life.

> *The goal is less to be a flutist*
> *Than to be a musician,*
> *Less to be a musician*
> *Than to be an artist,*
> *Less to be an artist*
> *Than to discover art,*
> *Less to discover art*
> *Than to discover life.*
> *One leads to the other*
> *And returns again.*

In practice, performance and artistic satisfaction the ideas in this book aim to become catalysts for further discoveries. May they spark more love for music, for flute, for the arts, for life. And may they bring more happiness.

1

Why Musicians Work to Play

"Musicians are the happiest people, don't you think so?"

It was the first thing he said as he slowly opened the front door a crack to delay letting me in. In surprise, I tipped back on my heels, searching for an honest answer, reviewing my life and music experiences as they swirled into place before me like some hastily assembled collage.

"Don't you think so?" he ardently asked again through the doorway as his beatific face gleamed above the artistically patterned Indian clothing he wore. I saw that he was eager for a reply before regular greetings could be exchanged. All the ups and downs of my past became like an untamed but ultimately supportive architecture that encouraged me to add it all up to...*hmmm...okay...happiness!*

"Yes," I replied. After all, I was anticipating the joy of a lesson with such a fine musician.

Annada Prasanna Pattanaik, who goes by the name Butto, is an internationally known bansuri flute player and composer from India. He was in Colorado's Boulder-Denver area to perform a series of concerts and teaching engagements. Even though my music background is mainly in the Western "classical" tradition, I was lucky to arrange a couple of lessons with him, knowing he would offer valuable insights about breathing technique and musical approach. An added joy was to play in call-and-response with him, trying to imitate his beautiful qualities of sound.[1]

In that moment, his greeting in the form of a question was a revelation. Although there can be plenty of trials along a person's path in music, ultimately I agree with Butto. Musicians are the happiest people.

The pursuit of music offers miraculous and fulfilling experiences and endeavors. The priceless and far-reaching treasures include:

- The privilege to work with sound
- To stretch and extend our capabilities
- To search for what has meaning
- To touch others and share that touch
- To travel in the imagination
- To discover new patterns of thought
- To appreciate and commune with composers
- To artistically collaborate with other musicians
- To have a sense of human history
- To feel and express a connection to the land

We can be overflowing with these riches! Happiness is ours.

Didn't Know I Had It in Me

IN WORKING WITH MUSIC, GRATIFYING EXPERIENCES come forth along the way. In seeking the satisfaction of playing a musical passage, we make many subtle choices in approach and expression while engaged in experimentation and a process of *trying and trying again*. While playing, something happens—the music jumps further into an inspired clarity. The nuances we aimed for pull together into a more complete picture. It is a thrilling experience, because another part of the universe within us is revealed, and we may think, *Wow, I didn't know I had it in me!* Keep that knowledge and that experience alive. There is a universe within us and around us. We use only a fraction of our brains, our imaginations, our spirits, our entire beings.

Why Work So Hard to Play Music?

IN CONTRAST TO THE CONTEMPORARY CULTURAL drive toward acceleration and immediate results, a musician will spend years honing creativity and capabilities in a progression that might seem painstaking and gradual.

Despite roadblocks and discouragements large and small, the excitement and joy of knowing that we are capable and full of potential helps us to build our art. The music evolves from what we hold in our heart, hands, body, and breath and from our values of truth and beauty. Accepting the challenges, feeling the progress, and finding joy, are some of the motivations to keep playing. The following observations provide a glimpse of subjects explored throughout the book.

Play Around in Sound

SOUND! WE DIDN'T INVENT IT. IT COMES FROM earth, sunlight, water, air, nourishment, fingers, lungs, waves, wave physics, orbits, vocal chords, gravitational fields, black holes, imploding stars, and much more. We live in a universe of color and light, just as we live in a universe of sound. How lucky we are to be able to study and gain insight from these parts of Nature. What a miracle that we are able to interact with sound, to actually *play* with sound.

Mystical Experience

MUSIC IS A WEALTH BEYOND MATERIAL MEASURE. Standing on a particular spot, in a particular moment, on a particular day, we embody an infinity of possibilities to create and generate awe-inspiring art.

Actively playing music is a mystical experience. Whether communing with a composer or improvising ideas occurring out of the blue, we are on an ethereal ride. Not knowing exactly where it will take us, we discover possibilities beyond what we were looking for. We play music to discover miracles in the music and miracles in ourselves.

Music is the divine way to tell beautiful, poetic things to the heart.[2]

—PABLO CASALS

Transform Your Life

PLAYING MUSIC DEVELOPS OUR CAPACITY TO persevere in something that changes us. Each day, each practice session, we make a transformation to a truer, more honest and clearer manifestation in sound and in being.

An opportunity opens to explore the deep underpinnings of humanity: *emotions*. Music gives us the flexibility to feel tenderness, assertiveness, gaiety, grief, and every facet of expression. Consciously and subconsciously, the practice of music transforms our attitudes, perspective, and approach to life. To become acquainted with these qualities in our lives deepens our ability to express them in music.

Hold a Treasure

Above the fray of our manic modern era, above the carelessness that seems to steam roll over the arts and dismiss them as nonessential, we keep music alive. The musician, the performing artist with beating heart, opens a treasure chest, releasing a cascade of refracted rainbow beams in experiences that are mystical and transforming.

The practice of music (and all the arts) is an avenue to insight, hard work, seeking, and appreciation. It can never be finished. We never really "arrive." Nor would we want to. Being truly present in it all is the best, actually the *best*—as in the highest—we can do.

A Meditation

Even though we may recognize that our lives are not rosy and there are tough problems outside of our control, the practice of music is a practice like meditation is a practice. The practice of music fosters patience and recognition that we human beings are ourselves works in progress.

Making music lights up aspects of our being and reveals glimpses of understanding, communication, and collaboration. Music offers a lifetime of building a more patient and long-range viewpoint.

Health: Body and Spirit

Playing music benefits health in body and mind. Chief elements of playing music are fine muscle development, sustained concentration, coordination, and stamina.

The breathing required for flute and all wind instruments is health giving. At the same time that the breath brings the fuel that oxygenates the body and clears the mind, it supplies the energy for the music, generating the singing quality of sound.

Building a More Awake Awareness

A musician's consciousness of sound grows, just as a person in the visual arts becomes more aware of color, light, shadow, form, design, luminescence, atmosphere, and perspective. Musicians benefit by observing qualities in the symphony of natural and man-made sounds in the environment: roaring trucks, washing machines, speech patterns, wind in trees, water flowing in a brook, subtleties of bird song, cricket rhythms, and sounds in snow. Being awake to the daily sounds of life brings a consciousness that can inform a musician's artistic approach.

Composer and music theorist John Cage (1912–1992) lived among the harsh sounds of New York City and loved them all. He heard them musically: traffic, sirens, jack-hammers, garbage trucks backing up—he accepted and included them all in his musical ear.[3]

Accompanied by the hums, buzzes, and mechanical sounds of a lonely soda pop vending machine in a college hallway, a couple of my fellow music students once improvised an amazing late-night saxophone concert.

Communication

When we are captivated by a music performance, whether a simple melody or a complex multilayered work, we may find the experience intensely moving. While playing or listening, an unexpected gift sweeps us up and pulls us into a moment that is timeless and sheds light on our existence. Perceptions open to a clarified beauty, and listener and player participate to experience it. This is a communication we all treasure.

Art is an expansion of perception, a freedom to roam in new ideas and depths of insight, to explore what lies under and beyond the surface of our lives. Music and all the arts hold the potential to "speak" to artists and listeners in a profound way.

What You Offer

SOME PEOPLE ACKNOWLEDGE THAT THEY WOULD love to play music but question whether they could add anything to humanity's achievements. They are shortchanging themselves; they may need to stop doubting their potential and consider a broader perspective.

Individuals are always unique, always interesting, always evolving in their life and music. It may sound cliché, but just as no individual snowflakes or fingerprints are alike, in playing music, our individuality will naturally bring something new and interesting. Even in listening to a child who is beginning to play, one can hear the unique sound of his or her development unfolding. Discoveries evolve from experience. We learn and grow by building on our life experiences just as we build on our musical experiences.

Music is your experience, your thoughts, your wisdom.
If you don't live it, it won't come out of your horn.[4]
—CHARLIE PARKER

Creativity and Creative Freedom

WE ARE ALL CREATIVE. WHAT WE FIND WITHIN ourselves allows us to invent our next action at any moment whether it is turning to look into someone's eyes, washing the dishes, or playing a cadenza. By staying true to our creativity, we know that we have what we need within us.

To keep our art alive, we must be ourselves. To be oneself is a tall order. Being present and creatively engaged enhances our experience even if at times the road is difficult. While it is true that negative experiences can entangle us in the hurt and confusion that are inevitable in life, in spite of these problems, we can search for our being, our human essence, in art.

We escape being stuck in a box by realizing our individuality. By offering the rare gift of being ourselves, we help others feel free to be themselves. People can learn from and value how we make them feel, both in our music and by our being.

Fame and Fortune

FAME AND FORTUNE MAY BE A PART OF THE MOTIVAtion for a musician to work to play music, but there are always decisions to make. We can take a good look at the real circumstances, the cultural environment, the competition, the commercialism, and the music industry, and we can choose our path through or around them. No choices are right or wrong.

It is important to remember what got us excited about music in the first place and keep blowing on that spark. Music is a friend. It talks to us as we play, and no matter what fame or fortune we achieve, music continues to have a lot to say to us on down the road.

Self-Discipline—Working Discipline

SELF-DISCIPLINE HELPS US AIM OUR ARROW WITH more precision. The freedom to say what we want to say musically is within our reach because of all we have taught ourselves and the abilities we have gained over time. Self-discipline is a noble character in our lives, a nurturing and supportive muse.

We need a new vision of self-discipline, one that rejects

the old model of a drill sergeant in our face ordering, "You should suffer, or you are not really working!" Our discipline is a slow process where we can look back an hour, a day, a week, a month, or a year and realize that we have been building our capacities for focus, concentration, and understanding. In our work we may not often recognize it, but we have been blossoming. Discipline as a whip will not bring a flower to blossom; nurturing will.

You can experiment and build on discoveries, using supportive and benevolent approaches. These foster the greatest insight and understanding toward achieving your aimed-for results. Aim your discipline, your arrow, with delight. You are the archer—perhaps a Zen archer or a Cupid. You might be both.

Cheer Up the World

As a young music student at San Francisco State College (now University), I splurged on taking a cab to play in an evening concert at the school. The cab driver asked, "What are you studying?" I told him I was majoring in music. He said, "Oh, you're going to cheer up the world." I thought that he was humoring me, but when we exchanged glances in the rearview mirror, I knew he was sincere. It jolted me awake. That was an encouragement I've never forgotten. Music does cheer up the world.

Not all music expresses cheerfulness. Music doesn't have to be cheerful to cheer our world. It is our perspective that counts.

Years later, when I came home from my day job, dragging and feeling stressed, I would listen to the outrageous, somewhat avant-garde music of Marc Ribot. Jagged and satiric, one would think this music would be stressing, but it felt like an acknowledgment, saying, *Yes, things are crazy.* It was actually relaxing.[5]

Hearing or playing something solemn can cheer and unburden the heart. Even if the music is dark or sad, there is relief in hearing an expression of truth. Darker music can feel relevant to our experience and bring a feeling of being acknowledged. It is said that the church music of Bach is often about death. Being beyond words, this music gives us perspective. Finding perspective and deeper understanding can give a lift to our lives.

To feel acknowledged, to have rapport, connection, perspective, and understanding—these are how we lift each other. These are the ways we recognize each other. To recognize ourselves and one another is to make life more fulfilling and more satisfying. Music can do this.

2

Body and Sound

"Be like a jackal."

Chogyam Trungpa Rinpoche (1939–1987), Tibetan Buddhist master and founder of Naropa Institute in Boulder, Colorado (now Naropa University), gave the welcoming speech to new students at the contemplative and inclusive liberal arts school. He told us to stay alert "like a jackal" and be responsible in scrutinizing teachings and influences. We should not blindly jump in but stay aware and thoroughly consider any teaching to determine if it fits us and our needs.[1]

The same vigilance is important in learning music from teachers. A music teacher gives suggestions, but the students must teach themselves. Genuinely try the suggestions that come from lessons, classes, master classes, and books, including those in this book, yet preserve the attitude that a method or approach has to fit, has to ring true.

Whether a technique or idea seems right may be evident immediately or only after working with it for a length of time. If you admire someone's approach and are convinced of a certain mode of practice, that's great. If years later you change your mind, you have not wasted your time. Stepping from one approach to another is your natural way of moving. Maintaining an attitude of staying as aware as you can will lead to improvements even if you "change lanes" along the way.

Like many flutists, I was taught that the embouchure must be formed with the corners of the lips drawn back as if in a smile or a grimace. Years later, I changed my embouchure to a more forward and relaxed approach, which allowed more flexibility and a variety of tone qualities without adding tension in the face.

In his master classes, cellist Pablo Casals encouraged students to play in the most relaxed and natural position possible. Early in his career, he revolutionized cello playing. When he began to play as a child, cellists were taught to keep the right elbow tightly down at the side. Students were even required to hold a book beneath the upper-right arm, squeezing it against the side of the rib cage. Casals rejected this method, advising cellists to play with a more free and flexible bowing arm and hand. This liberating approach bypassed a buildup of unnecessary tension and saved many cellists from repetitive strain injuries.[2]

Tune In to Your Body

MUSIC IS OF THE BODY, BY THE BODY, AND THROUGH the body. Music seems ethereal, yet every musical sound we produce is manifested through our bodies. The body in relation to music is a vast and inexhaustible subject. A natural and healthy approach allows ease and clearmindedness.

Posture is central to developing our capacity to reach what we want in tone qualities and to achieve a graceful dexterity. In every practice session, in addition to focusing on the many aspects of the music, we can be rehearsing our ideal natural posture. Feeling awake and energetic without unnecessary tension, we sound better, and our session becomes more fun. As we achieve what we want in sound, our ideal posture becomes a habit that will be the mainstay of our ability to play with skill and expression.

"Stand up straight!" Many of us have heard this admonishment. We tend to groan and feel reluctant. The effort to straighten our posture may seem like moving out of a comfortable position into something less comfortable, but good posture means fewer aches and pains from repetitive misuse. An aware-yet-relaxed posture helps us to breathe, stay agile, and avoid injury from tension. Being relaxed does not mean slouching but maintaining a natural physical and mental alertness. Naturalness of being produces naturalness of sound.

Balanced in Gravity

ALL INSTRUMENTALISTS HAVE POSTURE CHALlenges in having to hold their instruments or reach out to them (piano, harp, percussion). Flutists have a particularly difficult situation, because the weight is held to the right side of the center of the body. To some extent there is no getting around the unnatural awkwardness of holding something to your right hour after hour, but there are many helpful ways to approach the problem and forget that it is a problem.

Many flutists incline to the right as they play, leaning as if tired of holding up the flute. Maybe they are tired, but by continuing to maintain that angle, they become even more so. Many more muscles have to work unnecessarily, muscles not designed to hold the body up: neck, shoulders, and the left side of the torso. When the body is balanced and aligned in gravity, muscles can relax and move more freely.

If the head is held unnecessarily forward, eventually a significant amount of tension develops, causing pain in the neck and shoulders, and around the ears. Let the head be up and balanced on the neck vertebrae to avoid tension. Think of aligning or "stacking" the vertebrae of the neck.

Having the neck stacked informs the vertebrae in the whole backbone to be aligned and balanced. In finding your balance in gravity, develop awareness of the front and back of your body. Sway gently forward and back as you slowly narrow the sways to find the center, and stop where there is no strain in standing. It reminds me of the way people often move their heads around on a pillow until they find the perfect position to relax and fall asleep. You are finding your most relaxed (but not sleepy) stance in space.

With head up and aligned, upper breathing passageways are automatically more open, and the way is clear for air to the lungs and oxygen to the brain. The brain becomes more refreshed as we practice. With a clear mind, concentration improves. We make fewer mistakes and have more energy in our overview of the music. Our general awareness may expand to the space around us, the room, the hall, and the audience.

Stand with even weight on your feet. If you notice too much strain on the front pads by the toes, give some of that weight to your heels. Ideally the weight should be balanced in the whole foot. Your feet are your base of stability. Generally the most stability comes from a stance with feet approximately shoulder-width apart and a bit turned out. Allow the ankles, calves, and thighs to relax. Allow the knees to be slightly bent (not locked) and hips to be a bit forward. The pelvis and lower belly are engaged and united with the chest. This posture is a stance of stability, yet it includes freedom to move and not be locked in place.

The rib cage can also be relaxed in gravity. The chest needs to be allowed to move outward with the intake of air, not held out in a locked position but moving freely. I think of the image of a songbird singing with a puffed-out chest. I occasionally draw on the printed music a hieroglyphic design to remind myself to be like a songbird.

Alexander Technique and the "Carrot"

ALEXANDER TECHNIQUE, CREATED BY FREDERICK Matthias Alexander (1869–1955), teaches methods to improve posture and movement. They alleviate unnecessary, habitual muscle tension as we move and do ordinary tasks. Moving from standing to sitting and back to standing can be done with more ease and simplicity of motion than most of us use. We tax our bodies, producing extra tension and fatigue as we perform simple and complex tasks.

Accomplished pianist, piano teacher, and friend Carol Toensing includes Alexander Technique lessons for her piano students, instilling habits of ideal posture and natural use of the hands and arms. Her appreciative students play piano throughout their lives with no repetitive-syndrome problems.[3]

Flutists have their own set of challenges in finding their most natural posture. I am indebted to Carol for using her expertise in Alexander Technique to coach me to improve my posture with flute. The gentle energy of her touch guided me to lengthen the back and keep the shoulders down, chest open, and head balanced at top of spine. She coached me to find the best position for my arms and the angle of the flute in perpendicular relation to my body as well as a more open and stable stance for the feet and legs. After she "placed" me in this improved posture, I played a few notes and immediately noticed added depth and richness of sound.

To find someone who can coach you into a more natural good posture as Carol Toensing did for me is of great benefit.

There are helpful books about Alexander Technique for musicians, but to experience the verbal and physical instruction of an AT practitioner who works with musicians is of great value. Even if over time some aspects of your posture need adjusting, your body will remember the basic principles as a foundation to finding further beneficial adjustments.

An additional way to become aware of posture is to look in a mirror while playing or make a video recording. We can look for where our posture shows tension or where we are using unnecessary energy. Most importantly, we can listen and observe improved tone qualities as we adjust our posture. Those tone qualities are the "carrot" hanging in front of our nose. Our gorgeous sounds encourage us to play using better posture. The body begins to habitually gravitate to the best postural adjustments to achieve the most beautiful tone qualities.

Standing and Sitting

STANDING ALLOWS THE MOST FREEDOM IN PLAYING flute. For practicing, it is ideal to position the music stand high enough to see the music without bending forward. However, for a performance, it is necessary to lower the stand to avoid being hidden behind it or having the stand muffle our sound. The lowered stand also allows ease of visual contact with other musicians and the audience.

With the stand lowered, we must avoid bending forward or scrunching down and thereby compromising our best breathing and best projection in the room. If we look down at the music with just the eyes, we can maintain our more ideal posture. A good familiarity with the passages will help, as we will not need to look at the printed music as much, peeking occasionally for points of reference.

Sitting is even more challenging, because we tend to collapse the rib cage and crumple forward. However, sitting is necessary for some ensemble playing and orchestral playing. Any slouching while sitting will limit airways, lung capacity, and movement of the diaphragm. It also compromises our stamina, limiting the ability to get enough breath intake to keep long musical phrases alive. Playing with inadequate amounts of air interferes with getting enough oxygen to the brain, increasing the danger of mistakes and trip-ups due to diminished concentration. To avoid this, keep in mind that the same set of ideal standing habits applies to sitting posture. Make sure that the back is kept lengthened, the shoulders down, the chest open, and the head balanced on the vertebrae.

We must make sure we are not trapped by our position relative to other musicians and music stands. Flutists are able to twist and rotate the upper body to accommodate being crowded. Twisting and accommodating are not wise. We don't want to be contorted, looking out of the side of our eyes, rotated at the hip with the chest and flute aiming sideways. With these contortions, the shoulders, arms, torso, and neck must endure more tension. Adding more tension is the opposite of what we want.

Sound can be directed better when the whole body is aligned to the front, playing out to the listening audience. That means the arms are angled back a little in relation to the chest. Holding the flute up so that it is more or less parallel to the floor keeps the head centered and helps maintain a favorable angle of lips to embouchure. Holding the flute up this way also maintains an energetic attitude. *Energy* is of paramount importance even when playing music that is peaceful, quiet, and slow. In fact, quiet, slow music often requires more energy than lively pieces.

Shoulders, Arms, Hands, and Fingers

WHETHER YOU HAVE PLAYED FOR MANY YEARS OR relatively few, it is important to reassess your physical approach. Habitual ways of holding the flute may give a musician subtle disadvantages or, when improved, release a wonderful new ease of playing.

The shoulders need to be down, not hiked up in order to hold the flute. The upper arms can be relaxed as if hanging from a frame that includes an open chest. The counterweight of the shoulder and upper arm make holding the flute easy (or relatively easy). Take care that the left shoulder is naturally aligned with the body and not jutting forward. The right shoulder should not be raised in the effort to hold up the flute. Use gravity to help you relax.

The flow of energy through the wrists, hands, and fingers should be a straight extension of unbroken energy without roadblocks. Wrists need not be bent. However, the left hand will be naturally rotated toward the body and slightly bent to cradle the flute at the base of the index finger. The right hand is rotated away from the body. The wrist need not be bent.

For the fingers, the main thing to remember is that the fingers should drape in a relaxed way over the keys they commonly play. The following exercise was of great benefit to my students.

To find the most natural position for the right hand, stand with your arm and hand hanging at your side with the fingers completely relaxed. Do this while holding your flute with only your left hand as if ready to play. Look at your relaxed right hand at your side, and observe that your fingers are curved gently and naturally. Bring your relaxed hand, with the natural curvature of the fingers, just as they are, up to the flute, and slide it into position. You may find that the supporting thumb will naturally position itself so that the flute rests not centered on its padded part but more or less on the side of the thumb nearer the edge closer to the nail. This will vary for individual hands. If you attempt to turn the thumb so that the flute rests on the center of the pad, the other fingers must reach sideways for their keys, setting up unnecessary tension. No reach is needed when the thumb maintains its relaxed position and the fingers remain in their natural curvature and can hover over the keys they play.

The thumb of the right hand will be directly below and opposite the index finger or somewhere between the index and middle finger. *Voila!* The fingers are naturally draped over the keys with perhaps subtle adjustments necessary to widen the distance between fingers, based on the individuality of the hands and length of the fingers.

For the left hand, the ideal placement can be found in the same way. Hold the flute with only your right hand as if ready to play. Rest your left arm and hand by your side to see how the fingers naturally curve when they are relaxed. Bring your relaxed hand up to the flute, and slide it into position so that the fingers hover over the keys they play. Subtle adjustments must be made to slightly rotate the hand and allow the side of the base of the index finger, the "little shelf" of the first knuckle, to be part of the support holding the flute.

Maintaining relaxed hands and letting the fingers hover close above the keys gives a player a vital advantage. The fingers are perfectly ready for action without having to stretch or travel distances. Rapid passages can be played with greater ease. One can also avoid key-slapping noises (unless that is a desired effect).

Once when I was watching a televised orchestral concert, the camera zoomed in on an oboist playing a fast, lively passage. I noticed that his fingers appeared to barely move. In a light bulb moment, I realized how much of an advantage there is in keeping a minimal distance between finger and key. This offers more control in accuracy, smoothness, and touch. Fast passages can be played with more ease and evenness.

Everyone's hands are unique. Small adjustments may be necessary in finding your ideal hand position. In general, search for ways to eliminate tension. Some aching may occur due to temporary fatigue, especially in your earlier years of playing, but persistent pain may indicate you are not holding the flute in a well-balanced way. Tension that leads to pain should be addressed.

Check how you are balancing the flute. Are you assigning too much of the weight to one hand? Are you making the little finger of the right hand work too hard? Check on the points of weight and the points of direction in what I call the "wedge" effect (described below).

If you can't find the right shift or adjustment to alleviate muscle strain or tension, look for advice. You may find informative flute instructors online or local teachers who can help. It is important to address pain and tension early to avoid injury.

Balancing the Flute and the "Wedge" Effect

As discussed above, holding the weight of the flute against gravity occurs between the base of the left-hand index finger and the right-hand thumb. Further stability is gained by the "wedge" effect.

This helps to gently hold the flute in place. In positioning the flute against the lower lip, the natural slight pressure of the embouchure creates a subtle *forward force*, while the base of the left index finger pushes with a slight *back force* (in addition to supporting some of the weight of the flute). The right-hand thumb can exert a slight *forward force*. This three-point wedge effect makes playing and holding the flute feel more secure. We might visualize the wedge as follows:

- An arrow forward from below your lower lip
- An arrow back over your shoulder from the base of the left index finger
- A forward arrow from the right supporting thumb

Added stability comes from the little finger of the right hand, as it is almost continuously engaged in depressing the D# key. The advantage of the wedge effect is that it can create a confident balance that frees up the fingers. We can raise our fingers off the keys and the flute won't roll or, heaven forbid, fall.

The physical energy needed for the support points and the directional forces of the wedge effect are very gentle. It is important to make sure the pressure we use is light enough that we are not pushing too hard on the lower lip. The lower lip needs to maintain flexibility.

Flutist Murray Panitz spoke of the subtlety of the pressure needed against the lower lip and chin and the importance of keeping the lower lip flexible. He used a piece of paper pasted on the mouthpiece embouchure to help keep the flute in place.

> I use very little pressure against the chin. If one perspires, it is probable that you may start to press more, therefore, it (the piece of paper) enables me to hang the flute on the lip rather than digging in. I am never without it.[4]
> —Murray Panitz

Belly Engaged

BELLY MUSCLES HELP CREATE THE STEADY PUSH FOR an enduring stream of air, and they need to be flexible and relaxed, which may be a challenge to many individuals. If you are female, cultural hype tells you that it is ideal to have a flat belly. It's likely we have heard "keep your stomach in." Thus we try to renounce any natural curvature, attempting to disown our "faulty" belly by maintaining a constant tension to hold it in. This tension can be bad for our well-being in many ways. In ancient Japanese and Chinese culture, the lower belly, just below the belly button, is regarded as the *hara*, the center of the body. The hara is our center of gravity and our central field of energy. In females, the lower belly houses our reproductive organs. Sexuality is interwoven with creativity. The denial of the naturalness of this part of our being causes confusion. Our body is where we stand. Our center of gravity is our reference point, our generator, our hara.

If you are a man, "Stomach in! Chest out!" is the military drill. This looks like a posture of weakness to those who study Asian martial arts such as aikido, kendo, and tai chi. A lower center of gravity, based in the hara, gives a stronger, more stable stance. Standing relaxed and flexible, ready to engage one's center, is better than standing stiff like an automaton.

Balancing when crossing a stream, stepping from one rock to another, is made easier by focusing our center of gravity in the hara. Even a fall is handled better. With a lower center of gravity, a fall is absorbed by the lower body, closer to the ground. This means the arms, chest, and head are less likely to be impacted.

Appearance Pressure

Playing music requires flexibility and constant renewal of energy. It is a great asset to feel the freedom to move and to change position when needed. Maintaining good posture doesn't mean forcing ourselves to stay locked in a position. Being locked creates extra tension.

Conversely, there can be tension in feeling that we must *appear* to be moving—that we are on display and expected to move. Hollywood and YouTube music videos have given the impression that a musician should be a dancer, an entertainer while playing music. There seems to be an assumption that it is necessary to move around to create a certain "stage presence."

Stage presence can be highly individual. I believe it is not about *planning* but about *being*. As musicians, we are not obliged to try to move or to look any certain way. Here's my rant:

- Our art is music.
- Our art is not for entertainment.
- Our art is for the ears, for the soul, for listening.
- We do not have to fit an image.
- We do not have to *demonstrate* what we are saying musically.
- We are speaking from our core; our extremities need not create a separate show.

For musicians, some movements and facial expressions are natural, but if they are not natural to the performer, the listener, while appreciating the entertainment, may be distracted from hearing the music. Some people who grimace or dance while playing dissipate their energy and focus. Their music is weaker.

As listeners, if we close our eyes and ask ourselves if the music is as moving as the visual effect, the answer might be yes or no.

When performing, we need to stay with ourselves deeply and not allow our focus to be diffused. If we concentrate on the music, and we tend to play while standing relatively still, our music will naturally and confidently speak its presence and our presence. Our experience in playing, in performing, is more satisfying artistically if we can be true to ourselves.

Dancing and playing at the same time may come naturally to some, but that doesn't mean a musician is obligated to be a dancer. We can ask ourselves, *Where do I want to direct my focus*? Sure, we may be feeling the music in every pore of our being, but to feel that way, we might need to keep our feet solidly on the ground like David Oistrakh.

David Oistrakh (1908–1974) was one of the most spellbinding violinists I have ever heard. I was fortunate to hear him play in San Francisco in the early 1960s. He had a powerful presence. As he played, he physically moved in a natural way that emanated from his intense concentration on the music. Olympian melodies flew from the core of his being. With a solid stance, his body moved subtly from deep within.[5]

Once I listened to a radio broadcast of a contest among Celtic women, singing solo performances. I was thoroughly enjoying their beautiful singing, but one of them reached in and grabbed my heart. It was one of those times in listening to a musician when all thoughts about the merits of the music are forgotten, and one revels in the sheer beauty.

The radio announcer gave a little background on each singer, and I was waiting to hear about this extraordinary singer (sadly, I do not remember her name). He said that she was a great singer but shy and only performed in public with her back to the audience. Ha! So much for stage presence. Her art was amazing enough, really divine, with no need for stage presence.

Push Your Weight Around

PHYSICALLY AND METAPHORICALLY, WE CAN PUT our weight behind the music. As we generate energy, directing the phrasing and the melodic push and pull, we can do so with an inner feeling of physical weight. The weight of our physicality is behind our sound qualities. Music is ethereal, heady, but its life is also generated by physical and earthy qualities. A physicality could be present like the tones a person would use describing hiking up a mountain to see a meteor shower or seeing a whale from a kayak.

Cuban dancers appear to move very little when dancing to slower, rhythmical music like that of the Buena Vista Social Club. The slow dances derived from *son, bolero,* and *danzón* styles show little extraneous movement but a kind of glow from within. The moves are discrete and subtle, the steps minimal, but they emit a great and strong energy. The strength and beauty of this dancing embodies this feeling of "pushing weight around" possible in music and other arts.

Performance Space Is Your Space

FEEL YOUR OWN PHYSICAL PRESENCE RELATED TO the room or to the audience. Look for a way to feel anchored (in a safe harbor) where you stand. This reminds me of a story in Carlos Castaneda's *The Teachings of Don Juan: A Yaqui Way of Knowledge*. In his account, Castaneda was instructed by Yaqui shamanic sorcerer Don Juan Matus to find his place on the front porch of Don Juan's house. He couldn't understand the instruction and doubted that any place would feel particularly like his own. After moving around the bare porch nearly the whole night, trying different areas to sit, sometimes haunted by doubts, fears, and demons, he at last felt one particular spot as "safe" and protective and like "home."[6]

In practicing and performing, there are not exactly choices about where one can stand, but the feeling of claiming the space as your own can apply. It may not feel totally safe or like home, but it is *your* space for creating music.

Our space awareness helps us to work with the acoustics of the room whether it is our practice room or a performance hall. Prior to or during a performance, we can notice distances in the room as we check our sound and adjust to the acoustics. How is the sound bouncing from walls? How is it being dissipated or absorbed by the chairs or audience? In a large venue, you may need to project to the last row in the balcony. In a smaller room that may be duller acoustically, it may help to add "fresh air" to tone qualities. The space may reveal a need to direct the sound outward or keep it closer and more intimate. Based on the acoustics of our surroundings, we can focus the direction we are sending the sound. In any rehearsal or performance situation, there are many details that need our attention. Being present relative to the space can go a long way in creating the kind of performance we seek.

An opportunity to experience performance space was set up in a contemporary dance class I attended at Naropa University.[7] The exercise was to individually walk onstage, turn toward the audience—and—do nothing. Nothing was outwardly required, not one gesture. This was not a performance. We were encouraged to take the time to stand there and use the exercise to experience the space around us. In silence, each person, alone on stage, could allow herself or himself to feel and observe. We might become aware of the distances to the walls and perhaps beyond the walls, feel the space below our feet, beyond the floor and through the earth. We could sense the awareness of the people: the audience, the quality of their attention, and the atmosphere in the room. We were free to expand our awareness in as much detail as we wished—then walk offstage.

Being there without anything expected of you, without expecting anything of yourself except to observe and be aware, allows for less separation and more connection. You feel the energy of the audience and the room as part of your own energy in the moment. Your presence is not separate as a kind of intruder but part of the room and atmosphere. You are finding a friendliness. This exercise provides a rare opportunity to watch your nervousness and to observe your mind. Engaging one's curiosity to explore and find personal discoveries supersedes much of the nervousness of being in front of an audience.

In performance situations, extending our awareness to everything around us adds to the richness of our experience. We come to know the *feel* of our canvas as we get ready to paint. Playing and practicing while engaged in this kind of awareness can enrich our sound. The whole body is resonant, and the music reaches every space of the room.

Being aware of space and of our body in space brings a more satisfying whole body-mind experience that can benefit our everyday awareness. It is enriching to keep our awareness alive in all settings as we move through our day.

Free Up Your Eyes, Let Them Keep Moving

WE CAN EASILY FALL INTO THE HABIT OF LOCKING our eyes on the page, tracking the notes as they are being played in an effort to be correct. This habit can add much unnecessary effort. To see and play each note correctly is essential when one is beginning to study a piece. Soon it becomes possible to see ahead and anticipate whole phrases.

Trust what you see. Your visual memory is much better than you think. Try flashing a glance at some short series of numbers or letters. (I try this with license plates.) Take a glance and then look away. Say to yourself what you think you saw, and you will be surprised to discover, when you look again, how well your eyes registered exactly what was there. While you may have felt unsure that you read it correctly, your mind is more reliable than you may believe.

Our sound is generated from ourselves, not from reading the printed page. We often attach our attention to the written page because we are anxious to be correct. It is necessary to develop the skills to read correctly, but as reading skills develop, reading begins to demand less of our focus, and we can devote most of our energy to flying with the music. We have opportunities to be more sure of ourselves through repetition as our eyes, ears, and fingers become familiar with the patterns. The printed music becomes a light reference as we concentrate more on artistic considerations—playing how we feel it. Our eyes can relax. We can be free to look up from the page, communicate with other musicians, or close our eyes in concentration.

Actively Engaged

WHEN PLAYING MUSIC, AND IN LIFE IN GENERAL, WE MUST be relaxed and engaged at the same time. "Relaxed" is an imperfect but evolving awareness involving a calm physical approach and a cool and aware mental balance. Relaxed does not mean passive.

I have heard musicians who play as if they want only to be entertained by the music they issue. They tend to play in a more aloof manner, but the pitfall lies in playing too passively. Hearing a recording of themselves may help them observe that their music doesn't sound like they think it does, and they realize that they can't afford to be so passive. There's no sitting back to listen while playing. Yes, listen carefully but *actively*, not *passively*. To put more life into the music, it helps to realize that *I, as an individual, am doing the "speaking."* Then you can ask yourself, *What am I saying?* That helps keep the spark of life, the spark of melodiousness, the spark of creativity in playing whether scales, exercises, or compositions. More about this in chapter 10.

Fingers and Breathing

FINGERS CAN SUBTLY CHANGE PITCHES AS SMOOTHLY as the singing voice can go from pitch to pitch. When singing, vocal chords make smooth shifts while the flow of air of the exhale generates the sound. In playing flute, be conscious of your touch and how the fingers move. The transition from one note to another defines the timing and the grace and smoothness of a passage.

The quickness or slowness of a lift or depression of each finger in sync with breathflow can make infinite subtleties in expression. Where notes begin and end within their time frame, within beats (while keeping a steady pulse), most often depends on finger synchronization. To intentionally begin a note slightly before the beat can generate excitement. Initiating notes slightly late, playing broadly, can calm things down. To push the tempo or to draw out a few notes of a single run or other series of notes can create shape and purpose in the phrasing. When fingers make the transition from one note to the next as smoothly as possible, the music takes on a constant, unbroken singing quality. There are many more possibilities.

How we sing with flute is generated by our stream of air. The fingers, fueled from this same supply of air, are simultaneously shaping the music. Unifying our conception of the efforts of fingers with the stream of air avoids the pitfall of a purely mechanistic idea of our sensitive and willing fingers. The fingers are sculpting notes rather than simply "hitting" them. The flow of air supports our whole body as well as the music we issue forth. Feeling this unity of effort, we are more whole and integrated in our intention. We are giving the music body and spirit.

Directing Your Stream of Air

Subtle changes in formation of the lips and mouth can produce different tone qualities as they change many aspects of the stream of air. This stream can be visualized in various ways. Some people describe a "column of air" or a "ribbon." Advice varies about the formations of the lips and mouth in playing.

To form the mouth as if to openly pronounce *Ooo* (not *Eee*) directs the column of air more accurately and enables different tone qualities. The *Ooo* is more relaxed and allows for a more open jaw and what I call "cavernous mouth." This is the way we blow on our hands to warm them in freezing weather, saying, "Hoa, hoa." We might think of being an opera singer with a gigantic voice. These approaches allow for a tone quality that is warmer, larger, and more open. A forte will sound fuller, and notes in the low register will not sound crunched but have more body, substance, and ability to carry distances. These ideas are developed further in later chapters.

Physical Exercise

A FLUTIST BENEFITS, AS DOES ANYONE, FROM AERObic exercise: walking, running, swimming, dancing. With regular exercise, one's lung capacity can feel expanded, and breathing can seem easier. The head feels clearer and the body more coordinated.

A flute is not a heavy weight to lift or to hold, yet some arm strength and stamina are required for the long periods of time spent standing and playing. Good posture with shoulder blades down and arms "gravity relaxed" can help maintain support. Exercising and strengthening arms can further alleviate fatigue in sustaining the weight of the flute.

Exercise energizes circulation and brings strength and relaxation to the arms, shoulders, and hands. You can build strength by doing modified push-ups on the floor or against a countertop. Simply raising the arms up and down as if doing jumping jacks, with or without the jumping, can release tension in the shoulders and neck. It is fun to dance to your favorite music while holding a pair of one- or two-pound weights (or any objects of this approximate weight). These are some light and simple approaches. Any healthy and hearty exercise such as running, yoga, Pilates, rowing, basketball, or hiking can add a great deal to the art and physicality of playing flute.

3

Breathe to Sing

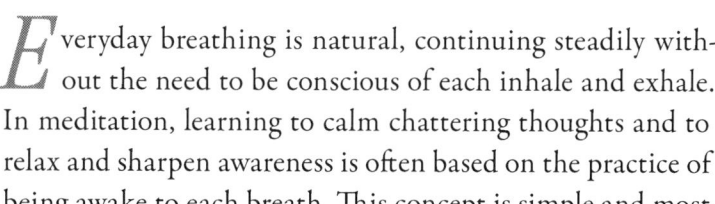

*E*veryday breathing is natural, continuing steadily without the need to be conscious of each inhale and exhale. In meditation, learning to calm chattering thoughts and to relax and sharpen awareness is often based on the practice of being awake to each breath. This concept is simple and most profound at the same time.

Breathing is life and awareness, and for the flutist, it is music. We breathe in enough air to keep ourselves alert, energetic, and tuned in to actions and thought. Our exhale through the flute is transformed into the expression of our energy in meaningful musical phrases and sentences. Playing flute requires a great deal of attention to breathing, and this attention expands and branches to have many purposes in our art.

Breathe to Paint Your Canvas

WHILE PLAYING FLUTE, WE CONSCIOUSLY MANAGE each breath. The inhale loads our "brush" with paint, and the exhale allows us to put our design on "canvas," using fine strokes, broad strokes, graceful lines, tiny dots, myriad shades, and color juxtapositions.

Flutists produce sound by blowing against an open edge. Hardly any resistance meets our stream of air, unlike other woodwind and brass instruments where one blows into a carefully crafted reed or a horn's mouthpiece. Even whistling has more resistance than blowing to produce flute tones. In playing flute, the column of air is directed against the narrow edge of the embouchure hole. The way the column of air is split sets the instrument to vibrate, creating sound waves.

To visualize this column of air directed against the edge, being split by it, and making the instrument vibrate is helpful, but realistically, this is a simplistic description of the physics of producing tone with flute. Experiments were carried out using photography and colored, visible gases directed to produce sounds with flutes and recorders. The photos showed that the physics involved in playing a wind instrument is wild and mysterious and cannot be measured as it can with strings or percussion.

> *...sound from a flute is the result of chaotic fluid dynamics, creating patterns as variable and unpredictable as swirls of cigarette smoke in air....flutes rely upon complex interactions of jets, vortexes and air pressure.... just how such wind instruments work 'is still not fully understood.'* [1]
>
> —William J. Broad

A Flutist Is Born

Teaching offers a great opportunity to learn. Learning how to assist an individual in playing music is a chance to consider many details and pick the best ones that gracefully guide a student through many steps. The first steps can seem daunting to a beginner, yet his or her abilities grow exponentially.

First-time flute players, whether young or adult, often start with a struggle to produce any sound at all. The flute doesn't speak, sometimes for a week. When it becomes possible to get some sound, there is a natural tendency to huff and puff, playing one tone per breath. At this stage, it is important to take frequent breaks, as it is easy to hyperventilate and get dizzy. Soon the player is able to direct and aim the column of air more accurately and less wastefully, channeling the wind power where needed.

No matter if we are beginners or more advanced, calm patience is our friend. In the beginning it may take months for the elusive tones to become dependable. Each attempt brings us closer. Over time, beautiful, focused, and varied tone qualities can be created.

To develop the ability to take in and blow a sufficient amount of air to play a short group of notes or a phrase of music takes time. We discover that to play a single long tone using the full extent of our breath can be the same amount of breath needed to play a number of notes. Stamina gradually increases for longer and longer phrases.

Another challenge for a flutist is keeping the wind power at a steady stream. The exhale is the basic generator of sound. After breathing in with an optimal inhale, the exhale must be directed as a steady stream under ideal pressure and with varied fluidity. The process of *trying and trying again* yields swifter and more satisfying results.

We don't arrive at a point where we declare, "Okay, now I know how to play the flute." We learn that by developing subtle changes in the focus of that column of air created by mouth, lips, lungs, and body, we find ways to create colors and qualities that bring the music to life. This continual development allows more subtle musical ideas to emerge. The artist is at work!

Whether we think of ourselves as beginner or pro, our position is rich with possibilities and the potential to find many interesting and new directions. Zen master Shunryū Suzuki Roshi (1908–1971) recommended in *Zen Mind, Beginner's Mind: Informal Talks on Zen Meditation and Practice* that we maintain an open, inquisitive approach rather than assuming that accomplishments mean a definitive arrival.

> *In the beginner's mind, there are many possibilities, in the expert's mind there are few.*[2]
> —Shunryū Suzuki Roshi

"Doo" Articulation

Many flutists are taught to articulate or tongue notes using the syllables *Te* and *Ta*. I found that using *Ta* tends to slightly open and close the mouth, which can be disruptive to the subtleties of creating the formation of the column of air. *Te* unnecessarily involves the back of the tongue and creates a narrower passageway through which the air must move. For articulations, I prefer the formation of the syllable *Doo*, which allows the mouth to stay calmer and steadier. In pronouncing *Doo*, the tip of the tongue contacts the gums behind the upper front teeth, briefly interrupting the flow of the steady column of air, allowing it to return fully for the next note.

The *Ooo* formation makes single, double, and triple tonguing flow and speak with greater ease. For years I struggled to master double-tonguing, having been taught to use the syllables *Te Ke/Te Ke*. "*Non!*" said my flute professor in France, M. Pierre Cazaux, "*Il faut qu tu dit, 'Du Gu/Du Gu.'*" With a long *ū*, it is like a short form of *Doo/Goo*. It works well for double-tonguing as well as triple-tonguing: *Du Gu Du/Du Gu Du.*

Variations of *Doo* can be used to create different-sounding articulations. For single-tonguing, the tongue touches generally behind the back teeth. A stronger attack can be created by using *Doo*, with the tongue hitting closer to the edges of the teeth. For a passage to sound soft and gentle, maybe a lullaby, the tongue touches the gums behind the teeth, and the articulation is more subtle. To create a stunningly strong articulation, try putting the tongue behind the lips and almost spitting as if propelling a seed off the tip of the tongue. Doing this with plenty of air support will produce a variety of strongly attacked notes depending on what strengths are desired.

Another kind of articulation is not to articulate at all. Only the breath initiates each note. The lips and mouth are openly formed as if saying "*Ooo, Ooo, Ooo*" instead of "*Doo, Doo, Doo.*" This not only creates a great sound but is a good practice technique, building the strength to play notes that arrive with immediate full sound the instant they are initiated.

Sound and Silence

EVERY NOTE HAS BODY OF SOUND. EVERY NOTE evolves from the previous note and leads to the next. Even if a note sits by itself between silences, it isn't isolated, as both the silence and the note evolved out of a context. Silence has body. It is not an absence between leaving a sound or beginning a sound—it is a great living space allowing all possibilities. In music, silence can frame or highlight the sounds and rhythms or provide a pause to allow the heartstrings to feel the message just expressed. Silence can be loaded with meaning.

There's an art to playing from silence when making an entrance while others are playing or when playing alone. In ensemble with others, to enter the music "in sync" rhythmically and avoid feeling that we are jumping in cold, it helps to listen as if we are doing the playing, and seamlessly add our voice. In a solo or ensemble situation, consider the music, the atmosphere of the room, the audience, and how to "bring up the subject." It could be a clear attack or a soft, diffused, subtle entry, bringing in a sparkling clarity or a calming contrast. These are a few of the many artistic considerations when initiating an entrance.

When looking for clarity in playing articulated notes (detached, not tied or slurred) in a phrase, the style of tonguing is important but should not dominate. I often hear flutists lose the body of their tone when they play staccato or fast articulations. What makes the line speak is the steady flow of air and the sense that each note is important and has a voice, a place in time, no matter how short.

We may believe we have mastered being able to play a fast passage of sixteenth notes, and yes, it might all be there accurately, but we need to listen more carefully. Are we rattling off that passage? Does it have a scampering quality rather than a singing-melodic quality? Every note, no matter how brief, should have body and quality. We can do this with our airflow, playing as if the passage is a held note, a note that may grow and change and has character. The whole line has a beginning, middle, and end, so it can have shape and expression.

I sometimes use vibrato for fast passages. Vibrato can give more life, more emotional tension, more fullness even if each note is brief and the series fast. Vibrato can create an increase or decrease in intensity and shape a line without having to rely only on dynamic levels.

Every note has a life. I like to think that each individual note of the composition might be the note that reaches someone in the audience with special meaning. It might be a brief note, poignant, pivotal, or it simply shines. I won't know which note (or notes) will touch someone, so I must make every one sing and radiate in meaning.

Breathing Is Healthy

FLUTISTS EXPERIENCE GREAT HEALTH BENEFITS BY exercising their skills and capacities to breathe. Inventor, musician, and composer Theobald Boehm (1794–1881) is given credit for designing the modern European orchestral flute. He claimed that playing flute restored his health, as he had been sickly in his youth. It is said that asthmatic children can strengthen their breathing by playing a wind instrument.

Advice varies about techniques for breathing for flute. Some advice is not ideal. The following are suggestions I worked with in the past but now would not recommend.

- Breathe from the diaphragm (the diaphragm is an involuntary muscle)
- Inhale to belly only (better to include lungs in the upper chest)
- Tighten the stomach muscles (no need to add extra tension)
- Push the belly out, keeping it tight on the exhale (extra unnecessary effort)
- Don't allow any movement in the upper chest (loss of a wholeness of body).

I seriously used each of these techniques for years until I tried new approaches inspired by Arnold Jacobs, Indian bansuri flutists, and others. Keeping in mind Casals' ideal that the best way is the most natural and relaxed way, I began to experiment. I found an improvement when I thought of fill-ing my entire lungs from lower to upper. There were immediate benefits to the sound quality and the energy in my arms and hands and head (brains love more oxygen). I had more stamina and enough air supply to complete longer phrases with less effort.

I found new freedom to be more connected with the emotional qualities I was able to express, because the music seemed to be generated more from my heart and chest, even breasts. We are mammals. Breasts are the physical manifestation of the "the milk of human kindness." In our culture, they are much maligned, debased, abused, and slandered, but if we found ourselves alone on a desert island, able to do nothing but survive and appreciate our existence before dying, we would probably tune in to a more honest assessment of our body and being. Instead of ornaments or jokes, we might regard breasts as essential keys to survival in mammalian evolution. We come from a long line of nursing mammals. In our consciousness of playing music, why not include a more complete energy from our whole heart-filled chest and compassionate breasts—our mammalian compassion—that has enabled our ancestors to survive for eons?

Breathing West and East

ARNOLD JACOBS (1915–1998), PRINCIPAL TUBA player with the Chicago Symphony Orchestra, was considered a master teacher of breathing for wind players and singers. His lectures and seminars were highly valued throughout the world. He advocated a natural, relaxed way of breathing using "airflow" rather than air pressure. He warned that consciously ordering the muscles to provide air pressure can lead to constriction of the air path. Many students equate air movement with air pressure and needlessly add tension to their musculature. Through his measurements, he found that only three pounds of air pressure are needed for airflow, whereas the contracted torso can support one hundred pounds. He advocated visualizing air as wind. As wind players, it helps to realize that we are moving wind out and in.

His helpful concepts include the following:

- *Breathe to expand, not expand to breathe. Body expansion is the result, not the cause of the inhale.*
- *Work to end conflict between breathing-out muscles and breathing-in muscles.*
- *The primary friction of incoming air is at the lips, not in the throat.*
- *Blow wind outward past the embouchure as if nothing is in the way.*

Jacobs recommended many helpful breathing exercises. One basic exercise he referred to often is a simple slow breath exercise done away from the music:

> *Inhale a slow breath for five beats at metronome marking, MM 42-48 (slower than one beat per second). Visualize a ribbon of air entering the body through the mouth. Exhale for five beats. Visualize the ribbon of air leaving the body. Sense the quantities of moving air.*[3]

Even without doing his exercises, just by understanding the concepts of his approach, improved natural skill in breathing will evolve through daily practice. There are a number of books about Jacobs' teaching written by his students. You can watch him teaching on YouTube by searching for Arnold Jacobs, "Almost Live."[4]

India's foremost classical flutist, Hariprasad Chaurasia, is miraculous to hear. To watch him in concert playing bansuri flutes seems like real magic. He plays long, complex phrases, intricately nuanced, with ease. No effort. No audible inhale. Exquisite music rolls out of him as if he is hindered by nothing, as if he and his flute barely need to be there, as if the music flows by itself. He is a master.[5]

At a concert he gave in Boulder, Colorado, I watched him closely. I saw he was breathing in through the nose and mouth. When there was time in a rest or pause in the music, he breathed in slowly and evenly. When a quick supplemental breath was needed in the middle of a phrase, he silently grabbed it, not interrupting the flow of the music. Listeners who are not wind players would not be aware of his breathing. He wasn't relying on circular breathing.[6] How was he doing it? I wanted to know, so I listened and watched carefully.

Years later, I went to hear the trio, Atmic Vision—Annada "Butto" Prasanna Pattanaik (bansuri flutes), Muthu Kumar (tabla and percussion), and Paul Erhard (double bass). They brought classical Indian compositions into shorter arrangements, perhaps easier for Western listeners.[7]

Butto, a master in his own right, studied with Chaurasia. After the concert, I had the chance to talk with Butto and mentioned how amazed I had been with Chaurasia's breathing as well as with his own. I boldly asked if he might have time to give me a lesson, and he graciously said yes.

For the first lesson, we met in a practice room in the music school of the University of Colorado-Boulder. We sat on the floor, meditation style, and he introduced me to a list of excellent breathing exercises. We played a raga scale and went on to exchange call-and-response riffs. I tried my best with my flute to have the warm and fluid sound of the bansuri. I pride myself on being able to imitate a variety of sounds on Western modern flute (I can even play an elk bugling). To sound like a bansuri flute, one must create a more open and voice-like penetrating sound. The breathing exercises he showed me helped to bring about ease and flexibility in my playing. The ease came from having optimal intake of air and managing the velocity of the outward flow.

Butto's exercises can be practiced anywhere, but the ideal place is sitting meditation style in a quiet room in front of an open window, so that you breathe fresh air. The exercises I like best are as follows:

1. Take in a full breath through the nose. Fill the back and sides of the chest. Blow out through the lips, and take time for this exhale as if blowing on a candle flame, enough to make the flame dance but not to blow it out. Repeat this for two minutes.

2. Take in a full breath through the nose, and blow out through the mouth in short bursts of exhale. Repeat this for about five minutes.

3. With the stomach in as much as possible, take a deep breath, and blow it all out quickly through the mouth. Repeat this four or five times.

4. Close your eyes. Close your ears with your fingers. Take in a deep breath. Hum on the exhale, making the sound come from the nose. Repeat this five to ten times.

5. This is a yoga exercise done through the nose with the mouth closed. With the index finger against the side of the nose, close off one nostril. Take in a full breath through the open nostril. Close that nostril, and hold the breath in for a short time. Open the nostril that had been closed for the inhale, and slowly breathe the air completely out. Breathe in

a full breath from the nostril through which the exhale has just passed, close both for a short time, and open the other nostril to exhale. The ratio in timing for the inhale-hold-exhale is 2:1:4 (or if you are counting faster, 8:4:16)

6. Breathe in deeply through the nose to the chest. Slowly (but not too slowly) blow all the air out through the mouth. When it is completely gone, bring the stomach toward the backbone, and hold for a short time. As soon as this is mildly uncomfortable, take in a new breath through the nose. Repeat four or five times.

These exercises bring many benefits to your playing, but one of the best is how good you feel after a session: awake, fresh, and clearheaded.

Breathing well for flute playing is more than vital; it has the power to give you everything you want. You can develop the ability to always have enough air for phrasing, dynamic range, continuity, and all the artistry of your musical ideas. In addition, a healthy air exchange helps keep the brain functioning clearly.

Breathe for Confidence

THE CONFIDENCE THAT COMES FROM HAVING plenty of air from each inhale is priceless. It allows us to make the greatest advances in our playing, technically and musically. There is much more pleasure when a stable supply of air is present all along the way. We can be confident that we have what we need as we play phrases and sentences, giving plenty of energy to our artistic choices.

Even with our best efforts, there can be times when we

find ourselves playing without enough breath. We realize that we have to find a way to push ahead in a phrase despite not having enough air. There are ways to get away with "running on empty," but there is an added danger. The lack of air and extra stress it causes is distracting and can lead to surprise mistakes. If this occurs too often, mistakes will be reinforced by repetition, and the resulting discouragement makes it even harder. The best approach is to look closely at breathing itself. Devote more practice time to issues of breathing: quality, quantity, and planning. Breathing exercises are a great help. Mapping and planning the ideal breathing places in the music may need more careful work. (More on mapping breaths in the next section.)

We need adequate air to play with plenty of "juice" all the way to the ends of phrases without "flatlining" on the last few notes or actually going flat in pitch for lack of air support. If we are running out of steam on a last note, we can roll the flute slightly outward to nudge the pitch up and prevent the note from sagging. This is often a last-ditch technique.

Sometimes it is necessary to accumulate more air by a series of short breaths taken quickly enough not to interrupt the flow of the phrases. It can work well, but there are pitfalls. Too many short breaths may cause too much backed-up, stored air in the lungs. When taking many small inhales between short phrases, unused air stays in the lungs too long and sets up carbon dioxide, which can starve the brain of oxygen. The remedy is to plan and practice our ideal inhale points. Our "map" can include longer stretches or shorter stretches between breathing places. Mapping has the added benefit of clarifying our musical intention, phrasing, direction, and overview of the design of the composition.

Mapping Breaths

AIR INTAKE IS A PHYSICAL AND A MUSICAL ISSUE. Rehearsing where and how we want to breathe is as important as practicing the notes of the piece. The best time and place to take in a breath can be at any point when there is enough time in a pause, a notated rest, or by cunning techniques of grabbing a short breath between phrases of a passage. I sometimes repeat a passage many times for the sake of rehearsing the breathing. I want to make sure that the way I breathe is workable and has grace in the context of the musical line. How we breathe and where we breathe is part of our art.

Breath marks are like reference points on a map. In some printed flute music, breath marks are edited in. Usually these indications are noted in the most natural places to breathe, but they are not "set in stone." It is common to discover that some areas of the music need more breathing places, and some need fewer. Some phrases can sound natural with a breath, and others need a continuous flow with no break. We can chart our own map according to what will allow the musical phrases and sentences to speak naturally.

It is common for a (V) to mark a place for a substantial breath and an apostrophe (') to note a place for a short breath. In addition to the common markings, I write and draw on the printed music with more details in my "map." I might put a capital (B) above a breath mark to indicate, "Take a really big breath for what's coming next." I use parallel slashes (//) with a line over the top to indicate abbreviating a note slightly to take a quick breath. It is important to take the quick breath gracefully. If the note previous to the breath is sung well and sent substantially out to resonate and hang in the air, it will sound natural and not as if it has been clipped off or "shortchanged."

Places for Large Breaths

Starting with the beginning of the piece, note where it will be possible to take time to fill your lungs. Some of these places will be:

- Before the first note of the piece
- When you have an entry after a long rest
- Sometimes in slower passages, by letting go of a long held note slightly early

Before playing the first note and phrase, hear it in your mind's ear. Settle your embouchure, and take in a full breath as a natural, slow, full inhale through your nose and slightly through the formed *Ooo* of your lips.

As you take in the full breath, you notice a feeling of more power and endurance emerging. This power brings a kind of clarity of purpose that includes the about-to-be-spoken first note and first phrase and beyond to the architecture of the entire composition. It sets up a feeling of having all the energy you need, a perfect amount, maybe even a surplus. Even if later in the composition there are places when getting enough air means carefully planned quick intakes, there is no panic, as you have taken full advantage of the places for larger breaths and will be coming upon more generous places again. Your playing gains consistency and confidence.

Be sure in long rests, when you are counting measures, that you calculate when to begin taking in a slow, full breath before your entrance. Plan when you need to pick up your flute, center your embouchure, and take in a big, relaxed breath while staying aligned with the music. It can help to enter as though you were already playing with the other musicians so that your new statements evolve from theirs (unless a contrast is the intention).

A quick intake of breath before beginning to play can sound and work fine in certain circumstances, but a slower, relaxed breath is far more effective in giving yourself balanced energy for the notes and passages that follow. The value of the slow, calm intake of air goes a long way to energizing your playing.

There are many approaches to taking in a quick breath in those parts of the music that offer little or no time, and I'll discuss these next.

How to Grab a Short Breath

How can a quick breath be taken in without sounding like a gasp? A noisy breath is okay at times and can even add to the expression to an extent. More often than not, a noisy breath can distract a listener away from the unfolding of the composition and interrupt the focus or meaning.

Many people open their mouth to take air in and then must reset their embouchure to play. Why would we upset our good, focused embouchure every time we breathe in? It is possible to keep the mouth and lips at, or nearly at, the formation needed to continue playing. It helps to breathe in through one's nose as well as the mouth. It takes practice, but breathing through both is refreshing, gets more air in quicker, and is less drying on the throat.

Whether breathing in or letting air flow out, keep the lips in the *Ooo* formation and the nostrils open. Keeping the lips in a more or less *Ooo* position and not opening the mouth too much stabilizes the relationship of the column of air to embouchure. Without holding the mouth and lips too rigidly, the embouchure stays relaxed and nearly at the position needed to play. The throat remains relaxed with an openness that will prevent a gasping sound. Practice taking in a quick and quiet breath by experimenting with these approaches.

If you are in a chamber music setting where you must signal or conduct an upbeat and downbeat for a piece, be careful not to get into the trap of trying to go along with the expectations of other musicians. They may wait to hear your quick gasp as you signal the upbeat and downbeat. Since you want a full breath to begin the piece and not just a quick gasp, work to make your gesture clear in another way. You may have to explain why relying on the "gasp" won't work for you. It is easy enough for them to take their cue from a subtle conducting gesture if you make it clear. You may want to look in the mirror and practice your slow, full inbreath and your precise nod (or other gesture) to conduct and play the downbeat.

You Are a Musician First, an Instrumentalist Second

I HAVE WORKED TO ACHIEVE A BEAUTIFUL QUALITY and flexible sound that projects different colors and characters. A great deal goes into it. For each piece, phrase, or note, there are many artistic decisions and discoveries. The aspiration is to have a natural sound, yet incredibly intricate work goes into producing natural sound. It comes from observation and study. After hearing me play, people who express that they thought it was beautiful often ask, "What kind of flute is that?" While it is true that a good flute is important, the quality of sound at every turn in every moment comes from the player's sensibilities and attention and the resonance of the body. People may view you as simply manipulating the instrument to make it speak, but your whole body and whole being are playing.

All instrumentalists are told to "play like you sing." It is one of the most helpful pieces of advice, but I'd take it further.

As a flutist (or any wind player), you ARE a singer. When you sing, your vocal chords are your instrument, but what makes it sound uniquely like you is your whole body and mind, character, and spirit. For a singer, sound comes mostly from the chest—a big resonator chamber connected to the heart. It is the same for the flute player.

Practice Breathing

INSTEAD OF THINKING OF PRACTICING AS LEARNING notes, practice *all* the vital aspects that go into playing. Devoting a practice session to breathing brings great advantages. Before beginning a piece, take some deep breaths as if preparing to play. Take a long, relaxed, huge breath to begin playing. Learn to disguise the in-breath by breathing through the nose.

Listen to phrases, and mark the obviously natural places for breaths. As you play, notice where you are going to need extra breaths, find the ideal places that will work with the phrasing, and mark those in parentheses. Where there is no rest in the music, figure out how to hide the extra breath you may need. If you give the previous note plenty of "juice" before leaving it slightly early to take a quick breath, it won't seem like an abandoned note. This can be done by working with the expression and character of the note through articulation, dynamic, accent, or vibrato. Imagine sending the note out to hang in the air while you take a secret breath.

For the smaller quick breaths, figure out how much air you need to end the phrase before you reach the next big breathing place. If you do not need much air, take only as much as is needed. This is usually easy to do quickly through your nose. If more breath is needed, shave a bit of time off the last note before the breath, as mentioned above, being sure that the last note has life in it to disguise its brevity.

The way we use breath to support the sound helps us to keep tones solid and in tune. Breath support will come to our aid when there are sudden, unexpected problems. If I am in the middle of a piece and there is an emergency like dry mouth, dry lips, or embouchure slippage, I revert to articulating without tonguing. I maintain good breath support through an open mouth and throat (like the way we form our mouth and open our throat to blow warm air to fog a window). This maintains moisture around the throat and keeps dry air from increasing the danger of coughing. I articulate the notes without using the tongue while keeping the *Ooo* formation of the lips. This way I can maintain a singing quality through the short emergency stretch before finding a place to reset the embouchure, swallow, and generally regroup. It helps to have practiced articulating without tonguing. Notes that are articulated well without tonguing can sound fine or even better than tongued notes.

Breathing and Intonation

THE MORE AIR SUPPORT WE MAINTAIN, THE LESS need to compensate for intonation problems by rotating or rolling. The techniques of rotating the flute outward or inward, away from or toward the body, are helpful for adjusting intonation. Rolling inward flattens the pitch; rolling outward sharpens the pitch. This is a blunt way to maintain true intonation. Fine-tuning can occur with subtle changes in lip formation.

Subtle lip changes can direct the column of air slightly high (to sharpen) or direct the column of air slightly low (to make the pitch flatter). Blowing stronger or weaker will also change the pitch but may compromise the quality of sound desired. Maintaining air support, using steady energy to generate the musical line, can make the above adjustments unnecessary, or they can be done more minutely.

The remedy for an intonation problem involves many variables, but imagine that you are playing a phrase where the top note has a tendency to sound flat. You could roll out when you get to that note. That would be a radical adjustment that may "overshoot" and be sharper than you intended. You could direct your column of air more upward, subtly changing the angle of your jaw or tilting your head up. That can help but still might change the color and quality of tone too much.

Using the pressure of air support is the most natural way. Using core abdominal muscles and allowing the rib cage to relax and push air out gradually can create the perfect stream of air. I have found that intonation improves if I think of the entire musical phrase as one steady push, as if playing a single sustained note. I tell myself, *Don't expect the flute to do it. It's you. It is your breathing and your energy.*

Although modern flutes are scientifically calibrated for nearly perfect intonation, each flute has idiosyncrasies. A flute may tend to be slightly sharp or flat on certain notes. If it is your own instrument that you play daily, you will become accustomed to what you need to do to play certain notes in tune. You will be able to readily make the adjustments needed to tune with other instrumentalists as you play. It is most helpful to remember that a steady push of air, a steady pressure throughout a phrase or sentence, can create a more consistent intonation without having to make adjustments for individual notes as often.

Be a courageous powerhouse of energy. Whether playing a quiet piece or music in full sound, energy must be kept up.

The steady push of air supports it all. Passages gain real life and expression and will be exciting, clearly spoken, and at times achingly beautiful.

4

Brilliant Practice

*S*tudying and learning through each practice session, rehearsal, and event, we can be present with ourselves. Creatively trying things invokes inner joy and pushes the envelope of delight in playing. Connections and opportunities appear inwardly and outwardly. Inwardly our joy connects to the development of our playing, and outwardly it influences our life.

- *Music is a practice.*
- *To practice takes practice.*
- *To perform takes practice.*
- *To practice is to perform.*
- *To perform is to practice.*

THERE IS A REFUGE IN THE SINGLE-POINTED FOCUS of exploring beauty and character in sound. The quality of our concentration in music can bring a feeling of balance. The speed in our daily lives seems ever increasing, yet we bear the stress and push ourselves to adapt, enduring multitasking, divided attention, rush hour, and half-hour lunches. Coming from this accelerated life into the realm of practicing music where progress takes patience is a different world. Practicing can be a time to pose questions and find answers within ourselves.

Is practicing being selfish? There are many people and duties calling for our attention, and we can feel anxiety and guilt about taking time out for music. It is helpful to remember that our dedication to our practice, our progress, and the music itself, contributes to those around us. The mental, physical, and spiritual health that playing music can bring to an individual contributes to family, friends, and society.

Make Plans

For each practice session, it helps to have a plan, even a vague plan, to consciously choose what we want to cover in the allotted time.

To warm up with scales can be helpful, but within the music to be studied, there are many patterns that offer scale practice. I often choose a portion of a piece and use that as a warm-up. I might make an exercise of long tones based on some of the wider intervals in the piece. Playing these intervals with accurate intonation and character pays off when I play the piece at tempo. The intervals are now familiar friends, beautifully in tune, ringing with greater clarity.

We might choose to warm up by focusing on a tricky passage—playing slowly and smoothly, relaxing through the subtle exchange of fingers from one note to the next. We may choose to experiment with the quality of tone for one high note and gradually include some of the notes around it, deciding how to approach, or to come from that note with its special quality. Soon the desire to play these small, slow excerpts in the context of the whole piece at a more natural tempo will be irresistible. We are well on our way; our explorations and artistic decision making are activated for a productive practice session.

Playing with Ease

Practice with ease to play with ease. The key is to practice slowly at first before gradually bringing the piece up to its natural tempo. Playing slowly helps us relish each note and listen for potential expressive qualities that we may want to bring out. There is time to develop smoother finger transitions from note to note. At a slow tempo, we can easily play the correct notes, which allows us to be free of fear. We relax into playing the correct notes as we increase the tempo by gradual increments.

Feel free to *play,* to have fun with the music. Work with a phrase without looking at the printed music. Rather than feeling that the origin and authority of the music comes from the page, become free to feel it directly from the flow of your breath and your artistic choices in phrasing, color, etc. This needn't be formal memorizing. It is an exercise to lighten your regard for the printed page and focus your attention more on your sound. Enjoying the freedom to feel the music, to discover its messages, allows you to bypass barriers before they have a chance to block your way. It is practicing with ease in order to play with ease.

To train the fingers to play a rapid series of notes smoothly, it helps to "play around" with them. Speed them up, slow them down—play all staccato or all legato. Play around but at a speed comfortable enough to avoid frequent mistakes.

Enjoying a flexibility that allows for play in no way contradicts our serious efforts to develop and improve. Playfulness is part of our committed dedication to excel musically. Control and flexibility are not in conflict. We are working toward mastery of both.

Make Exploration Your Goal

Active curiosity propels progress in practice. Our best friends are exploration and openness to discovery. Even if a piece seems prepared and ready for performance, each time we play it, we discover new ideas. That is the joy of the art: new options, new directions, and fresh beauty.

By way of illustration, imagine you are studying a short, fast passage. It's interesting yet is not a solo part. It serves to outline harmonies while the other musicians have more melodic parts. You are in a supportive role, yet the passage needs to be heard, for it provides rhythm. You feel that it shouldn't dominate yet shouldn't be lost. You might experiment with playing the notes more detached or more connected or shaping it so that it appears clearly and later blends in quieter. Maybe you experiment by slightly emphasizing one or two notes within the pattern or varying the articulations. Your exploration may lead to a combination of approaches. Your part is not background. When a supporting part is distinctive in the weave, it contributes life to all the parts.

With an exploring and curious mind, we are equipped to work with shifting situations. Maybe the acoustics of the room mean that this passage will need more distinct and detached articulation. Maybe at the concert, the other musicians play at a different dynamic level or tempo than they did at rehearsal. We must transition into new options to come into balance with the other musicians. We can be confident that we are good at this. Because we are accustomed to exploring, we find within ourselves a treasury of options.

Build Confidence with Confidence

Lightening up on difficult passages and making them fun lets our fingers and mind trust that we are not going to drill them like some military exercise. Fingers relax and can assimilate the feeling of playing correctly without unnecessary fear and tension getting in the way.

If there are a few problematic notes, play those notes slowly. Are there two or three notes within the passage that should be even but tend to be uneven? Sometimes one finger can be slightly ahead of the others, interrupting the smooth singing flow. In that case, try purposely making the finger that always plays slightly ahead now be slightly behind. Keep tuned in to the sensation of your finger pads on the keys as you do this brief reverse exercise. Practice this three or four times, and then play the phrase straight. Often you will find that the problem is resolved, as the fingers now know what you want.

Conversely, in a spot where one finger is coming down slightly late, do the reverse exercise by purposely making it too early. Try that a few times, and then play the passage evenly. The problem will often have been corrected. If it is not resolved right away, leave it alone, and try it later or in another practice session. The passage will soon come naturally.

For passages that are difficult (finger transitions, difficult interval skips, unusual rhythms, articulation changes, dynamic changes, etc.), isolate the hardest parts, and practice the simplest unit. This simple unit might be the two hardest notes out of a longer passage. Play these notes in various ways: as lengthened, beautiful notes, softly and slowly focusing on the finger and breath transitions, and play them as smoothly as possible. Then broaden to include more of the context: the notes that come before or come after these notes. Broaden the line by degrees to include the whole passage.

Know when to stop. It never helps to pound or force the passage by pushing ourselves to play in frustration. We have all been there, petulantly thinking, *Why can't I do this?! I should be able to do this!*

Pushing ourselves in frustration yields diminishing returns. Mind and body receive mixed messages, and we work against ourselves. That kind of frustration builds up a feeling of inadequacy that we then associate with that piece or portion of the piece each time we play it. We are practicing our anxiety and our mistakes.

A healthy break or a change of focus is more helpful. It would be better to shift our attention to other parts of the piece or a different piece or stop for the day. Even though we may feel tempted to try to fix all the glitches in one session, giving ourselves a break is the best idea. When we return to the passage, it will be with fresh energy and a better attitude. In the end, we save time and energy and avoid discouragement.

Gently allowing fingers, breath, and attitude to get accustomed to the patterns, repeating them slowly, simply, and correctly, yields results beyond our expectations. Within a few days, the passage comes with greater ease, and our fingers are ready to try it faster, moving closer and closer to the natural tempo desired. It is amazing how obliging and smart fingers are. They learn patterns easily with a bit of coaxing on a regular basis. This kind of practice builds confidence with confidence.

Added magic happens in the hours or days from one practice session to the next. When we begin a practice session, we may find that improvement has taken place. Is there consciousness in the body that assimilates our practice while away from the flute? Was some part of our being dreaming about it? I often hear the pieces I am working on in my mind's ear—sometimes one phrase stuck on repeat. Instead of feeling stuck in a rut, I am thankful for its presence. The ghostly repetition can inspire me to start to sing or whistle segments, bringing about more ideas for phrasing and approach.

One approach that has helped me to get fast, difficult passages "in the fingers" is to play the entire passage in dotted rhythms: *long-short* or *short-long*. In other words, a passage of eighth notes will become approximately dotted eighths and sixteenths, and a passage of sixteenth notes will become dotted sixteenths and thirty-seconds. Reverse the pattern by making the short note come first before each longer note. Triple-patterned passages can be adjusted the same way by lengthening and shortening chosen notes (i.e. *short-short-long, long-long-short, short-long-short, long-short-long*).

Try a *long-short* pattern the entire passage, at slower tempo, and then play the reverse *short-long* throughout. Then try the passage straight as written, at tempo or nearly at tempo, and notice how much ease you have gained. Remember that this exercise should be tried and then left alone to come back to later. Don't bash yourself with it. Never beat yourself up with your music practice. Music is to help you fly, to help you soar, to help you be at peace. It's not for self-abuse. Work *hard* but not *nasty*.

Metronome

PRACTICING WITH A METRONOME IS USEFUL. THE mechanical precision is highly informative. It can help us to internalize the feel of a steady, consistent beat. We can use the metronome to spot places in a composition where we have a tendency to rush unnaturally or where we slow down inappropriately. A metronome also allows us to experiment with deciding on a best overall tempo and to note our choice with precision. We can use the metronome to gradually build our skill to play up to tempo by increasing the speed by small increments.

It is helpful to practice a new piece with a metronome to feel the placement of each note. Practice the entire piece slowly with the metronome set in subdivisions—for example, one beat per eighth note—to get every note seated, taking care not to play mechanically. Playing at a slow or subdivided setting helps reveal the accurate proportions in the seating of each note. Then we can gradually increase the speed, playing only as fast as comfortable with no mistaken notes or trip-ups.

A metronome can seem like a terrible taskmaster. Eliminate this feeling by abandoning the idea of the metronome as a trap. We don't have to succumb to playing in a mechanical way. Use the metronome as a grounding to stretch against. Once there is comfort and confidence playing in a steady beat, we can use it as a foundation to experiment in shaping the rhythmic line.

Within the space between one beat to the next, a single note can be fuller or sparser. It can be intentionally placed slightly before the beat or held beyond the next beat, and the time can be made up for by rushing slightly or shortening another note. A group of notes can be subtly rushed or slowed between beats, or one or more notes can be lengthened and the others quickened. The possibilities are endless and enjoyable.

Exact, enthusiastic, and alive rhythms keep the music moving and meaningful. When we know confidently the exact placement of each note in its rhythmic context, we can decide to push and pull in subtle ways for expression.

Sight-Reading: Useful Conflict

EVEN THOUGH I WAS MODERATELY GOOD AT IT, sight-reading felt like a betrayal of my principles. Why would I want to play something in public that I hadn't had a chance to study? The skill of good sight-reading is useful and essential for many types of careers in music such as orchestral and recording. There are some practical considerations when teaching ourselves to sight-read. I found out the hard way that being good at sight-reading is not a talent but an acquired skill.

The shock came when I was in high school and auditioned for a city youth orchestra. Any orchestral audition is a tough competition for a flutist, since an orchestra may have only two or three flutes. Often the flute section has only one chair open and many flute players who come to audition. I was excited by the possibility of joining this excellent youth orchestra in the San Francisco Bay Area. I did well in all aspects of the audition except for the sight-reading, which disqualified me. Even though I scraped by in the sight-reading portion, I felt ashamed. *If only I had had one more chance to play the piece*, I thought, *I could have played it at least 85 percent, maybe even 95 percent, better.* However, that is what sight-reading is: playing correctly and musically on first sight.

After that, I made discoveries about sight-reading. Some will seem obvious to the reader, but sometimes hearing specifics about how someone else struggled is more informative and valuable than hearing about their successes.

The first discovery was that sight-reading must be practiced regularly with other people or alone with a metronome. It must be done with the self-discipline to keep going onward no matter what notes or phrases you trip over. Sight-reading helps to loosen up the eyes and train them to be flexible in looking ahead to what is coming next.

When you must play a piece at first sight, take a few moments to look it over before playing. Scan the pages for the first information needed.

- Quickly observe the key signature(s), time signature(s), and tempo indications such as andante, allegro, or a metronome marking.
- Look at the first few measures, and sing them to yourself silently. Even if you do not imagine the pitches correctly, the rhythm will be there.
- Peek at the last few bars of the ending.
- Page through the music, and notice any changes of tempo, time signatures, or key signatures that occur in the middle of the piece.

Above all, when you begin, play with confidence, even a bit of "braggadocio." Act as if you know the piece. A confident mistake is far better than stopping and going. Keep playing no matter what. Use your best tone qualities. Don't retreat into a shy whisper or play in an uncertain, sketchy manner. Draw your lines confidently, like Picasso. Play with full breaths and conviction. Even belt out your mistakes, and leave them behind as you regain your balance. Your balance can be regained by concentrating on your best tone qualities and the notes and phrases ahead.

We can trust our sight as well as our ear and our musicality. The practice of sight-reading is a compelling project of discovery where we can appreciate the art hidden in the composition. Trying only for correctness is the more difficult approach. The easier way is to play from musical motivation. Being involved in the musicality increases our focus, because it engages us more completely and directly. As we use more of our creativity, we experience more pleasure, more adventure, more fun, and more natural focus. The music will sound with character as well as clarity and correctness.

Our active playing and active listening are one and the same. We should avoid passive listening and not allow our outwardly critical mind to interfere with the *now* of active playing. While playing we are not in the "armchair" but in the "command chair." Command your playing along with commanding your listening. You are sending out your message.

I used to resent sight-reading and consider it not really playing music. Why would I want to hash something out when I could make it 90 percent more musical after a few read-throughs? More familiarity with the piece would mean I could make it multiple times more exciting.

Developing the valuable skill of sight-reading can help us become more alive and musical. True, the musical decisions we make on the spot may not be what we would choose after weeks or years practicing the piece, but they can be good enough for being in the moment on our first read-through.

One aspect feeds the other: the studied and the unstudied. The more we have explored music in general, the better explorer we will be in unfamiliar territory. We will not just be reading notes but bringing our best sensibilities to shape phrases and contours of lines. The more we have challenged ourselves to play something new on sight, the livelier our artistic explorations will become in our approaches with the familiar. It's like traveling. When we venture into new lands and cultures, we are enriched. When we come home, we see our culture in a new light with added possibilities and added understanding.

Charting Breaths

IN STUDYING A NEW PIECE, MAKE YOUR MAP EARLY on. Along the way, as you discover the phrasing, observe the most natural places to take a breath. Keep a pencil handy to make notes on the printed music. The music may already be edited with breath marks, but often only a few are indicated in obvious places. You may disagree with the placement of some of the breath marks, finding that they interrupt the line unnecessarily. Feel free to revise the printed indications and change your mind regarding your own markings. More on breathing and mapping breaths in chapter 3.

Time and Energy

FINDING PRACTICE TIME CAN BE PROBLEMATIC. It is often hard to fit a session into our busy schedule, so we must try using shorter and more frequent times and design the session with more intention.

Our short practice session might proceed like this: Launch into the music, the piece(s) being studied, right away. If there is time to feature only one, play it through. Identify areas that need work. Play those areas slowly, trying unequal rhythms (the long-short, short-long technique mentioned earlier). Find the tone qualities you want in those sections. Visit other areas that need review and ironing out. Play through the whole piece undertempo. Play through at tempo. Take pleasure if you can hear that you have made advances, and leave it there until your next practice session. Write notes about what you want to work on next time; they may help you focus more quickly on specific things you are developing.

If you have limited time, try the following:

- Fifteen minutes: Work mostly on tone quality
- Thirty minutes: Tone quality and slow work
- Sixty minutes: Tone quality, slow work, one or two pieces

- One and a half hours: All the above, plus review new pieces for fun
- Two hours: All the above, plus record yourself and listen back
- Four or five hours: Be sure to take breaks!

There is such a thing as too much practice. I once had a teacher tell me to stop playing for several days to a week. I was twenty years old and had been practicing four or five hours a day. Although I may have been practicing in all the best ways, I hit a barrier where I couldn't achieve a good quality of tone. The lips can tire from too much work for the fine network of muscles and nerves. It felt like I'd lost flexibility. Taking a break of a week helped. I came back to it with renewed flexibility and energy, and I was more aware of avoiding overdoing it.

Flute practice can seem like extra work on top of intense life burdens. The efforts of having enough wind power to reach the end of a long phrase, catching enough air for the next phrase, the intense concentration, and standing for one, two, or more hours can seem exhausting. Thankfully and paradoxically, expending energy increases endurance. People who train to be runners know that the more they do, the more they *can* do.

Take short breaks in a practice session. Set your flute down for a moment, ideally in an uncluttered and honored place in the room. Your flute is a vehicle for extraordinary musical travel, and it needs a safe parking spot. After setting down the flute, stretch a little to shake out your arms, twist from side to side, stretch your legs, or walk to the kitchen to get a glass of water.

These breaks make a big difference. It is like standing back to look at the painting you have been working on. You renew your outlook, and fresh ideas will occur to you when you return.

Embrace Change

EVEN IF OUR PRACTICE METHODS SEEM RELIABLE and reasonable, it is helpful and artistically exciting to remain open to change. Perhaps our methods are fine but need tweaking, or perhaps there is an entire next step to be taken. Practice embracing change. Each time we begin to play is a new moment, a new experience. We embrace the given of the moment and build on that moment.

Art Lande, internationally acclaimed jazz pianist, was teaching a class on improvisation and gave a great demonstration. He advised that if you are improvising and trip on a note or play a note that seems out of context, use that moment as an impetus to go on. As he described this, he got up from his chair but faltered, almost fell, caught himself, and created a humorous step to regain his balance. It was a composition in movement and a funny but meaningful illustration of accepting a surprise moment and using it to create something new.[1]

Can we be "on" every day? Yes, in our own way. It is helpful to honor our mood and at the same time be aware that our mood transforms how we play. A sad, contrary, or angry mood might give our approach to the music a plainer, straightforward expression that is not interrupted by manipulation. By manipulation, I mean "pushing the river," forcing something unnaturally such that the playing becomes, for example, cloyingly sentimental, technically virtuoso without musicality, or any number of other forced affects. Playing while in an angry mood (or any other mood) might reveal to our ears a more natural approach to the music.

When do we know we play well? Although we may achieve confidence in our abilities, it is never a solid thing, as each time is unique. A performance can be a kind of arrival, yet we don't know if we have officially *arrived*. It is nearly impossible to be objective about our own playing even when we listen to a recording of ourselves. Then again, we are not rigid entities. We are not products; we are works in progress.

Go with What Inspires You Most

Planning a single practice session, planning the year, or planning a career, we can choose what interests us most. Choices can be made in our long-range view as we work on favorite and non-favorite material. If we must play non-favorite pieces, we can enjoy every corner of good in them that we can find. If we have a long-range perspective, we might notice that the non-favorite pieces grow on us and even become favorites.

To work on a piece means that the music is taking shape in us. In selecting pieces to work on ask, *What do I want at this point? What abilities? What understanding? What enjoyment and satisfaction in playing?* We may think about what kinds of expression we want to feel and explore or what styles to embody. Would it be jazz, baroque, romantic, modern, contemporary, world music, or a broad mixture? What strikes the deepest "chord" (pun intended)?

If music is our job, our career, we may find ourselves open to play whatever is placed in front of us. Listening carefully to a large variety of performers in a variety of genres of music is immensely helpful no matter to what genres of music we end up committing our energies. Listening is our greatest inspirational teacher. To perceive the range and details of expression other artists achieve consciously or subconsciously awakens us to interesting possibilities in our own art.

Even listening to ugly music can be interesting. If you are stuck waiting in line or trapped on hold on the phone, and dull or obnoxious music is being piped in (Muzak), instead of wishing you could shut it out, try paying attention to it and asking yourself why it is so repulsive. What elements make it that way, and what would improve it? What impressions and manipulative messages is it designed to give? What influence is it trying to impart? When you can be awake to its ploys and direct your focus to how it could be made better, it becomes less wearing on the nerves. You have moved away from being a victim of the music to becoming an astute observer.

Good Begets Better

OUR PRACTICE SESSIONS DESERVE OUR BEST TONE qualities every time. We might need to experiment until we find the qualities we seek. For example, at certain points in a piece, we might say to ourselves:

> *This area needs a frank, clear quality.*
>
> *These quick notes are not just speedy; they have to sing.*
>
> *Those low notes must project melodically as a bass line.*
>
> *That top note is not so much a loud forte climax as a poignant, conscious climax that says, "Now I understand."*

The music might become a story, not necessarily a story in words or images but in emotion expressed in qualities and character. We shape the new insights and information into our playing. When an idea comes our way, it's not enough to intellectually acknowledge it. It will become real and beneficial only when we play it and sculpt it in our own way. As we work, some aspects of our sculpture will bring life to the music, and those that don't will fall away like the chips of stone that are chiseled off.

The quality of a musical passage might be profound peace, light playfulness, fiery passion, mystery, or reverence. As we, in our own ways, develop our abilities to produce those qualities through our sound, we are connecting with those qualities from life. In a parallel way, because we have been with them musically, we experience the same qualities in our lives with more depth and understanding. Being more attuned and observant of life and of people will inform what we bring to our music.

Stay Present

IF WE PLAY NOTES ABSENTMINDEDLY, WE ARE PRACticing being disinterested and training ourselves to have a "turned-off" attitude. To be present, we must *be* present. If we drift or daydream, we can look for more challenges—try for better intonation, tone, expression, or phrasing. Practice is habit forming. Good habits can lead to better habits.

We possess self-discipline to wake ourselves up, to use our time well. We can create something interesting instead of clinging to a dull routine. It is unnecessary to be stuck with our assumption about how this or that *must* be done. We can explore how it *can* be done. In our explorations we will then love what we are doing and regard no corner of our practice as a "grind." We look forward to each practice session with renewed interest.

5

Avoiding Practice Pitfalls

The choices we make when we pick up our instrument for a practice session are important. We may have been taught that it is best to begin with scales and exercises in order to warm up, to exercise fingers, and to become familiar with common and uncommon patterns.

Exercises can be beneficial but can also be counterproductive. When they are played as mechanical drudgery, they can be dangerous. If we believe we must drill ourselves on exercises even though they are uninteresting, we are no longer fully engaged and more likely to play in a mechanical, monotonous way as if performing a disdainful chore. Half-consciously going through exercises turns off the ear, turns off our motivation, and can start our session off on a wrong footing.

Playing in a detached, passive way can also produce more small trip-ups and promote repetition of mistakes. The accidental repetition of mistakes, even if it occurs only here and there, has the effect of poorly training our reflexes, leading to frustration and discouragement.

Playing dully and mechanically becomes reinforced in the ear, trapping us in a deadened musicality. Conceiving and manifesting these drills as dull and dry, imprints our mind's ear with a degree of ugliness we accept as normal. To "play ugly" was probably not our inspiration when we decided to take up playing music. Why be nonmusical with such a beautiful instrument, such a potentially expressive voice, and our own capacity to bring music to life? Scales and exercises can be played with as much expression as possible, and the benefits of playing them increases exponentially.

Scales

IN PLAYING SCALES AND EXERCISES, WE CAN'T BE slouches, physically or mentally. The more respect we give them, the more we receive in the development of our understanding and musicality. Any series of notes played as if mechanically resting on them will seem like music taken for granted, as if lazily draping an arm over the shoulders of someone we love. No! Ours should be a genuine embrace! Scales and exercises can be played as if the most beautiful music ever heard. Then no aspect of our practice will seem like dull drudgery. Practicing patterns can be exciting and fulfilling.

Play scales with a flourish even if you play them slowly. Make them interesting by playing them in different patterns. For example: from 1 (being tonic), play each note of the scale up to 9, then down to 2 and up to 10, and down to 3 and up to 11, etc. Play slowly to explore using different tone qualities or in dotted rhythms (long-short or short-long). Stay awake and engaged in challenging yourself. If you feel bored and detached, play something else. It is more productive to play the scales well than to push yourself to keep playing them when you have lost interest and they sound routine and bland. This way, each time you decide to practice scales, you will be unburdened of the conflicted feeling that you are pushing yourself to do something you dislike. Instead, it's all part of your delicious banquet. You are continuously motivated by the beauty and variety you can create.

Here are some different ways to focus on practicing scales:

- Play slowly in your most beautiful tone qualities.
- Be sure the airflow support is strong and consistent.
- Try different dynamic levels, crescendos, and diminuendos for single notes or series of notes.
- Play with different rhythm patterns.
- Be sure the high notes grow out of the energy of the lower notes so they are not "punched out" in a separate effort.
- Play the arpeggio (the 1, 3 5, 8 of the scale) for two octaves up and back down for each scale, working to play the transitions between intervals with utmost smoothness.
- Use the arpeggio for long tones by playing the first degree to the third degree and back to the one. Play the first degree to fifth degree and back, and onward from the first degree to the next notes of the arpeggio and back, with each widening interval played in a smooth and liquid way.

Carnival of the Animals by the Romantic composer Camille Saint-Saëns (1835–1921) is a humorous suite scored for small ensemble including two pianos. One movement, "Pianistes," is a parody of the way piano students study scales. The scales are set in patterns similar to the well-known exercise books of Carl Czerny, used extensively by piano students to gain facility in playing scales. Saint-Saëns instructs the two pianists to play as though they are beginners. There is a sense in the music that the musicians are struggling with a burden, a kind of drudgery, recognizable to any musician.[1]

The Tyranny of Downbeats

WE LIVE IN A TYRANNY OF DOWNBEATS. WE HAVE all experienced stopping at a stop light and being assaulted by the subwoofer of someone's car audio system jolting our brain in a monotonous imprisonment of uniform pounding. Why must every beat be the same dull, mechanical, plodding thud with a relentless insistence that is lifeless and bleak?

Conformity, offering no variety, is acceptable in our culture. There is Pablum-like security in having no danger of being embarrassed because everyone knows it's cool (at least the recording companies know that the sales are cool). People are afraid of sex and of creativity. They feel that unimaginative, insensitive thuds of regularity are how it's done. Hammering away mechanically gives a sense of detached power. It seems to say, "I'm impervious and nothing can affect me. You're not going to catch *me* being human."

Even if the music is not pop music, it is easy to hear the overemphasis of downbeats that permeates our culture. Thus Baroque music becomes "sewing machine" music. If the focus is on punching out the downbeats, does anyone hear the rest of what could be going on? In playing music, there are so many possibilities, explorations, and experimentations that make it endlessly fascinating.

The beat, the pulse, and how to feel it is an interesting question. How do you feel it in each circumstance? If defining and emphasizing each downbeat is musically warranted, fine, but the music may have a chance to speak better if you stop the "pulse counting" and fly. The melodic lines should not be chopped up by the beats. Find ways to bring out the more meaningful beats, and then soar gracefully through the beats that don't need emphasis. They are naturally present without being punched.

Stay steady with the melodic lines, and they will stop being broken up by relentless downbeats. There is more singing and more life in the long phrases. We can look to where we are going as if there were long distances between certain downbeats, leaving the intervening beats felt as part of the soaring. There is more room for grace and beauty. Our wings are soaring while our heart beats a quiet undercurrent of rhythm under our feathered breast.

This might mean feeling the rhythm in our whole body. We may have been taught to tap a foot to keep a steady beat, but sometimes this can feel too artificial like the foot is being used to impose another "tyranny of downbeats." Somehow detached from the rest of the body, the foot is trying to insist that we obey what it tells us. This can bring conflict and distraction within the body. We want to be wholebodied and wholly involved, not to impose a separate role for our foot. Foot tapping can create an unnecessary bodily disconnect and dissipation of energy.

Instead of making our foot work so hard, we can put energy into listening and having more trust in our ability to naturally feel the beats. The beat becomes steadier, more direct, and more accurate. Have you ever watched a cat react to a sudden noise? It will startle so immediately that it appears to be "pre-immediately," almost a nanosecond before the noise. In playing music, staying alert with a tiny amount of anticipation helps to keep the rhythm accurate. Alternatively, variations of anticipation and delay (even tempo changes) could be part of your intentional color palette.

When playing in an ensemble, foot tapping is bothersome to others. No one wants to see, out of the corner of their eye, someone's foot tapping. People tap differently. Some tap eagerly, slightly before the beat—it's their personal body messaging. Others tap in a laid-back delay. Even if a fellow musician is tapping perfectly in sync with our own sense of the music and the desired "tightness" of the group, it is *still* visually distracting.

If you have a habit of tapping your foot, you can tap a few toes unseen within your shoe, and no one will be bothered. Another reason not to tap one's foot is that it can physically add to tension. Standing is the best position for playing the flute, and good posture begins with stability in the feet and legs. The legs and feet should be as relaxed as possible. To lift the front part of a foot to tap can mean shifting more weight onto the other foot. Tapping is a repetitive motion and can be a waste of energy. A sense of the rhythm can be felt in a variety of parts of the body and needn't be imposed only on a foot.

Polishing—Make It Whole

THE CIRCUMSTANCE OF AN UPCOMING PERFORmance can be stressful, but we can disentangle our thoughts about the situation from our dedication to the music itself. As much as possible, make them two different worlds. The music will please us the most, and our concentration in that beauty will result in the most gratification. The details in the arrangements of the event are important, but dwelling in the music must be the main focus.

When a piece can be played from beginning to end yet small mistakes still occur, there are methods to find a more steady confidence. Foremost, we must be sure to have an adequate intake of air in all areas of the music. Often mistakes occur when we are "running on empty." Practicing the piece for the sole purpose of practicing our best breathing in every passage goes a long way toward "smooth sailing."

Start at the end. It is natural to play the beginning of a piece more than the end. This tendency, as well as dealing with fatigue at the end, means we must be extra attentive to keeping the last portion of the piece vital and alive. We can devise an approach to practicing the end. One approach is to practice the last two measures, then the last six measures, then the last twelve measures, or the last quarter of the piece, moving up to the last half of the piece.

We can remind ourselves of our goals in each movement by writing a directive at the top of the page for our expressive goal (for example, "steady," "calm," "walking," "angelic," or "mercurial."). This might seem like a silly idea, as with all the practice we have done, we surely would remember the feel of each movement. Yet in a performance situation, seeing these words can help refocus when jumping from one movement to the next.

To have an overview of the piece, we might think of the expression, "The whole is greater than the sum of its parts." In reality, every detail of the "sum of the parts" is important, while the trajectory of the whole movement and the whole piece can be constantly felt. To thoroughly get the sense of the direction of each phrase, we can play over passages until they seem like one even-flowing line. The entire work can become one flowing line no matter the changes and silences along the way. After playing the first phrase or two, we can ask ourselves, *Can I hear the ending from here? Can I hear the whole ride to the end?* Or we might imagine one sound, a foundation that is the rails beneath the train, a continuous direction.

Make sure there are no "holes" in the energy and direction of the piece. Holes can appear when we lose the drive, perhaps in a quiet section. The energy drops out! Energy must be kept up even in a contrasting section. Even a silence must have energy.

In the practice session, sing the piece, paying attention to how one phrase connects to another. Singing the piece shows us the spots where we lose energy. If there is a long rest in which others play, sing those parts too. Study a silent rest, and ask what kind of energy gathers here. When we make our musical entrance, we will be in context.

It helps to make a recording of ourselves and listen for areas where we may be letting the energy down. Observations and ideas can be penciled on the page. I sometimes draw a long arrow over the top of a line or phrase to indicate *keep directional energy going.*

Phrase by phrase, feel each gesture, and be guided by where it goes and where it lands. Feel long "sentences" and the relationships of the phrases to the larger whole. Locate the climaxes. What kind of climaxes are they? Loud, poignant, speedy? Play the sentences from end to beginning (start with the last phrase, then the previous phrase, etc.).

Be careful not to lose the energy in slow pieces or slow sections. Slow pieces often require more energy to play than fast music. You can't be passive. You can't assume, *These notes are easy.* The music may be quiet, dreamy, and contemplative, yet you must remain alert, awake, and actively creating. You are inside the music, and you are generating it. Keep plenty of air support. Keep the tempo and rhythms precise, or if you are playing more rubato in places, keep your artistically decided placements of notes precisely where you want them. You are slowly and deliberately saying something important. Slow music is surprisingly harder to play than fast music, because every detail of expression and emotion can be felt, making you and your artistry exposed. Be alert and tuned in, and you will say it exactly how you want to say it.

Technical Difficulties

When we find ourselves frustrated by a difficult passage, we must throw out the bitter brew of fear, doubt, and frustration. Focus on love for the music at hand and music in general. Replacing fear with love maintains a more relaxed and confident attitude. It generates a more musical approach, which will enhance our methodical approach. We can dwell in our art as we calmly practice.

By practicing slowly but correctly, we are training our reflexes. Impatiently playing a passage faster than our workable speed, even if we make only a few mistakes, trains our innocent reflexes to include and accept mistakes that may show up again even though we consciously know the correct notes. We need to slow to whatever speed necessary (using a metronome) to assure ourselves that we can play every time without mistakes. Gradually, we can bring the tempo up a little at a time. With patience and lots of good practice, we will soon be at the tempo we seek.

Flutist Roger S. Stevens spoke about how we learn consciously and unconsciously:

> *The unconscious portion of the mind is what the flutist is constantly training as he practices. Because of the inability of the unconscious mind to discriminate between correct and incorrect, it is essential that everything the flutist does in practice be absolutely accurate. This is the reason for slow practice.*
>
> *If the player is already an accomplished performer, but, for some reason, lacks confidence in his playing, he may be unable to turn over the job of negotiating a difficult passage to his "computer" (unconscious mind). He will try to do the job at the much slower conscious level, 'getting in his own way,' and countermanding the neural patterns established by his preconditioning (practice).*

He will spoil the passage for two reasons: even though this conscious mind is precise, it is slower than his unconscious mind; there will be two sets of impulses going to his fingers, tongue, or embouchure with an inevitably confused result.[2]

—Roger S. Stevens

A surprisingly effective approach to a technical problem is to forget the technical problem and play from the inspiration of the musical character and meaning. The technical problems will often self-correct with our impetus toward the expression we are seeking.

Depression and Discouragement

Depression has many facets and depths. One facet is the feeling of being disconnected—a longing to feel engaged. How can we engage ourselves in spite of being depressed? Playing music can help. Flying with the music can invoke a vision that our ability to soar allows us to rise up and see all around. Fresh viewpoints and expanses are available to us.

Depression can be a natural response to many issues in our lives, one of which might be haunting memories. There are ways to transform the feeling of being stuck. In his book *Walking Your Blues Away: How to Heal the Mind and Create Emotional Well-Being*, Thom Hartmann describes ways to lighten the burdens of stuck memories. By gently focusing on one small element of your memory—one detail of your perceptions of the event, perhaps the angle of your view, the detail of one color, noticing a smell—what was once a static memory that was almost "carved in stone" has a slightly new view. This subtle change in perception can make the memory less haunting.³

Sometimes being depressed influences our playing in a profound and insightful way. At the beginning of the Gulf War, I was so depressed (not knowing that it was only the beginning of our current endless wars) about the oil greed and the resulting human tragedy, grief, and misery of yet more war, I could not play. I tried. I leafed through music and could not find anything that I could focus on. I could not connect with any music that I had in my files. In my two volumes of transcriptions of Bach's solo cello suites and violin partitas, I found *Prelude to Cello Suite No. 2* BWV 1008. I had worked on it before, but now it spoke to me and I to it. I played it again and again not only to learn it but to feel its noble and expansive perspective.

Perspective is the key. Happiness is a perspective. It isn't always the click-your-heels kind of happy but an overall love for life. For example, when we think of our own death, we all face a daunting mystery. We know it ends the life we currently live. We can feel fear at the reality, but since the present contains us living, breathing, and seeing, why not do these with gusto? Playing music, watching light on the land and sea, giving each other acknowledgment and support—these are the things we are here for.

We can be depressed by the thought, *Nobody cares that I am working so hard to be a good musician*. We would be right. Our culture does not acknowledge the work; it thinks only of so-called "talent" (disembodied from the actual work) and commercial success. In contrast, in India, the life-work and practice of a musician is widely respected. In the United States, we must rely on ourselves for respect. It is our responsibility to hold up our end. Our long-range effort offers something beautiful, while the work is highly individual and alone. It is possible to honor and enjoy being alone and not be lonely.

Some days we may be discouraged with our playing. If we keep playing in spite of this feeling, we may be surprised. A "bad day" offers the opportunity to analyze why it is not our best. In consultation with our mind's ear, we can reach for an idea, *What would make it better?* If we come up with one idea and run with it, that one idea could bring sunlight and life to the music. Perhaps we will find ourselves coming up with a wealth of ideas. A practice session that starts out with dissatisfaction might become an important turning point for us, and with discovery built upon discovery, the insights may be exponential. A bad day can be more valuable and satisfying than a good day.

It takes supreme gentleness not to berate yourself when you are feeling down. Remember that you would not be so unkind to another person who is feeling low. Have respect for the growth of human capabilities: your own. You are:

- Capable of manifesting what you hear in your imagination
- Capable of intuiting what will make it work
- Capable of discovery
- Capable of experimentation
- Capable of "loosening up" and finding more freedom
- Capable of patiently trying again

In disciplining ourselves to practice each day, we have the privilege of working with colors of sound. We must keep working, keep practicing. If we are downhearted and uninspired, we can hold on to a kind of faith that we will work through it. Nothing is everlasting except changeability itself.

We might begin by choosing a few tones, slowly making large adjustments and gradually making finer adjustments until the tone becomes clear and satisfying. Those adjustments might be to relax the lips more, change the angle of the column of air as it divides against the edge of the embouchure, lengthen posture, hold the flute parallel to floor, keep the head balanced on the axis of the spine, relax the neck, and open the throat. Replace any heaviness in the heart with a flexible, mercurial energy. With this energy, the music will come alive, and so will we.

Practice Gaps

It is important to play every day, but if practice is not possible for a long period, we needn't be afraid to pick up our instrument again. Instead of assuming we are hopelessly behind, we may find ourselves amazingly ahead. Life influences music, and music influences life. As life development matures us, our physical and mental approach to playing improves. Perhaps this is because attachment to rigid expectations have eased, and we have become less habitual and more relaxed. We are open to more discovery. Work may be required to reactivate reflexes and regain flexibility in tone qualities, but there is also the pleasant surprise that our attitude and musical insight have matured along with us. This outlook will be a large motivation that propels our learning and our inspiration. With joy and without fear, we can pick up our estranged instrument and delight in it anew.

6

Aware Care

A person's practice space should include a safe surface to open the case and assemble the instrument. Musicians commonly neglect to provide themselves and each other with a small table to open a case or briefly set down the instrument. We fill our living spaces with objects that gather dust while providing no space for an instrument we use daily and value so highly.

The instrument is a beloved friend, a personal treasure as well as an expensive object. Even a "cheap" instrument is not cheap in terms of its value to the life of the person playing it. An inexpensive instrument can sound as good or even better than an expensive one depending on how it is played—a fact easily proved in the hands of an experienced flutist.

Whether it is made with nickel, silver, gold, or platinum, along with their alloys, a flute is made of soft metals. A flute can be dented by even the gentlest of taps. Although an accidental dent can be repaired and appear to be fixed, the intonation may be permanently compromised. The instrument is no longer in tune with itself or with others. The frustration of trying to adjust to an impaired instrument might bring discouragement and lost interest. What do you do if you can't afford to fix the instrument, and buying a new one is out of the question?

For these reasons, I lived in mortal fear of harm coming to my flute, and I would hold it rather than risk placing it anywhere. However, it is occasionally necessary to use both hands to adjust a music stand or do another brief task. Care should be taken to set the flute in a safe place, not where people will be moving around it and are unlikely to be aware of its presence. I shudder when I see someone set a flute on a chair with one or both ends sticking out beyond the seat. It would be easy for anyone walking by to accidentally knock it off.

If you must ask someone to hold your flute for a short while, be sure it is someone who understands the care that should be taken. That person needs to know not to hold it around the assemblage of keys. Keys, rods, posts, and springs can get bent out of adjustment. The flute should not be held solely by the head joint. If the fitting is relatively loose, the weight of the body could allow it to fall away from the head joint and land on the floor.

One should never set a flute on a bed. As a kid, I often set my flute down on my bed. One day, in a playful tussle with my younger brother, I lost my balance and fell, landing on top of my flute, bending it near the foot joint. It was repairable, but the foot joint never fit perfectly. I was devastated, but the accident made me careful ever since.

In the 1970s, I was teaching flute lessons at a music store in a small studio near its instrument repair shop. Part of the arrangement for renting the space was a trade whereby the repairman would occasionally ask me to test the flutes he was repairing. I would see the before and after. Flutes from the local school bands would arrive with the most nightmarish damage: huge dents and twisted keys. The repairman could work wonders. I often felt as if I were a nurse in a "flute hospital." I once woke from a bad dream in which I was trying to stop a childish play-fight where a group of kids were wildly brandishing flutes like swords!

Assembly

WHEN WE OPEN THE FLUTE CASE TO ASSEMBLE THE beautifully made instrument, we should honor what this "object" means to us. Among all the objects we may possess, this one is a part of ourselves. It is our voice, our inner world, and our ticket to travel in discovery and beauty.

Be observant that the assembly is not done as a mundane chore but with care and awareness. Make sure the tendons are clear of dust and grit. Avoid gripping the flute over the key system while fitting the tendons together. It is best to hold the flute only on its body without putting stress on the key assemblage or the lip plate. To join the head joint to the body of the flute, hold the body near the joint fitting. To join the foot joint to the body, hold the foot joint at its end, away from the keys, and again hold the body near the joint fitting. Each joint or segment should be lined up carefully and fitted together with minimal rotating to avoid unnecessary wear and tear. One small turn should be all that is needed to slide it in place. The fittings should not be excessively snug or loose.

Take the time to let the assembled flute warm to room temperature (or warm it quickly by holding it close to your heart). Blowing warm air into it can help but can produce too much condensation as the warm moist air hits the cold metal. A cold flute will sound flat and require many adjustments as you play until it reaches a more-or-less steady temperature and can remain in tune. In any performance or rehearsal when you have a tacet or lengthy rest in the music, be aware of keeping the flute warm to avoid coming in flat on the next entrance.

When not playing, the safest place to put the flute is in its case. The dangers of leaving it out are many: people moving around it unaware it is there, someone deciding to move it or try it out, or children or pet animals moving about. Knowing it is stored in a safe place gives peace of mind. This might mean that when other musicians leave their instruments out (say, during a rehearsal break), they may wonder why you put yours in its case. In addition to being a safety measure, putting your flute away offers a good opportunity to swab out moisture and wipe clear the lip plate.

After a practice session, rehearsal, or concert, cleaning and putting away a flute requires care. A cleaning cloth that is not textured or abrasive will avoid wearing, scratching, or dulling the surfaces. Soft, absorbent cotton cloth works well to swab out moisture. I use cotton jersey. The cloth must not be bunched too widely around the cleaning rod, or it could cause friction against the key pads (especially those that remain closed like the G#, E♭, C, and the trill keys). Friction against the pads could wear down or break the delicate membrane. Avoid scratching the inside wall of the flute with cleaning rods (or floor stands). As you look "down the barrel" to make sure you have dried all moisture, check that the inner wall is smooth and polished. Some people laugh at me for being fussy about the inner bore and keeping it smooth and unscratched. I base my judgment on the finest Japanese shakuhachi flutes, (made from the lowest segments of giant bamboo), in which the inner bore is highly polished.

> *Lacquering is a very delicate procedure most crucial in establishing the correct tonality. The urushi is applied with long human-hair brushes in several layers. This is a process which, on the finest flutes, may take as long as*

> *a year to complete; these instruments vary inside by no more than the thickness of a piece of newspaper. Differences are so subtle on flutes of this quality that they are discernible only to players who have many years of experience behind them. Meian shakuhachis, being more simply constructed, are not inlayed and are lacquered with only a thin coating of urushi. On both Kinko and Tozan flutes the bore is polished to a glass-like finish.*[1]
>
> —MONTY L. LEVENSON

When swabbing, fold a portion of the cleaning cloth over the end of the cleaning rod to keep the rod from gouging or scratching. Keeping the cloth over the end helps to wick moisture from the mouthpiece near the fitting for the cork. Avoid using too much pressure against this fitting, as any shifting of the cork will change the flute's general intonation. A friend who works on flutes once did a repair on my old Haynes flute. As a gift, he made me a wooden cleaning rod fitted with a leather loop at the end to hold the cloth. I have used it ever since, assured that I am less likely to scratch the inside with these materials.

Leaving the damp cleaning cloth inside the case can cause mildew problems and compromise the pads. On the other hand, in a dry climate, a small piece of clean cloth dampened with a small amount of distilled water can be left in the case near the mouthpiece (not near the keys) as a short-term humidifier. I use distilled water, because tap water is full of chlorine and other chemicals, and bottled water may have minerals that are fine to drink but not so good for a flute.

Dampen a clean piece of cotton jersey cloth with a little distilled water, and clean the oily smudges made by the fingers and lips. This maintains the flute's polished appearance and prevents corrosion caused by acids from the skin. It helps to have a plentiful supply of cloths for cleaning, enough to use a clean one (or two or three) each day. Avoid washing them with harsh detergents; use milder soaps. Q-Tips come in handy. Dampen them with distilled water to remove fine lint or dust from around the assemblage of posts and springs.

Before playing, it helps to have clean teeth. A flutist I knew (who was also a fine flute repairman) mentioned to me that certain toothpastes are better than others and less likely to cause stickiness in key pads. I am not sure which toothpastes are better. Perhaps it is wise to avoid those with sodium saccharin, a petroleum-based sugar substitute. All toothpastes have sweetener. To rinse the mouth thoroughly may help with this problem. Having a clean mouth makes the subtle work required of the lips, tongue, and breathing feel clear and smooth.

Sticky key pads are annoying and can lead to ongoing problems. One method to silence a "tacky" pad is to blot it with a piece of cigarette paper. Gently place the paper (avoiding the edge of glue) between the troublesome key and its tone hole ring. Gently and evenly depress the key. Avoid pulling on the paper, as it should be only placed there as a thin blotter. This may need to be done more than once to get rid of the clicking sounds of stickiness.

Molecules and Vibrations

AN OLDER INSTRUMENT DOES NOT SOUND THE SAME as it did when it was new—it sounds better! It acquires certain qualities from the player. It was explained to me that with the vibration of fine tones played over time, the molecules line up in certain ways and cause the instrument to take on characteristic sound qualities. Perhaps it is more the atoms, ions, and/or electrons. People laugh when I talk about this, but we live in vibrations of molecules, which is what sound waves are. Perhaps this could be one more reason the fine violins of the sixteenth, seventeenth, and eighteenth centuries, built by Stradivari, Amati, Guarneri, and their apprentices, sound as beautiful as they do. Their extraordinary sound may not be solely because of the fine wood, unique carving, and mysterious finishing techniques of the master luthiers. Added to these extraordinary attributes is the physical influence of the beautiful sounds made by past musicians who held and played these instruments. The vibration produced by playing with beautiful, singing tones has given the instrument a certain structural alignment of atoms and molecules.

The enriched and finer sound that an instrument can acquire through playing is acknowledged by master Japanese shakuhachi flute makers.

> *Older, well-played shakuhachis are far superior in quality to newer instruments. The longer the flute has been around, the more it has been played, the better it is.*[2]
>
> —MONTY H. LEVENSON

On a coarser vibrational level, it is important to protect an instrument being transported in a car or other vehicle. Some padding under it may help to mitigate the vibrations and bumps of the road so they don't cause unnecessary wear. The case can be placed on your lap or on a folded blanket, pillow, jacket, or piece of foam, or set within another case that is padded. Make sure the case is right-side up. If there is a slight possibility of the flute shifting inside the case, keeping the case right-side up will avoid weight or repetitive stress, however subtle, on the keys, posts, and rods.

Be mindful of the temperature in any situation where your flute is stored temporarily such as in a car on a hot summer day. Being kept in a place that is too cold or too hot can wreak havoc on the pads. After a rehearsal, if I need to stop for errands, I take my flute out of the car and carry it with me. It is small enough that it fits in a briefcase, large handbag, or backpack.

Everything that is has a history. A flute once existed as ores, in veins in the Earth. It is well acquainted with soil, water, minerals, elements, magnetic and gravitational fields, and ancient stars. It helps to think of a flute this way instead of thinking of it as a commodity or a product. A flute is of the Earth and the stars in origin and in spirit.

7

Approach and Perspective

What is strength? Not brute force but strength? The mistake of using force instead of strength causes deficiency and disappointment in our playing. Forcing causes a loss of range of expression, a loss of smoothness and clear articulation. To play from our natural strength allows us to be heard and understood even when we are playing quietly. Natural strength is a type of energy.

An aikido exercise illustrates the difference. It is called "unbendable arm." If you stand and lift one arm, extending it out to the side and parallel with the floor, and challenge another person to bend your arm at the elbow, the other person can accomplish this easily. Try it again, this time extending the arm using all your muscle strength to keep the other person from bending it. The person should use reasonable pressure, not in a manner that would cause pain. With reasonable effort, the person succeeds in bending the arm despite your muscular resistance.

Extend your arm and your fingers to point at an object or spot on a wall, something you see across the room. Direct all your energy to that object, aiming your focus and your concentration—in other words, your *chi* energy—channeled through the arm and fingers. Maintain concentration in directing your energy through your arm and fingers to the object as the other person tries to bend your arm. Now the person is unable to bend it (with a reasonable and sincere effort, not brutal force). It is a revelation how this works. You have enduring strength. Life energy or chi is stronger than forced strength.

Chi is the concept of a life force like "may the Force be with you" of the *Star Wars* movies. It is an important concept for many ancient cultures and is used in medicine and healing as well as in martial arts such as tai chi chuan, qigong, aikido, kendo, and kung fu. "Unbendable arm" is one of the popular demonstrations of chi energy. Others are "immovable body" and "unraisable body."

Strength can come from focusing and directing energy, and directing energy can be the foundation of playing an instrument. For flute playing, using chi can be a way of keeping presence and direction throughout a musical work. Energy and focus are always *on* whether the music is fast or slow, simple or complex, loud or soft. To crescendo to a peak and segue into a tender melody shows no loss of power or energy. On the contrary, keeping the energy directed produces a kind of transformational power. Chi can generate strength of conviction be it love, tenderness, or other emotional qualities inherent in the musical statement.

To "extend chi," that sense of directing life energy, of aim, of concentrating consciousness and purpose, can help guide many aspects of our playing. One vital aspect that extending chi can influence is tone quality.

Keeping Up Your Energy: Your Chi

To create qualities of strength in flute tone is not necessarily an effort to be loud. Strength can be carried by having a more openly broad "extended chi." Think panpipes.

When played well, they have an almost whispered quality, yet the sound carries with astonishing strength. When one of the fine groups of musicians from Peru, Ecuador, or Bolivia is on tour in North America, they sometimes grace an outdoor public space with their incredible sounds and beautiful melodies. The whispered sounding tones of the panpipes magically carry for long distances and over noisy city spaces like a strand of mist traveling to your ear.

When playing panpipes, we automatically adjust in order to produce the sounds with a more open mouth and relaxed lips. This same openness can be applied to playing a modern flute to achieve a deep, broad sound that carries "far and wide." It is a big sound and can be heard clearly without force, without being loud. The quality of the tone is large and colorful, not forced through a narrow, pinched, metallic, or labored approach.

Perhaps this difference between loud-yet-sounding-narrow and relaxed-yet-projecting-broadly is what flutist Murray Panitz (1925–1989) meant when he said,

> *I have found instrumentalists whose tone seems really big close by, but when you walked away from them, the tone did not project as far, but the smaller tone that you heard next to you traveled farther. I don't know what the physical processes are but that is an observation on my part.*[1]
>
> —Murray Panitz

The Japanese shakuhachi, an end-blown flute made from the lower segments of giant bamboo, has a sound that carries broadly and is powerful without sounding forced. Sound qualities and tone colors of the shakuhachi have a rich color palette in the hands of a fine player.[2] The sound has an uncanny ability to be *inclusive*. By inclusive, I mean it can be so present in the moment that whatever else is happening—bird song, street noise—feels like part of the broad, open presence of the music rather than an interruption or distraction. No wonder shakuhachi is associated with Zen.* The sound is so natural. (More on Sui-Zen in chapter 10.)

Chi energy can focus and extend airflow to maintain a steady stream of windpower. In our playing this generates a feeling of life energy, steady purpose, and direction. It can give a feeling of always moving forward, always being *on*, with never a drop in our energy. A steady airflow is the foundation of our musical energy. *Breathe through the phrase*. By "breathe through," I mean push air continuously through each interval, each line. Sing a *steady sing*. This steady sing, through our constant flow of air, generates energy whether we are playing legato, staccato, large intervals of pitch, contrast of dynamics, or long-range phrasing. We generate everything with it.

With the steady generation of energy, a long phrase can be played as if it were a single sustained note moving toward a conclusion (which itself may be another beginning). The whole piece may be played as a *beginning* that flies in one big sweep of motion to the *ending*. While being present in every detail, you can maintain an overview that extends your consciousness to the shape of the entire architecture. You are the master cathedral builder, giving placement and balance to every structure in an overall design. From the first note to the conclusion, you maintain energy in that overview.

Feel each gesture, and sing each "word." Phrase by phrase, reveal the arc of each sentence: beginning, middle, and end. Feel the potential ending in each beginning or in each ending the potential beginning. Space is important in our cathedral. Feel the life in silences that are full of existence.

Maintain strength and aliveness in the end of a phrase and in the last note. The last note speaks of all the life in the music that was just present, and it creates energy that moves into being finished and complete. It may not necessarily be the length that gives a last note impact but the energy with which it is spoken. This is not a time to think, *Well, here is the inevitable ending, and now I'm done.* Stay with the meaning of the last note. Let it ring out as part of what was spoken, and let it influence the following silence. The music that spoke so eloquently is slowly walking away.

Playing Flute by Not Playing Flute

IT IS POSSIBLE TO QUIT THINKING OF YOURSELF AS AN instrumentalist. To directly find your expression and send it out, it is helpful to bypass the mechanics and even your thoughts of how you operate this instrument. You *are* manipulating the instrument, but it is *you yourself* doing the singing. You are a voice. It is your body that creates the depth of sound and your artistic will that expresses the meaning. You are playing the flute by not playing the flute. You might tell yourself, *Don't lean on the instrument*, meaning don't rely on the instrument itself to make the sounds work. It is you. It's your desire to sing out and express your music, not a desire to be instrumental.

Through years of practice, you have given your body the know-how to reach for what you want artistically from moment to moment. You have trained your fingers in the right touch, smoothness in transitions, and agility from note to note. The breathing, the lips, the posture, the chest with emanations from the heart—your whole body is resonating and allowing you to produce colors in tone and expression. As you play, you can trust that your body will unite these abilities and respond to your specific direction in artistic expression.

Even if there are imperfections, let your artistic musical desire guide you in learning the technique. While you are concentrating on the "story" in sound or the "sound dance" that you are expressing, the mechanics, column of air, posture, adequate intake of air, finger transitions, etc., will follow your inspiration. Practicing is more fun and creative when along the way you give yourself real glimpses of your expression and how cool it will eventually sound. Run with that motivation, and your abilities will grow exponentially.

You might say to yourself, *This series of notes is a challenging pattern, but what quality do I want? Is it joyful, racy, dancing, driven, playful, sparkling?* Okay, now, every time I use techniques to practice this passage, like playing it slowly, parts of it isolated, backward, different rhythms, whatever it takes to get it in the fingers, I must foremost work with the colors, the qualities, and the feel.

Unnecessarily separating the technical from the artistic makes two modes of practice out of what should be one. If we are playing technically as a separate exercise, at some point we will wonder, *Will I be able to pull this off when the time comes to play it musically?* This doubt can displace a more positive, one-pointed motivation: *I am aiming for the best musical quality.* A difficult passage practiced separately as an exercise should retain its living musical qualities, never to be played one dimensionally. To play in a mechanical, lifeless way removes us from the music and turns off the inspiration, the magic, and the fun of discovery.

"Mechanicus"

IN A LETTER TO HIS FATHER, MOZART CRITICIZED the pianoforte playing of the well-known pianist and composer Muzio Clementi.[3]

> *Clementi plays well so far as execution with the right hand is concerned; his forte is passages in thirds. Aside from this he hasn't a pennyworth of feeling or taste; in a word he is a mere mechanician.*[4] *(in another translation: "mechanicus")*
>
> —W. A. Mozart

Why is it that some of us relinquish our naturalness to a mechanical approach? Perhaps it is because we think machines are infallible, always performing as expected. The assumption that playing must meet an expected standard may be part of the problem. We may be clinging to an ideal of how to be "correct."

Too much of an academic approach in an effort to be correct can result in coolness and distance. The notes are all there in their places, but they lack meaning. On the other end of the spectrum, music that is played too melodramatically can become cloying and sickly sweet. Being too mechanical or too cloying can sabotage the natural ability for the music to have meaning. The key word is "natural."

Flutist Jean-Pierre Rampal spoke about finding this naturalness within yourself:

> *If some people overblow on the flute, they should be asked, 'How would you sing this phrase? Not as a singer, but naturally, without any effort—for the pleasure.' Try it out with a man who has a bad style, and he will not sound the same because he is singing naturally. You cannot force something which is natural. So listen to your playing, listen to your singing—that is the thing, to play like you sing or like you act, like you speak. Then you will find the truth.*[5]
>
> —Jean-Pierre Rampal

Love: The Larger Motivating Force

THINK OF LOVE NOT AS A LONGING, NOT AS A NEED. Think of love as rejoicing or a kind of respectful exploration. The love of life that is rejoicing, accepting, and involved in rich exploration wants to know, dares to ask questions, and finds the encouragement to be creative. This love enjoys a respect for gentleness and growth of human capacities. Sure, these open sensitivities can be exhausting, overwhelming, and even painful at times, but they serve a person in all aspects of life including a capacity to feel, to notice, to be open to discovery in music, or any other art or endeavor.

Rejoicing, accepting, exploring, asking questions, and finding encouragement all inform our progress in music. The pathway can be rocky. Many times when we show up for a practice session, a rehearsal, or a gig, we may be feeling less than large. Our energy may be low; we may be sad or angry. Just by beginning, by dipping a toe into the clear, lively waters of our art, we soon find ourselves swimming or maybe flying, walking, skipping, dancing, or running. One kind of energy can morph into another.

Listeners are listening for our musical, nonverbal encouragement. Our musical presence resonates with them and touches them, because they also have these same emotional capacities. They are able to connect with what is a part of their conscious or subconscious experience or thought. They can even venture into some aspects that are relatively uncharted territory. Musicians help bring about a kind of harmony, actually as well as figuratively.

The musician and the music are not "products." Music is not divorced from the creative process and the experience. A concert or a recording leaves the listener with feelings. Later it is possible to access memories of how it sounds and remember the joy of hearing it, but these are *experiences*, not products. As performers and as listeners, we are not merely consumers. We are fellow travelers in life.

Your Artistic Realms

WHAT IS THE TRUE PERSONAL PROGRESSION FROM the years of practice? What is the true expression from within of the love, the work, the fascination, our unique experience, our voice? Contemplating these questions can lead us more deeply into our artistic nature.

When we play, the life of the music comes through our life and all the subtleties we perceive that are a part of our growth and imaginative character. We can let certain musical influences be part of our approach, or we can carve out a unique path. In any case, we are on our own life journey as a musician.

Why not gravitate toward maximum expression—to say what means the most to us, to step out in the world and the universe imaginatively? Let our voices be heard! Enter the noble realms of delicacy, the realms of vistas, the realms of change, the realms of searching. We can sing our heart to the sky. We can be with every note nakedly. It is *our* voice in the universe or, better, *with* the universe.

Music Helps People Think

WE HEAR ABOUT STUDENTS DOING BETTER IN THEIR studies when they listen to recordings of Bach or other Baroque music. Music helps us think, but why? Perhaps it has to do with the thought patterns of the composers—not their verbal language patterns but their nonverbal musical explorations. Where do these come from? Partly they come from ancestors.

Partly it is their cultural inheritance carried forward. Partly it is their receptiveness to Nature and human nature. Partly it is their individual inspiration and genius. Some would say that perhaps part of their thought patterns come from the visiting muse that seems to move through them.

Russian composer Aram Khachaturian wrote his famous *Violin Concerto in D Minor* during an inspired two and a half months:

> *I was writing it with strong enthusiasm. I was overflowing with musical ideas, surpassing the speed of their writing on the note paper.*[6]
>
> —ARAM KHACHATURIAN

The great violinist David Oistrakh, to whom the concerto was dedicated, gave a premiere performance on September 16, 1940, in Moscow. Here Oistrakh speaks of the concerto:

> *I clearly remember the summer day of 1940, when A. Khachaturian came to our residence in the country. He was so seized by his new composition that he dashed to the grand piano right away. Playing with his inherent ardor and inspiration he fascinated all of us. The music seemed to be sparkling–sincere, original, witty, full of melodic beauty and national coloring.…the Concerto still gladdens listeners with…an unforgettable impression. A new outstanding work was obviously born and would have to live a great life at the concert stage.*[7]
>
> —DAVID OISTRAKH

In 1968, Khachaturian encouraged Rampal to transcribe the great violin concerto for flute. Rampal had been a pioneer in solo flute performance in an era when it was not common to see a flute virtuoso on stage, and there were fewer works written for flute. The Khachaturian concerto is one of the first contemporary major concert works for flute soloist. Today, the recordings of Oistrakh's performances of the concerto are an enormous inspiration for flutists who are learning the work.[8]

Thought Patterns

My commute to work, driving along the foothills of the eastern slope of the Rocky Mountains in Colorado, took about thirty-five minutes. It was an enjoyable ride with views of the hills and plains, passing ranches with beautiful horses in their fields. One of the best parts was the chance to listen to some wonderful music on the sound system, improved and updated by my husband.

A recording of pianist Andras Schiff playing two Mozart piano concerti (Nos. 20 and 21) became my favorite. Schiff's phrasing is awake, conscious, and sensitive. Night after night for almost a year, these concerti accompanied my drive home. I noticed that my dulled brain, tired from the day's work, would be revitalized, almost as if the music was clear, fresh air allowing my mind to fully breathe. The music drew me into its diverse compositional wonders stated with depth and imagination by Schiff's fine playing. I began to analyze why it had such a transformational effect and to observe in the moment what was happening as I listened.[9]

I noticed that the music seemed to be speaking in thought patterns. These were Mozart's and Schiff's musical insights. The nonverbal subjects, places, and directions were broad and varied, spanning depths of sadness to heights of joy. I recognized that I was listening to thought patterns that were melding with my own. It became apparent to me how thought patterns could move from the familiar to more fluid landscapes. Not only were there readily understandable thoughts and feelings, but I felt I was being led to new pathways and introduced to better realms.

How do we explore these musical thought patterns in our own playing? When alone, we can enjoy being alone, looking for honesty by relating closely to ourselves. Individuality gives meaning to the music. Music reveals thought patterns when the weave of the composition is brought to light by the musician in his or her individual way. Our music is free to move into insightful new realms of musical thought when we step out into the world and stay true to ourselves.

Body Tone

THE THING THAT GIVES BODY TO OUR MUSICAL tone is our body.

I attended a master class with renowned flutist and conductor Ransom Wilson.[10] He had many helpful suggestions, one of which was to listen to and observe great singers. He said that he had learned a great deal from attending performances of opera star Montserrat Caballé.[11] I kept this in mind, as over the years, I observed singers in concert and online.

A friend invited me to hear Shlomo Carlebach, popularly known as "the singing rabbi." He sang while accompanying himself on guitar. His voice was enormous, as if there was a sound chamber in his chest. I began to think, *Yes, there are vocal chords there, but there is the chest and whole body generating the sound.* It inspired me to try this approach with flute.[12]

Philippe Jaroussky, the French countertenor, is one of the finest singers I have heard. He sings with heavenly shaped phrasing, relaxed huge, undetectable breaths, and complete focus dwelling in the grace of the music sung from his whole body resonating. To hear and see him can inspire an approach to playing the flute that is based in calmness and poise emanating from a kind of unity.[13]

A calm, unified approach is a full approach that produces resonant sound from the entire body. Some of the elements of that unity are as follows:

- Relaxed feet on the floor
- Balanced weight on the legs
- Engaged belly
- Backbone lengthened and tall
- The "big home" of the chest
- The feeling heart
- Shoulders using gravity to be relaxed downward
- Arms relaxed with energy flowing to the fingers
- Head balanced with no tension or constriction of neck or throat
- Jaw relaxed and open
- Eyes flexible
- Ears open with sensitivity
- Mind alert and brain oxygenated with great breathing
- The top of head held gently by a chord from the sky

These elements help form a unity. Play from that unity.

Learn from Everything, Everyone

We can learn from nearly everyone. Even when we listen to people whose playing leaves a lot to be desired, there's plenty of information there. What aspects work well? What aspects do not work, and why? As we listen, we can respect where that musician is on his or her path. Individuals who are actively involved with the art of music deserve respect for their engagement and their process. Even if with their best efforts they are not able to arrive at their own desired results, aspects of their approach and attitude can shine through. Their process can be beautiful and enlightening.

We can learn from everything. We can learn from hearing patterns of speech and ideas, expressions and actions, motion and movement, and even noise. Composer and music theorist John Cage loved noise. He enjoyed the sounds of busy city streets and felt that he was musically informed by noise.[14]

We can learn much from musicians who play other instruments, not just flutists. Some of the best lessons were given to me by violinist Maurice Bourg.[15] He was an octogenarian at the time, still in fine form after a long career in music in New York City and Los Angeles. I was playing at a small restaurant in Ashland, Oregon, one evening, and after he and his wife Julia dined, he approached me to let me know he liked the way I played Bach. I had read in the newspaper about his career as well as hers as a singer and about how they had chosen to retire in Ashland. I asked him if he might be willing to give me a lesson. Over about a year, I came to their house for lessons regularly. I also took singing lessons with Julia. Studying with Maurice was a joy, hearing his beautiful playing, laughing with his unusual sense of humor and receiving his generous critique and suggestions. Some of his violin students who were friends of mine envied me that I was able to enjoy his lighter side without enduring his well-known harshly critical side. Perhaps I was lucky I wasn't a violinist.

During a lesson, I was finishing a piece by Claude Debussy, playing the last quiet, introspective note, when the wind blew the front door wide open. We wheeled around in surprise to see the gaping doorway. Without skipping a beat, Maurice said calmly, "Oh, hello Claude, come in. She played it well, didn't she?"

Maurice emphasized the practice of dynamic range. On one occasion, he was playing an amazingly long *diminuendo* on the final note of a piece. Using the full length of the bow, he slowly drew the beautiful note quieter and quieter to almost nothing, right to the tip of the bow. He lifted the bow slightly, leaned forward, and blew a gentle breath on the tip as if to send the music on its way. It was funny and extremely beautiful.

In this era, a wealth of information is shared worldwide on the internet. We can attend some of the best performances, master classes, and lectures on YouTube. We can learn from pianists, guitarists, trumpet players, and percussionists. We can learn from everything and everyone. Something beautiful, something not so beautiful, something familiar, something novel—all can inform us and our music.

Meditation

LIKE MEDITATION, PRACTICING MUSIC IS JUST AS much working with the mind as working with the specifics of the music. Practice sessions are a focused meditation that can provide opportunities to grapple with the workings of our mind.

Even when we are well directed in our concentration on the music, distracting thoughts can easily arise. We can learn to let them go, but that also takes practice. Whether they are daydreams or demons of unwanted thoughts, we can choose how we want to deal with them. In time, we can learn to navigate through them more gracefully and quickly.

I once saw a poster at a Tibetan Buddhist center in Ashland, Oregon. The image was from a painting of a lion-faced Tibetan demon, fierce but almost smiling. Pouncing forward, the demon appeared about to leap out of the poster toward the viewer. The caption was a story about a man who was having a nightmare that a demon had chased him, overcome him, and was on his chest, pinning him down with crushing weight. Feeling that he couldn't breathe, the terrified man cried out in anguish, "Whatever shall I do?" The demon replied, "I don't know. It's your dream."

We need not be stuck if we remember that we have options. Our nagging thoughts may threaten to bring us down, but we can work with them. We can find ways to let them go, or set them aside by writing them down for later consideration. There are options. Thoughts are not permanent. (More on dealing with distraction in chapter 12.)

A practice session can be one of becoming more aware. Creative ideas can expand, and an inspiration may float your way when you least expect it. I have sometimes discovered a fresh new idea when I was completely tired out and about to stop practicing for the day.

Stuck in a Standard

Many flutists have a characteristic sound. A characteristic tone could perfectly reflect the natural and true character of the player. A consistent mode or style of playing could also be a stuck mode. Some flutists benefit from finding more variety.

A flutist's approach and awareness can be heard in his or her general tone quality. I have noticed and characterize some general tone qualities in these ways:

- Playing a metallic instrument—as if the instrument is doing the work
- Flowery, saccharine—flute as affable and cute
- Airy, fuzzy—unfocused
- Open panpipes—broad, diffuse
- Brassy, generally loud—steamrolling, domineering
- Biting, pushy, and edgy—trying to be a trumpet without the noble largesse
- Clear and cold—shivery, remote
- Urban jazz—under pitch, the lower quadrant of a pitch, almost flat
- Old fashioned—a dusty sound as if viewing antiques

These are not "wrong" tone qualities, but in my view, when a flute is played in just one of these modes, it can be a stuck mode without flexibility.

Aim to forget the instrument. The flute is not a flute but our own voice. We wouldn't want to use the same tone of voice to say, "The view is spectacular from this mountain top" as we would to say, "I'm all alone and sitting in this dingy, dark bar." In music, we can say all kinds of interesting things, but we wouldn't use the same voice for everything.

It is good to feel expansive, to perceive ourselves as being more out in the world. While playing music, we are stepping out into the world and into the universe. We are in space and talking with space actually and imaginatively. Our idea of space can vary—we can be speaking up close and intimately or be on a mountaintop, sending soaring tones outward. In reality, our bodies and minds and the sound vibrations we send forth travel in space. Even when privately practicing in our room, we are "out there" moving at gigantic speed as we stand on the blue planet.

Lightness

Lightness is having and cultivating a mercurial attitude in playing. It is being flexible in thought with an overview and interest in everything about the music—the joys and delights as well as the shadows and depths.

This attitude gives us range of sound and expression. We are freer to find a wide-open range of sound qualities instead of feeling "dug in," trying to have a consistent sound. The "dug in" quality is an effort flutists often make to homogenize their sound to make it standard, be more in control, or have a certain "bite" or "edge." This one-dimensional effort can defeat the purpose of bringing forth varied and expressive music.

"Digging in" narrows the tone and can make it harsher. You may want this "bite" quality for certain passages, but listen carefully. Hear the difference between a "harsh bite" and a "full-toned bite." Violinist Maurice Bourg helped me with this. He demonstrated for me by playing on his violin a single note very loud, very short, and very full toned. Slightly before this note, he was bearing down with the bow on the string. With a brief stroke, the note would explode with richness and color—it was musical, not just loud. I could not do it on the flute at first, as the quality of tone was lacking. He suggested leading to it by playing three chromatic notes descending scalewise and "exploding" the fourth note. This approach helped because the embouchure was in place and focused for the three previous notes and naturally still there for the fourth. The three-note approach helped to establish a relaxed yet energetic lead-in to the final attack. Eventually I was able to make a single note speak loudly with full body and musicality.

This exercise was a musical eye opener (or I should say an "ear opener"). Being able to articulate a rich exclamatory note, a note with body, depth, and color, is useful in different ways depending on the music and expression desired. When using this quality in a piece, it doesn't have to be a big explosion. It can be several smaller bursts used for clarity and emphasis, always with rich color. This is not just an accent. Accents can be played in many different ways other than loud. This ability to bring out notes articulated with full body can be incorporated into a general way to create emphasis in phrases.

Teachers

MY MOTHER USED TO TELL US ABOUT THE CLASSES my grandfather, sculptor Ralph Stackpole, taught. He was one of the first professors at the San Francisco Art Institute in the early 1930s. She said that he was a fine teacher in explaining concepts and ideas but even more so in his great enthusiasm. He would help the model settle into a pose, stand back with the students, and inspire them to observe the beauty of form, the ample shoulder here, the strong foot there, the continuity of torso to hip to thigh, the angle of head and face. His sculptures were sought after, and he was considered one of California's prominent artists.[17]

I got to know him in his later years. Through his eighties, he continued to produce beautiful, abstract sculpture in stone. With a physique that was lean and spry, he worked with massive pieces of granite or volcanic stone. From stone quarries, local and distant, he arranged for pieces of stone, sometimes weighing tons, to be transported to the enclosed stone yard at his home in the village of Chauriat in Auvergne, France. I recall the arrival of a huge piece of pink granite that came all the way from Finland. As he worked, he frequently repositioned the stone using chains and ropes arranged in a block-and-tackle pulley system rigged from the old, Medieval-looking stone pigeon tower. He did not spare any effort and moved the enormous stone often in order to see it from different angles, in different light, or to arrange one upon another. Then he would take away the rigging and continue with hammer and chisel. Months were devoted to the slow and patient process of chipping away fragments or tapping rhythmical light explosions of mineral dust to bring out sensuous or angular shapes in the design. His sculpture was shown in prestigious art events such as the Salon de Mai in Paris.

The village was surrounded by vineyards, fields of garlic, orchards, and sunflowers. His neighbors did not always relate to or understand his abstract art, but they held him in great esteem as they saw and heard him working long hours inside the old walls of his stone yard. When weather was rainy or snowy, he was in the kitchen near the woodstove, working on a painting or reading poetry.

He criticized academia and institutional learning as interfering with an artist's development. I did not understand this at first, but over the years, I came to understand his viewpoint. Modes of thought that cling to a standard of assumptions, that repeat what others have said, can block or destroy an artist's ability to create from his or her individual true being.

Leonardo da Vinci railed against the practice of quoting Greek classics, prevalent among the educated elite of his day. He was deeply interested in talking with and learning from philosophers and mathematicians, but he complained that many people, especially among the nobility, only repeated what others said in the classics. They did not think for themselves or speak from their own experience.

It is the same in playing music. You are not quoting someone else. The depth of what you are saying even while playing a composed piece comes from your own experience. In Leonardo da Vinci's art, his discoveries are present in his original approaches to light, shadow, atmosphere, delicacy of line, character, and the multilayered glow of life in a face—just as much as his discoveries are present in his drawings that illustrate his scientific observations, innovations, and designs for inventions.

> *My intention is first to consult experience before I proceed any further, and then by means of reasoning to show why such experience is bound to operate in such a way. For this is the true rule by which anyone who wishes to analyze the effects of nature must proceed; for although nature begins with the cause and ends with the experience, we must follow the opposite course, namely (as I have said before) to begin with the experience and by means of it investigate the cause.*[18]
> —LEONARDO DA VINCI

Teaching by Analysis

INFORMATION CAN ENGAGE OUR THOUGHT, BUT inspiration engages our whole being. Analysis in studying music is useful for recognition of patterns but shows only structure. Knowing structure can help us conceptualize the form of the piece, the design of the composition. As musicians and performers, we search for how to make it speak and sing, to convey meaning in nuances, to imbue it with presence and character, to translate it into our own humanity, to make it be alive with us.

All patterns can be analyzed and played by a computer, but a computer doesn't have the spontaneity of discovery, nor the presence to feel the context of the moment. A computer rendering is absent the heart, breath, cells, muscles, circulation, the quiet or thundering thoughts, and the flexibility of tone qualities that a human being creates with an actual instrument. Computers are by nature formulaic. Human beings come from the chaos of Nature.

Sometimes our desire to be academic, to fit it all into a mental system, brings separation from direct experience. A fine teaching approach includes enthusiasm demonstrated directly by playing and by attitude and observation. A teacher can spark a desire in a student to continue to reach for more agility, more life in the music. Much of this learning and awareness cannot be expressed in words. Analysis cannot recreate experience, yet the richness of life experience can be expressed in music.

Imitation Is a Great Teacher

When we lived in the Southern Oregon countryside, we sometimes heard the calls of screech owls at night. They have a beautiful, low-pitched whistle of repeated and slightly descending notes in an articulate rhythm that starts slowly and quickens before trailing off. They sing variations of this. Screech owls sound cozy and friendly. Theirs are the voices of beings who know and appreciate the woods and fields. They are poets.

I became adept at projecting an imitation of their low whistle. I stood outside in the darkness and listened. There were lovely silences between their poetic statements. I learned to wait in the silence, listen to the call, and after a polite pause,

I tried to repeat what I had heard. It was uncanny. After each of my bad imitations, the owl repeated the exact pattern. If I got it right, she or he would go on to a slightly different pattern and seemed to correct me until I got that one right!

Sometimes the silence was a bit long, and I humorously thought, *I guess I said something terrible in screech owl language, and she has flown off.* I was about to quit when there was the call again, only closer. She came closer!

This went on for an hour or so: the call, the imitation, the correction, the long pause, and the screech owl calling again from closer. I felt I was being visited by a night spirit capable of perceptions beyond my own. How brave of the screech owl to come to the edge of the clearing right next to our cabin.

The more we listen in Nature, the more we are treated to intricacies, variations, subtle changes, and development of composition as in the flute-like melodies of the western meadowlark. We have to wonder what our human ears are missing. By developing sensitivity, opening our receptivity, could we learn to hear more?

If we sit still in an open meadow or other natural place and make ourselves as peaceful and aware as possible, we will observe many life forms. Often wild creatures will come closer, not having noticed us, or approach with less fear as they sense our peaceful state. These experiences are gifts.

Even in a man-made place such as a city, we can stop to listen to the rhythms of traffic, construction, conversation, the exclamations of children playing. There is no need to look for a way to incorporate these into our music but to practice feeling present and include the discoveries as part of our being. To be aware is to participate in a feast that is living life. It is a feast that nourishes our music.

Echolocation

THERE ARE ACCOUNTS OF BLIND PEOPLE WHO CAN perceive aspects of their surroundings through their capacity for echolocation. Typically we associate echolocation with bats, whales, porpoises, and other animals. They locate food and objects by sending out sound waves that bounce from the object back to the animal's sensitive ears.

Daniel Kish, who is blind, teaches this technique for blind people. He travels the world independently thanks in great measure to his ability to use echolocation. It involves making clicking sounds with his mouth and processing the sounds that reflect off objects. He can interpret the reflected sound in the visual part of his brain, allowing him to "see" the world around him in his mind's eye. Through his work with the organization World Access for the Blind, he has helped many blind people to achieve what he calls "self-governed movement," which allows more independence in their lives.[19]

One person he met was Ben Underwood, a blind teenager who had taught himself the clicking technique. Underwood excelled at shooting hoops, riding a bike—even doing bike tricks—and skateboarding. He perceived things in great detail, even drops of water on a tabletop. He had the bold spirit of pushing past barriers and moved so freely and gracefully that it was easy to forget that he was blind. Sadly, he died in 2009 at age seventeen when the cancer that had claimed his eyes as a toddler returned to claim his life. He was considered the most capable self-taught human echolocater in the world.[20]

What does this mean for musicians? It means that our sense of hearing is far more subtle and far more inclusive than we have imagined. There is so much to discover by listening to the details of our environment. Being tuned in helps us be in the present as we reach our attention out to the details, the actualities, the space around us, our footsteps, forests, meadows, city sidewalks, rhythms of speech, even machine noise. Much can be learned by imitation of birdsong, owls, coyotes, and voices. The whole tapestry of life in hearing, as well as all the senses, can become vivid and vital.

Variety in Tone Color

Just as individual words can bring associations, individual notes and phrases can have their own characters. This one is tangerine, this one is a warm meadow, this one sizzles white hot, this one is calm like a cello. It is helpful to try different tone qualities.

Playing with a variety of tone qualities brings great expression. Listen to other instruments, and try to imitate them on flute. You will find many qualities of sound and ways of phrasing and articulation. Here are some instruments I have imitated and the quality of sound I reached for:

- Shakuhachi flute—open, mysterious, weighty flow of air
- Panpipes—open, spacious, outdoors, loud whisper yet with a center
- Violin—clear articulations and strong attacks, singing, vibrato
- Trumpet—noble, fanfare, playing out, golden
- Oboe—concentrated, searching, penetrating
- Cello—humming leaps, large sweeps as in Bach Cello Suites, substantial bass

Arriving at a note is not enough. A note that is correct and in tune is fine, but it may not be saying anything. What makes it speak and have significance is the quality of how it is *sung*.

Every manifested note has its own color, weight, and character and acquires more meaning by its context among other notes.

A flutist must aim for his or her artistically desired tone quality and intonation for each note, making subtle choices within the context of the line and the playing of the other musicians. We can trust our abilities to adjust, because we have trained ourselves to be tuned in and to hear subtleties and relationships. Our artistic approach and perspective are in continual development. It is a big adventure!

8

Experimentation and Discovery

Violinist Isaac Stern said about his pathway in learning:

> *I studied with Naoum Blinder until I was seventeen, and after that I never studied with anyone. I was responsible for my own mistakes. It is a process of intellectual and personal involvement with music as an idea and a way of life, not as a profession or career, but a rapport with people who think and feel and care about something. You have to find your own way of thinking, feeling, and caring.*[1]
>
> —Isaac Stern

Teaching Yourself

THERE IS A TENDENCY IN OUR CULTURE TO ASSUME that there is an exact way to play that comes from instruction given by authorities. A great teacher can point the way and reveal so much to a receptive student that the student is set for years, knowing what he or she wants to pursue in the art and practice. Hanging out with other musicians can bring new insights. However, most learning happens in the practice room when we are alone with ourselves. The artist is at work.

In a process of experimentation and discovery, we are searching for ways to fulfill our artistic sense, our internalization and embodiment of the music. It is not done only by exterior standards. The form and composition, the pitches and rhythms, have to be executed correctly, but there are infinite ways to create the sculpture on the framework and make it come alive.

Honor what is personally right, what resonates with your own sensibilities. Ask yourself, *What are the qualities I would like to bring out?* You have your own palette and paints. Part of your inner dialog could be, *If I make this section light and this section dark, that offers a better contrast, but I want to balance these with another section over here.* As you talk to yourself, you are trying things out, making decisions, and building and changing approaches. These are personal activities, your investigations, experiments, and decisions.

We can learn much by imitating. However, if we want to sound exactly like someone, try as we might, it won't be exact. We can't succeed in producing a perfect imitation because of our innate individuality. When we realize this, what we do next is important. If we think, *I'll never be that good,* we are short-changing ourselves and creating a dead end. If we think, *What can I add to this person's approach? What else does the music suggest? Maybe I'll try the opposite of what this person does,* that experimentation is fertile ground for new discovery and helps us find our way to artistic achievement.

From the Top

PRACTICING MUSIC IS AN ENORMOUS AMOUNT OF work, but it can be approached from a broader outlook. We think that to work hard, we must feel battered and worn down. *This passage is so hard, I'll drill myself on it. As they say, no pain, no gain.* This assumption is a limiting trap. We might find a more inspiring and satisfying approach by thinking, *How will this passage sound when I play it in the most beautiful way I can imagine?* If we hear that beautiful way in our mind and sing it, we can try it on our instrument. Suddenly we have a boost that brings forth amazing ideas and abilities.

I call this the "approach from the top," meaning that we already have in our mind's ear the beautifully played passage. The conception of the way we want to hear it is apparent to us as if it is in front of us in plain view, and it is only a question of realizing we are not too distant from playing it at this level. It is almost magical how this works in allowing progress to occur by leaps and bounds rather than tiny steps. The excitement in hearing the music come forth the way we intended is fuel for further development.

Conversely, an "approach from the bottom" is more burdensome. It is the mistaken belief that we must drill ourselves on these notes until we have them right, and only after we play them correctly can we make them sound musical. The "bottom" approach places our awareness at the bottom as if we are looking up to a distant musicality that is not formed yet and difficult to reach. Our goal appears farther away than it naturally and realistically needs to be. The "bottom" approach places us beneath our goals, where our hard work reinforces false perceptions of not being able to play as we would like to because we are stuck at the drilling stage—perpetually "woodshedding."

The top approach begins with feeling that we can already play. The music is present in our mind's ear and our whole body. Technical challenges are more easily resolved with this approach, because the musical expression is so attractive and compelling that our efforts are unified. It is as if our artistic *will* is all we need, and the rest comes into place naturally.

We dwell in the art as we trust our ability to use various techniques to straighten out problems. We can slow down, isolate difficult parts, play around with them, or vary rhythms on certain sections while artistically trying subtleties of expression. We are dancing close to the art we are seeking, delighting in discovering new expressive ideas and at the same time working out technically difficult parts. Art and technique become unified.

While we are creatively searching, the music is taking shape in us and evolving. A piece might be a light, lilting, pure, and innocent tune, but to convey that nature may take a great deal of artistic concentration. Every note is exposed and naked, and every nuance of our feeling is apparent. We will not approach this one with an academic attitude but with our whole being—upholding joy, purity, sweetness, tenderness, poignancy, mystery, reaching, dancing, and soaring. These are some of the qualities we discover, become, and sing out.

As you practice, make your artistic experiments and decisions with confidence. They are your personal performance. You can change your ideas later, but they need a place to evolve from. They need solid footing to take the next step. One step leads to another. You may have heard the adage, "Life is not a rehearsal." I say even a rehearsal is not a rehearsal. When you have a chance to sing out, play out! Even your practice room can be a stage. Go ahead and sing!

Act on Your Inspiration

HAVE YOU EVER HAD AN IDEA—PERHAPS AN IDEA for a poem or song, a drawing, a way to explain something—and because you didn't write it down, it disappeared and never returned? I once heard a singer-songwriter say that he felt that ideas came to visit him, and if he didn't write them down and begin working with them, they would go on down the road to visit someone else.

You may encounter the same situation. At some point in a practice session or rehearsal, you experience a breakthrough. A general insight might be, *Ah ha! I don't need to push so hard or manipulate so much to make a piece come alive. Just stay inside its energy.* A specific insight might be, *If I take a greater breath at this place, I won't need so much when I get to the next phrase.*

You can write a note about it, and that definitely helps, but often it is such an experiential insight that it is vital to act on it right away and work with it in your playing. One day at a rehearsal, I had a breakthrough. I found a new way to understand an aspect of the music. It was about an approach to playing the turbulent part of the Schumann "Three Romances"—something that made sense and was exciting. I went home to my busy household and launched into daily tasks.

I thought later that what I should have done was to play first, even five minutes. I needed to act on the inspiration to reinforce what was learned. I wrote a note, *You are the center and the source.* It's like the saying, "If not you, then who? If not now, then when?"

When we have ideas, we should explore them and not censor ourselves. There's plenty of time to refine and edit later. Like creating a sculpture, we can create the general form first and discover bit by bit how to refine it. I saw a similar process when watching my grandfather's huge stone sculptures emerge over months, under the hammer and chisel in his patient hands.

Discovery

THE REAL ESTATE PROFESSIONAL REPEATS, "Location, location, location." For a musician and other artists, the central approach is "discover, discover, discover." With an attitude of adventure, with experimentation and discovery, we can be at home with our curiosity and natural insight.

We may be fortunate to study with many fine teachers along our path, and what they give us is of paramount importance. The aphorism applies in a slightly twisted way: "You can lead a horse to water, but you can't make him drink." In other words, we (being the horse) have to experiment and discover how the information from the teachings works with us. What we learn must be incorporated into our being by our experience.

The joy in music is in discovery. Art is discovery. As players and listeners, we experience what is and what we are. We are part of the universe, a sweeping continuity of transience and transformation. Even while we sit eating our morning cereal, we are out there in the universe. Whether through galaxies and nebulae or veils of human tenderness and passion, we dance as part of the plasma of the universe. As artists participating in the great soundscape, we can trust that we have the "right stuff" and that our voice has meaning.

Children innately discover. They test, taste, and examine details. Toy manufacturers ignore how children observe. Toys are manufactured as oversized plastic forms with characterless features. In reality, children are keen observers of detail. What are we telling them about human culture when we present them with a nightmare of commercial objects and images in gaudy, bright colors with no subtlety of form and feature? When they are allowed their natural inclinations, children always find something of interest. In a natural environment, they delight in playing with a stick, a pile of sand, or a few leaves. They create interesting games, fantasies, and experiments. Their experiments and observations are scientific and creative, and their curiosity is crucial to their education and survival.

For an artist, being curious generates our continuing development. Exploration is our goal. With a more child-attuned attitude, we will feel alive and present in a practice session or in performance. Childlike discovery includes the following:

- Curiosity—everything is interesting
- Process is more important than outcome or product
- Freedom to be comfortable without understanding, because who of us truly understands
- Delight in new awareness and ability
- Desire to communicate. Children say, "Look at me! Watch this!" This is a universal way to communicate. It is not self-centered, as adults often misjudge.

In a practice session, we can playfully think up something to try as an experiment. For example:

- *What if I play it ultra-staccato or all legato?*
- *What if I try walking while playing an andante movement to feel a walking tempo?*
- *What if I try opposites, the quiet part more forte and the forte part more quiet?*

It may take only a few seconds to try our experiment. Even if the idea isn't precisely what we want to implement in a piece, it may indirectly lead to a different idea that may be perfect. Experimentation and discovery are thrilling and fulfilling in art.

Learn from All the Arts

I'VE NOTICED COMMON PITFALLS IN PLAYING FLUTE, and I did them all until I began to find other approaches. Playing well and speaking clearly in music can include a broad range of choices and approaches.

One area that can benefit from varied approaches is in playing the highest notes. Many flutists who have beautiful tone qualities in the middle registers start to sound artificial when they approach the high register. Often the high notes sound forced or punched out. To have plenty of air support before reaching the high note goes a long way to solving this problem, but there is more.

As a young teenager, I took great interest in practicing, but I struggled with the notes at the top of the third octave. I was extra shy about high notes because of criticism from a family member. As I tried to eke out the high notes quietly and inoffensively, they emerged but always flawed. I was trying hard to play them and, at the same time, trying hard to suppress them. Sometimes I skipped playing them—a silence in the piece instead of a note.

I gradually improved the sound but felt that my high notes were treacherous and touchy and not up to the better qualities I was getting in the other registers. Surprisingly, the answer to my trouble came from a dance class.

After graduating from high school, I was fortunate to spend a month as a music student at the Sun Valley Summer Music Camp in Idaho. The camp provided a confluence of great teachers and serious students of music and dance. In addition to our music classes, we were required to take early morning ballet classes. I found the ballet exercises energizing, and seeing the real dancers gave me a huge admiration for the work and the art of ballet. I was not a dancer but had briefly participated in a few modern dance classes in San Francisco given by my cousin, Diane Robertson, who danced with the Merce Cunningham group in New York. In the Sun Valley ballet classes, I was learning important lessons of balance, extension, body consciousness, grace, and beauty.[2]

The arts are related. I like to look for connections in creative process. An approach in one art can be translated to be beneficial in another art. One of the best translations I found was from ballet into playing flute.

To stretch into a ballet *relevé,* standing tall and rising onto the balls of the feet (demi-pointe), we find more stability by extending our awareness down through our center. As we rise, we extend our awareness down, down beyond our feet, beyond the floor—perhaps to the center of the Earth. Conversely, in a *plié,* as we bend our knees outward to lower the body, we send our concentration upward to the sky so that we are not merely sinking but maintaining an uplifted posture. We feel lighter, balanced on our legs with less effort while maintaining a stable and strong posture.

I began to think about high notes and low notes on the flute in the same way: *Think low to play high, think high to play low.* The revelation allowed me to enjoy the more beautiful tone I could reach in the higher register as well as bringing more freedom in the lower.

While playing high notes, imagine you are playing the same notes an octave or two lower, or think of one low-pitched note as a kind of drone. By thinking low while playing high, the tone quality in the upper register becomes rich and grounded. You will hear more openness, relaxation, and singing quality. The high notes can evolve naturally in the musical phrase with no extra effort. High E‴ through C‴ and even D‴ can be sung well with more freedom to feel delight in the character of these high notes. You can play like the famous solo sung by the Queen of the Night in Mozart's opera *The Magic Flute*—singing lightly and flexibly at the top of your range.[3]

The flute's lowest notes are gorgeous! Flutists often make an ardent effort to make these beautiful low notes resonate and be heard. If extra effort means extra tension, the flutist might make the mistake of leaning too hard or backing off to avoid cracking the notes. These efforts are counterproductive and can produce a forced, brittle, or sour tone quality as well as intonation problems. To alleviate this strain, think high while playing low, and the lowest notes will be allowed to speak more naturally with better intonation and projection.

As you play the lowest notes D′, D♭′, C′, and B′, imagine you are playing notes an octave higher, or imagine a single high note floating above the passage. The notes will sound rounder and broader and come forth with ease. That broad sound, like panpipes, will be heard much better than a sound produced with tension. Panpipes are played with an open embouchure, and their whispering yet focused sound can be heard a long way off. They are relaxed and powerful at the same time. Likewise, the flute can be played in an open and robust way. The low notes will stay energized and in tune. They speak strongly without being forced.

Practicing Wide Intervals

WIDE INTERVALS, SLURRING LOW TO HIGH OR HIGH TO LOW, are helpful to practice. Carefully listen to the first note as a reference point. By hearing in advance, in our mind's ear, what the next note needs to sound like to be in tune with this first note, we can trust that we will reach it. Like a bird approaching a branch from beneath, we have to have more energy than just enough to reach the branch. We must fly slightly above the branch to land on it. Therefore, we must prepare our energy with more than enough breath support to land on the higher note. A bird flying down to a lower branch carefully extends her talons to grab the branch. Likewise, our aim in playing a low note needs to be accurate. We hear where we are going and anticipate what it will sound like when it is in tune with previous notes.

When practicing octaves or wider intervals, teachers often advise making changes in the lips and jaw. These changes come into play, but I advocate thinking of them as subtle shifts. Better yet, don't think about them at all. With a relaxed embouchure and plenty of air support, we can trust we will reach the pitch. Just as when we whistle a tune, any subtle lip changes necessary to get us to the desired pitches will respond to our motivation, and if any part is out of tune on the first try, we can easily and immediately self-correct. When we revisit that interval, we are more likely to get it perfectly in tune consistently.

When we sing naturally, we aren't concerned with what we need to do to reach that note—we just go there. Keeping air pressure steady allows a high note to *evolve* from the previous low note. Even if the higher note is played more quietly than a lower note, the energy remains steady for both. That steady support, energy, and intensity will keep it alive and in tune.

Developing Ear

ENCOUNTERING INTONATION PROBLEMS CAN BE frustrating in any context. To treat it as a learning situation, whether you are the one learning or the one instructing, is helpful. Too often it is viewed as, *You either have it or you don't.* Sadly, the person who is having difficulty is dismissed and ends up feeling inadequate and incapable. Perhaps realistically there is no time in the immediate situation to coach all the corrections, but the larger truth is that the ability to develop the ear is real. It is a process.

In John Holt's book *Never Too Late: My Musical Life Story*, he describes when at age forty, he took up learning to play cello. The book combines insights from his lifelong career in education with his experiences in music. In one account, he tells the story of how he was on a car trip with a friend who loved music but had unhappily concluded that he could never become a musician because he was tone deaf. Holt believed that people who claim they are tone deaf are not. People label themselves unmusical only because of a faulty educational system. In music classes that offer insufficient time and explanation, some students do not get the extra attention they need to understand concepts such as "high and low" or "up and down," terms used to describe tones and registers. Nor are they given extra time to try matching their voices with tones. Because they are not able to do these things, they are judged and labeled and asked not to sing with those who can.[4]

Holt set out to prove to his friend that he was capable of perceiving and matching pitches. While traveling in the car, he sang tones one at a time and encouraged his friend to sing the same pitch. It was at first difficult, but each time Holt sang a pitch, he then sang his friend's pitch and compared them, advising his friend to keep trying as he got closer. They were delighted that he was soon able to imitate pitches well. Holt's friend went on to sing in a choir and became an excellent cellist; one of his cello instructors advised him that if he chose to, he could become a professional musician. Although he did continue playing cello, he pursued a different professional career.

Holt later realized that they might have had quicker results if he had shown his friend how to slide up or down to the pitches. This "slide" idea is practical for learning pitch and intonation. If at times we are uncertain where our pitch sits in relation to being in tune, we can slide it up (sharper) or down (flatter) by making subtle adjustments or rolling the flute out or in, purposely sliding our pitch briefly above or below the pitch we are intending to meet. Hearing our overstep, we instantly clarify our orientation helping us aim for the center of the pitch. Like adjusting the tuning peg of a violin, we can tighten too high, loosen too low, and then tighten just the right amount to slide up to the in-tune pitch.

In an abstract way, there may be another kind of grace in the idea of "slide." It might be useful in adjusting our expressive musicality. If while practicing we decide that we are not expressing something well, instead of stopping to analyze why, we can try sliding toward our musical goal. It is a graceful feeling to think, *I am not far from how I want to say this. I'll just slide over to it.*

9

Character and Emotion

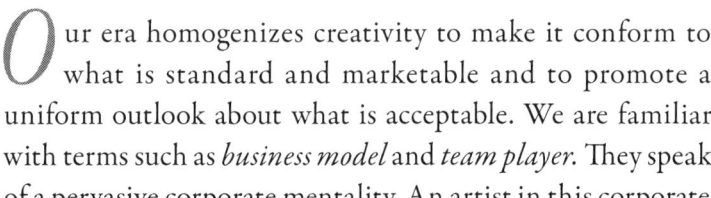

Our era homogenizes creativity to make it conform to what is standard and marketable and to promote a uniform outlook about what is acceptable. We are familiar with terms such as *business model* and *team player*. They speak of a pervasive corporate mentality. An artist in this corporate environment is expected to have the ambition for his or her art to be a successful product of the market, to conform to what is standard, formulaic, and marketable.

Things that are machine made and mass produced are held in high regard. In a great deal of pop music, there are constant mechanical and electronic sounds strongly encroaching on our ears, leaving an indelible synthetic mark (drum machines and electronically altered voices). This may influence people to feel that there is perfection in music that comes from a slick, "lean and mean" machine. The trouble is it *is* like a machine.

Mechanistic music has its place, but it is remote and cannot touch the heart. It asks, "Aren't we clever?" instead of asking "How can we tune into the universe, reality, and humanity?" Fascinating as it may seem in our era, I believe human beings will get tired of what I call computer/mechanical "gadgetosis," the overadmiration of the artificial. Appreciation and interaction with Nature and what is natural helps people thrive in body, mind, and soul. Without this, there is a large disconnect and loneliness.

Music that comes from a mechanistic, commercial approach is designed so that everyone is entertained in the same way. The aim is less to reach the individual listener than to produce the same experience for everyone. This creates *a look* or *a sound* that is marketable. Along with producing standard-issue music and art, this outlook makes manipulation and propaganda easier. Propaganda wants you to believe one thing to the exclusion of others, to limit and control and give you no choice.

As musicians, we could play a piece correctly according to a standard as if our only wish were to ace a typing course or to paint by numbers to achieve a uniform result. The result would not offer heights or depths, variety, or subtleties of emotion and therefore no choice of experience. Music dressed in a "uniform" is a representation without individual motivation, without choice or individuality.

Music is most exciting when its character and spirit come from the freedom of creativity. How does music engage a listener? How does it make you feel? The meaning in the words "make you feel" involves choices the performer and the listener make. How you feel belongs to you as the individual you are. Your unique experience gives you capacity to feel. The music comes to you, and you bring yourself to the music.

Outstanding art and music can stop us in our tracks. Famous visual examples of masterly works that give us pause and lift away time might be *Mona Lisa* by Leonardo da Vinci, *Guernica* by Picasso, or the sunflower paintings of Vincent van Gogh. In music, it might be the Khachaturian violin concerto performed by David Oistrakh or shakuhachi flute music performed by one of Japan's master musicians, considered in their country "National Treasures."

You might be tempted to say, *Yes, but those are master works. They are not what I can do.* You can! Maybe you will not achieve such an exquisite masterpiece of finished work, but you will experience elements of it, especially those elements that have touched you when you listened. They are in your experience. The fact that you deeply felt so much of what was said musically or visually means that those possibilities were and are part of you. The expression "it takes one to know one" applies here in the most positive light. The possibilities are present in you. They are ready to be shaped with your own hands and your understanding.

That means that artistic communication goes much deeper than we generally acknowledge. This communication is not merely entertainment but brings forth models for learning that transfer from one person to another. Mozart mentioned this in a letter he wrote when he was twenty:

> *We live in this world only that we may go onward without ceasing, a peculiar help in this direction being that one enlightens the other by communicating his ideas; in the sciences and fine arts there is always more to learn.*[1]
> —W. A. Mozart

That is why diversity is so important. We have what is innate to us yet also build on the discoveries of others. A musical artist can find great advantage in listening to diverse sources, learning constantly from everyone and everything, and at the same time learning to understand his or her individual true nature. These endeavors are no different than those needed in living. Music can be a way of life and life a way of music.

Perfect Irregularities

UNIFORMITY CAN BE DULL; NATURAL IRREGULARIties provide sparkle and life. Artists and art critics observe that the landscape behind Da Vinci's *Mona Lisa* is higher on one side, lower on the other, bringing the human figure to life and giving her the fresh air, atmosphere, and depth of a spacious world in which to exist.

Irregularities in images catch the eye and draw our attention. In sound, they also capture our focus and attention as they imbue music with more life, more naturalness. Musical irregularities make use of subtle imperfections that can sound more perfect than perfection. Some irregular perfections in playing might be the following:

- *Tempo*: Rushing and slowing subtly within the context of the steady beat
- *Vibrato*: Uneven vibrato, slightly changing speed
- *Trills*: Making them slower or faster or subtly changing speed within a trilled note to express a quality in the moment
- *Intonation*: Playing a bit on the sharp side within the pitch, adding excitement to certain notes, or playing on the subtly flat side to express loneliness or sadness
- *Phrasing*: Unexpected expressions, accents, and dynamics
- *Tone*: Variations in tone color, voice, and dynamic

Kristian Bezuidenhout

DUTCH KEYBOARDIST KRISTIAN BEZUIDENHOUT performs on Baroque and early Classical keyboards. He made a series of recordings of the solo piano works of W. A. Mozart, which he plays on replica-built fortepiano instruments from the late 1700s. Performing on the instrument that the composer worked with, his insights and approaches in playing

Mozart's music are unique and different from pianists who play the same works on modern pianos. He reveals a glimpse into how Mozart conceived the music and likely how he approached performing. On the eighteenth-century piano, the music does not sound antiquated but bright and moving with Bezuidenhout's vibrant and natural playing, revealing many dimensions to Mozart's music that we don't commonly hear.[2]

> *[Phrases must be]...expressed caressingly, lovingly,... played as drawn out, to come across as revolutionary as they really are. [Playing Mozart is],...not just a question of following instructions. It's about making very strong and vivid decisions about interpretations...a road map that's not quite set in stone.*[3]
> —Kristian Bezuidenhout

Bezuidenhout points out that Mozart relished variety. The timing, the stretches, the pauses would be of great importance as they are in his operas, since much of Mozart's music is "speech-like." For his operas, Mozart worked closely with the librettist to make sure the words and the drama were carefully created so that the music could convey the intention and meaning or even lift the meaning to a new dimension. The musicality in how a part in the opera was sung elevated its meaning beyond the words. The words and stories of his operas were revolutionary, tuned in to the Enlightenment era in which he lived: ideas of tolerance, education, opportunity, equality, progress, and feminism were emerging. Mozart's operas supported and brought to life these enlightenments.

What does this mean for our own musical language? In our playing, we are honing our musical language, how we speak. Language and music are learned by listening and doing. Educator John Holt compares how we learn language as a child with the process of learning music. He observed that we learn language and music by trying and subsequently revisiting our efforts many times as we make small improvements. In music, we not only revisit our efforts to learn basic technique but also in endeavoring to bring the music to life. It is an ongoing process of making finer and finer decisions in creating expression.[4]

Embody What You Are Saying

"You have to be happier," he suddenly told me. Bill Douglas, composer, pianist, and music professor at Naropa University, listened to me play the passage again. I made an effort to make it sound more cheery. "No. You actually have to *be* happier." I thought, *That's a complex requirement. I'm not sure how to suddenly be happier.* I then thought, *Why not? You can always be sad about something, and you can always be happy about something. What if I abandon the "about something" and embrace the quality?*[5]

Many things can be troubling us about life and still we can be happier. Happier doesn't necessarily mean happy-go-lucky or jolly all the time. Happy can be a perspective, an overview. Happy can mean thankful for what is, problems and all, and not taking anything for granted. In the end, playing "happier" makes us happier. It is the capacity for happiness that broadens our perspective.

We can try to be happy despite many things, but how can we be really happy? Can we turn it off and on? Within ourselves we can, to some extent, choose our response to situations, our own way of being. Experience is so momentary and changeable. Momentary and changeable: that is what music is. It is one more way that life and music are the same.

Embody the intention of the music instead of just standing beside it and representing it. Decide where it is or where it could be emotionally, and let it touch your own heart. Make it real rather than artificially imposed.

A character, not a caricature.[6]
—MARCEL MOYSE

Your Natural Treasure Trove

IN LIFE WE ARE CONCERNED WITH HOW WE RESPOND, how we react. In playing music, we generate feelings from our experiences. Our individual reactions, our responses, and the spectrum of qualities in emotions that we have found in life, are our natural treasure trove in music.

What capacity for happiness do you have—or does anyone have?

I will never forget an interview I saw on a news program on Link TV. A woman in Columbia, South America, was speaking of the violence, devastation and loss of human life caused by the drug cartels. She had lost family members, and her adult son had disappeared. It was heart-wrenching to hear. Even with her grief and horror, she generated something extraordinary—a kind of upbeat, generous attitude. The interviewer, moved by her positive demeanor, asked her how she seemed to have found strength and know happiness through it all. She said, "Happiness is the best defense."

In the worst kind of experience, the kind that could break a person's spirit, she located this strength within herself. She knew in the depths of her being, the power of this strength, and the power of happiness for generating improvement in the world.

The shadows and lights of experience, expressed musically in emotional qualities, can come from our overview. Whether our happiness is confident or tenuous, it can be a *defense* as the Columbian woman expressed. It can be motivation for music that we are playing in the moment as well as for our continued commitment to playing.

We live in a culture that has many "bestselling" formulas for happiness: drugs, shopping, and material wealth. We also have many stories, classic myths, and contemporary examples about how materialism and drugs do not bring happiness. From the ancient myth *The King Midas Touch* to the work of comedian, author, and advocate for freedom from addiction, Russel Brand, we learn that the bestselling formulas don't work.[7] Happiness can come from building a broader perspective based on wide-ranging experience. This broadened insight can bring more depth and quality of life for ourselves and those around us. In this natural way, our music making is enriched and becomes enriching.

On Playing Bach

BACH CREATED MANY RICHLY WOVEN EMOTIONAL qualities in his compositions. Oddly, our culture tries to separate reason and emotion. Emotion *is* reason and intelligence. We have been steered wrong by the prevalent talk of the mathematics and technicalities of Bach's harmonies and designs. I believe the theoretical musical patterns were for him well-cultivated tools that served his imagination and spirit. He was born from a long line of musicians and grew up surrounded by music. His great palette of technical tools was a means to an end, not the end. The end was to create music that beautifully expressed responses to existence. They are not feats of cleverness but keen, lifetime searchings and explorations.

Many performers do what I call "playing Bach with a scowl," in a monotone color that is dark and serious, or they play as if calculating a math problem or as if wielding a hammer. As long as all the notes are correct and in place, one can get away with being a hammer or being dour, and it will sound amazing because it is Bach! Bach will sound great in any context. The music can be quoted badly or tastelessly, and it will still turn heads with its masterful creativity. The *Mona Lisa* with a mustache or any silly alteration is still captivating.

In playing Bach, many musicians miss the composer's intention. The intention is inventiveness in a universe of possibilities. Inventiveness implies nonstatic exploration and flexibility—not a hunkered-down "scowl" of correct mathematical answers but a seeking of truthfulness of being. In Bach's music, there are many surprises, unusual harmonies, simultaneous melodies, and downright abstractions. There is grandeur, intimacy, grief, celebration, exaltation, dance, and peace. How does a musician pare himself down to the honesty and energy needed to play Bach? We are deeply moved by Bach's music when it is played with insight and honesty.

On the opposite end of too much "scowl" is the mistake of too much "sticky sweet" sentimentality. Perhaps it comes from a desire to bring out the obvious or to make it cutesy. Both scowl and cutesy seem a distraction from the clarity that the music is designed to express. This is music that puts the musician at the core of a sweeping yet intimate understanding. It expresses the precise and particular yet with a deep and broad overview. Bach's music ponders death, music of joyful dance, music of magnanimity, music that goes out to the stars, music that comforts—limitless variety.

Listen to different performers, and notice which ones pull you in and compel you to listen and which ones are all right but don't engage or touch you. Some of the best Bach performances I have heard are recorded by Marc Beaucoudray playing the Bach flute sonatas. Beaucoudray takes liberties in solo works but gives them the contemplative time and space that I also admire in some guitarists. Guitarist Raphaella Smits, in playing the famous Bach *Chaconne*, has personalized the famous work but has made it universal as well.[8]

With Bach, it seems unavoidable that a musician must reckon with himself or herself on issues of pure honesty, to be deeply felt and not imposed from some dictate. It cannot be one size fits all in interpretation, because it comes from one's interior and individuality. It is open for the individual to access what is in his or her pureness of heart and bring it out in Bach's music.

"In the Know" versus Individual Insight

I OFTEN HEAR PEOPLE SAY, "I DON'T KNOW ANY-thing about music." Perhaps they think they must know music history or technical stuff. It is not necessary to "know" about music to be able to hear and appreciate, be emotionally moved, or feel like dancing. Perhaps people who say they don't know anything about music feel they are "supposed" to hear it in a certain way or that they should have a standard response. In our culture and institutions, we are not taught the benefits of enjoying and engaging in our own individuality. We are not taught that fresh individual insight is welcome at the table when appreciating art.

We need to recognize how much we thrive on diversity. There are many kinds of beauty. We should rejoice that there is no standard. Understanding this can free our creativity in how we approach our playing and our listening. Our capability to communicate comes from our individuality, not from trying to fulfill a seemingly standard requirement.

Baby Talk

BABIES ARE MORE OBSERVANT AND CAPABLE OF communication than we generally believe. Adults often assume they can't communicate with babies as if a baby is incapable of hearing and discerning. Research is indicating how early in their infancy babies can communicate with mothers and fathers.

> *Within a day or two after birth, babies recognize the first beat in a sound sequence; neural signs of surprise appear when that initial 'downbeat' goes missing. Classical music lights up specific hearing areas in newborns' right brains. Even more intriguingly, babies enter the world crying in melodic patterns that the little ones have heard in their mothers' conversations for at least two months while in the womb.*[9]

> *Psychobiologist, Colwyn Trevarthen,…rejects the notion that babies passively absorb adults' googly-eyed gab. Instead, he holds, infants intentionally prompt musical exchanges with adults, and infants know when they're being invited by a grown-up to interact. Here, the currency of communication consists of coordinated exchanges of gestures, facial expressions, coos, squeals and other sounds. Trevarthen and like-minded researchers call this wordless conversation 'communicative musicality.' Babies' natural musical aptitude gets them in sync*

with mothers. Within weeks of birth, mom and baby compose brief musical vignettes that tune up a budding relationship.... moms and tots vocally express and share emotions in finely calibrated ways that differ in some respects across cultures.[10]

—Bruce Bower

    Learning language is a musical endeavor. Tone, rhythm, musicality, and context help children learn vocabulary. With my own children, I consciously tried to use unfamiliar words casually now and then in conversation without explaining (unless asked) and without putting a didactic burden on them. I included a new word in a sentence, and by the context and tone, I hoped they got the idea. They did. They naturally were interested in finding more nuanced ways to express themselves, and they tried out new words. Sometimes learning existing terms could not happen quickly enough. We lived in the country, and at around age four, my older son loved identifying plants. He was so eager to learn the names of plants that if I didn't know the correct name, he would invent one. Wild larkspur became "Blue Hummingbird-Tongue-Flower."

    Metaphorically, each child learns to the tune of his or her own music. "Watch me!" is a call children make everywhere in the world. There's more to this universal child's request than wanting attention. The child is sharing a new and interesting discovery. It doesn't matter that others have made the discovery before. Every child's "watch me" is unique, a real "first." The innate fact of individuality makes it true that what the child is showing us has never been done like this before. It is a new discovery.

Emotional Transformation

THE SIMPLEST GESTURE CAN BE THE MOST PROfound. We can surprise ourselves by touching our own heart in playing "Twinkle, Twinkle Little Star" or "Frère Jacques." A moment can offer a turning point.

    I was in a rotten mood, despairing over a falling-out with someone I loved. I had those familiar thoughts: *Everything I thought I knew was wrong.* In the early morning light, I walked down the road and happened to approach a woman tending her garden. "Good morning," she said in a melodious, uplifting voice. In an instant she caused me to feel indescribably encouraged. My wheels of depression turned a corner to perceive new ways of thinking, and I was able to work more clearmindedly with the problem. The simple music and spirit of her greeting created a turning point.

    Another turning point I shall never forget came when we lived in the country in the 1970s. I woke up at first light hearing the footsteps of our neighbor's cows "clop clopping" on our back porch. Our neighbor's farm had open-range rights, and since our land was not fenced in, their cows were free to roam through the woods and over to our property. They wouldn't come often, maybe two or three times a year, but when they did, they could cause discouraging destruction, especially to our two large vegetable gardens. Angry at such a rude early awakening, I threw on some clothes and rushed out to herd the cows home via a trail through the woods to the green hillside above their farm. I was uneasy about leaving the kids alone but hoped that if I hurried back, they would not have awakened yet. After ushering the cows back to their farm, I ran home along the trail. Still angry about the cows, I began to hear miraculous strains of flute wafting through the woods.

As I reached the cabin, there was my younger son who had climbed out onto the roof (he knew it was forbidden) and was playing a set of panpipes that friends had given him. His sweet notes uplifted my spirits. I had to reprimand him about sitting on the roof but, by then, not too harshly.

Examples of music that transform a mood are many. East Indian music is spiritual and sensual and allows us to look deep into our imagination. Native North American music pulls us outdoors into a natural, vast yet intimate landscape as it celebrates respect for Nature. Irish music invites us to dance in fresh ocean-blown air. South American Indian music offers lively yet poignant melodies that call from the vistas of the high Andes Mountains. Music offers the potential for important emotional turning points and transformation.

Falling Out of Love

There was a time when it all came crashing down. I saw through music and art, and it seemed merely manipulation, just a way we try to direct ourselves and each other. I didn't want to hear any music. It was toxic and sickening. Why was this happening? What was it? My mother had just passed away. In my grief and depression, I perceived music and all human arts as manipulative, just so much subtle and not-so-subtle propaganda, people saying, "See it—hear it—my way." Even when done well and beautifully, for a time, it was all manipulation. This shocked and terrified me, as I felt I had slipped through a veil, and there was nothing redeeming on the other side.

I know the arts as being essential and providing unlimited pathways to human growth, understanding, and enlightenment. I also acknowledge a possibility that art is nothing—temporal in the Buddhist sense. Knowing that everything is transient makes all in life even more valuable, even more worthy of love, even more important to take notice. The result is that I am more passionately interested and in love with all the arts.

How do we get through our darkest days? A dark time can be a time to become more honest and to more fully appreciate suffering worldwide. In the face of tragedy, music can create a counterbalance in beauty and allow time for tears. At the one-year anniversary of the September 11, 2001, attacks in New York City, a worldwide event took place: The Rolling Requiem. At the exact hour of the tragedy, Mozart's *Requiem* was performed, starting in Auckland, New Zealand. From time zone to time zone, countries and municipalities participated with hundreds of performances, and the *Requiem* was heard around the world, the last performance given on the island of American Samoa. I attended the performance in Boulder, Colorado, where the audience members were given some of the choral parts to sing. To hear everyone singing this exquisite music together was extremely moving and beautiful. In dark times, it is more important than ever to uphold color, emotion, and empathy in music.[11]

Emotional Perceptions

EMOTION IS HOW WE RELATE TO EVERYTHING. IT IS how we perceive, learn, collect, and remember information. Even work on a mathematical equation might start with anxiety, move into curiosity, and end with a feeling of triumph. The memory of those calculations is tied to the memory of the emotions that comprise the experience of making them. A technique often used for memorizing a long list of random words is to make a story about them. Memorizing is easier because of associations attached to our emotions. It is an effective method, because the driving force that creates confidence in the memory is emotion. *Confidence* itself is an emotion.

What are emotions? I believe they are qualities of perceptions. When I see the green of sunlight filtered through a tree, it makes my whole being feel a certain way. Playing and listening to music is emotional. Phrase by phrase, we feel the emotional quality of each musical gesture. The meaning in music is perceived when we allow the music to move through us, when we resonate with each sound, when we reach an empathic network with other musicians in eloquence and playfulness—not necessarily for the end "product" but for the emotive touching. That is the joy.

The experience of listening can be soothing, but the experience of *playing* soothing music is to be alert and energized in every detail. It takes great energy to play something sweetly and purely. We feel soothed while hearing the simple sounding melody, yet the musician is involved with generating the energy, precision, sense of direction, and the tonal colors. The performer looks deeply within and states emotional qualities in his or her most honest ways.

This is what British conductor, author, and Mozart scholar Jane Glover meant when she wrote of Mozart:

> *With all his performers his standards were extremely high, and his condemnation of musicians who did not match up to them could be absolutely withering…What he constantly sought was that extra ingredient of emotion and passion, not falsely or superficially applied, but fired from within the very soul of the interpreter. When he found anyone who could convey this, he was ecstatic.*[12]
>
> —Jane Glover

10

Creativity—Nakedness

While we are playing, there is a delicate balance between listening and playing. Listening while playing is not the same as listening while listening. While playing, it is important to avoid having an attitude of sitting back and being too passive. Although we remain receptive to the sound coming forth, we must be the active and responsible generator of the music. We are engaged in pursuing where we will go next and how we want to speak.

If caught in the passive trap, the music becomes what I call "representative." It represents something instead of *being* something. Everything in the representation can be technically perfect, but involvement, passion, character, creativity, and the feeling of the person present—are absent.

It is easy to fall into this trap. It's like the education we had when we were ordered to sit at a desk and memorize what we were told. It was all academic and not engaged. Ultimately, it was not "the whole picture." Real knowledge is not just intellectual. It encompasses an infinite spectrum of life experience.

Crisis in Creativity

HAVE YOU EVER EXPERIENCED WHAT I CALL A "crisis in creativity"? *What am I doing? Am I doing it for effect? For affect? Do I allude, pretend, bluff, or act? Am I just manipulating, or is there an honest core from which an utter truth or beauty might emerge?*

A personal experience helped me with this question. Music had been of central importance to me, and through my teens and early twenties, my primary focus was playing flute. In the era of marriage in my midtwenties, having two children and moving to the country, I played flute occasionally. We had little by way of possessions, but when we inherited a record player, in a moment when I was alone, I put on a recording of the Khachaturian violin concerto played by David Oistrakh. I had listened to it as a teenager, but now it was so full of indescribable energy and beauty that I sank to the floor in tears. I realized those tears were partly my longing to make music again.

The children were growing beyond the toddler age. I began to play again and tried to make it an acceptable and graceful time for the children, stopping when they tugged at my clothes to get my attention. At ages six and eight, they began to play music themselves; piano, guitar, clarinet, and flute.

One night in our cabin, the kids were in bed and, I thought, asleep. My older son, about six years old, appeared on the stairway, saying, "Will you play your flute? It helps me go to sleep." That was the sweetest request for music I've ever had.

In our country home in the 1970s, we were trying to be a self-sustainable farm with all the hard work that entailed. We were "back to the landers," in an era when many young people, disgusted with the war on Vietnam and the corporate system, sought to live a more peaceful and natural life. The property had as its centerpiece a beautiful, sloped meadow nestled in forested hills. Our cabin sat at the top of the meadow at the edge of the forest. Being tucked away in forest allowed us to feel private and free.

One summer day, I was pondering how to be honest in playing music, how to play from the core of my being. The family was away. I decided to play outside on the path beyond the back porch of our cabin. Playing outdoors had been recommended to me years earlier by my teacher in France, M. Pierre Cazaux. He suggested that occasionally playing outside builds projection of sound, adding that to play in front of a tree helps to provide a little reflective bounce-back of sound, which otherwise flies away dissipating to a large extent in the open air.[1]

I had tried practicing outdoors in previous years and found that it was helpful in learning to play out, to project my sound. On this warm summer day, alone in our private forest hillside, I challenged myself with another issue. Would my playing flute outdoors be more honest if I were naked? To me, on this occasion, *naked* meant a state of being part of nature with no pretense.

With the many ways our male-based culture objectifies the female body, anyone might easily visualize this from an exterior viewpoint as an observer, perhaps imagining it as some sexual fantasy. It was not that for me. This was an important personal quest for understanding myself in relation to the essence of music—in Nature—to be at the core, free of pretense, free of assumed obligations to society, free of my delusions, free of the "wrappings."

I was the human being in Nature looking for reality, looking for being true. It was Bach in the buff.

This experience showed me "the way" in many respects. Yes, underneath we are simplicity bursting with possibility. We are naked underneath our material or imagined layers. This was no place for an arrogant or egotistic approach, just honesty. Bach is beautiful out in Nature.

I wanted to continue remembering this experience to inform myself of what was basic to my nature. I wanted to remember how it feels to play purely without any false pride.

I recommend, in a private time, practicing naked. You are not so much "facing yourself" as *being* yourself. This core being, *your* core being, is expressing your essence.

We needn't be shy to ourselves. We needn't hold back behind feelings of inadequacy. We can be kind to our body, appreciating its strengths and weakness, accepting it all, and nevertheless allowing it to excel at the powerful creative capacity that is ours.

> *Hey Jude, you'll do.*[2]
> —The Beatles

We can know we are good, and we can uncover more good. There is a difference between good and good. I'm not talking about the ego's "good" but about recognizing basic goodness. This is *goodness* not as a virtue but as an element of nature.

What is real? When we encounter a crisis in creativity, we can ask, *Is it more satisfying to play for effect and affect? Or is it better to try to tune into true nature?* In that light, we are not seeking tricks of cleverness but engaging in keen searching and exploration, looking for truth.

Sui-Zen—Shakuhachi

IN OUR LATE TEENS, MY BROTHER AND I WERE interested in Japanese music and culture. Tim took up the art of kendo (sword fighting). He and a friend also worked to restore ancient samurai swords using traditional Japanese methods, with patient polishing by hand over weeks and months, gradually revealing the beautiful temper cloud-patterns on the edge of the blade. I listened to recordings of shakuhachi flute and koto music and tried to imitate the melodies and inflections with my flute. In an open-air tea house that Tim built over the small creek below the family home, we held tea ceremonies, talked over what we were learning from *The Three Pillars of Zen* by Philip Kapleau, and sat in meditation.[3] Tim became an excellent kendo student, getting high praise from his teacher-Sensei. We began to scheme with ideas of how we might go to Japan. Ultimately, our lives took us in different directions, and we didn't get to Japan, but our interest continued.

Sui-Zen is an ancient Japanese tradition of meditation, healing, and enlightenment based on compositions played on shakuhachi flute. Dating from the ninth century, it is the only music associated with Zen Buddhism. Sui-Zen shakuhachi music is considered a pathway of enlightenment, and it expresses the "music of the original self."

> *This is music dedicated to the expression of Peace in all its forms: as a source of comfort, and end to conflict, a way of transformation, and a path of realization… Traditionally this music is not performed for an audience, but is offered in hope of enlightenment for both musician and listener.*[4]
>
> —Bob Seigetsu Avstreih

In 1975, I purchased a shakuhachi from Monty Levenson, an American who has continued to make fine shakuhachis since 1970. Levenson's craftsmanship and methodology are authorized and praised by the International Shakuhachi Society.[5] When my shakuhachi arrived, I took it into the woods to be alone, to begin to learn to play. I was able to get a soft and even tone and again experienced what I consider the miracle of shakuhachi sound. The nature of the sound is extraordinary in that it seems to be at one with everything. The tone qualities have a perfect naturalness that does not shut out other sounds and occurrences. This inclusiveness gives a feeling of acceptance of the moment and incorporates the larger sound environment as equally interesting and equally real. The sound quality of shakuhachi seems to expand the mind.

As I played quietly in the woods, a strange whispering arose, a sound I did not recognize. It was a delicate crackling like many small animal ghosts gently approaching me. Was I in a dream? Watching the ground keenly as the phantom creatures came closer, I was baffled for some moments. I realized that dappled sunlight was coming through the trees and warming the brown leaves that carpeted the hillside. As the leaves warmed, they curled slightly and emitted exquisite crackling sounds. I had never heard this beautiful sound in nature before, and I felt blessed by the shakuhachi for leading me to it.

Follow the Recipe or Follow Intuition?

MUSIC IS WONDROUS, AND ONE CAN BE AWESTRUCK by the enormity of the art. What great fortune to be involved—to be a musician—but how to approach learning?

We can "knuckle down" and work hard to follow the guidance of a teacher, and we will learn a great deal. There is an additional important aspect to sort out. We must make a distinction between how much we approach our practice as if following a recipe and how much we rely on our own intuition. The recipe approach can help to a great extent, but at some point it can also be a crutch that holds us back. The intuitive approach can be a more streamlined arrow to the kind of playing we desire to make.

In the movie *Amadeus*, the insults made to the character Salieri, an adversary of Mozart, were also critiquing his approach to music as being a methodical, dogged approach. This was the movie's portrayal, and in reality, we are limited in knowing who the man really was. The movie's contrast of the two composers, Mozart and Salieri and their music, illustrates the distinction between a dry, methodical approach and allowing musical intuition to flourish. Intuition can be trusted in creativity and cultivated in practice. We need to value our insights more.[6]

Children have fresh insights and intuitions. They do not take anything for granted as we adults do. Parents may feel that their children take a lot for granted, but children are out in the world vulnerable and wide eyed, and for them every moment is important. Their natural position of dependence means every moment can offer them more stability or less. Having fresh insights and intuitions helps them survive the inevitable onslaughts of life as they mature.

A key to allowing more freedom of thought and freedom of intuition is to take nothing for granted. How do we access our intuition? One way is to have constantly listening ears. Listen to lots of music. We can allow ourselves to be moved by our favorites and branch out to listen to other genres and world music.

Besides listening to music, listen to sounds. Distinguish among birdsong and bird calls in detail. It's not just "chirp, chirp" but quick little melodies, sometimes elaborate and complex. The same kind of bird can have a variety of tones and patterns. Can you imitate them? Listen to the wind in different trees, their different kinds of whispering. Listen to the rhythms and the rise and fall of speech in a cafe. Listen to the sound of your footsteps in one room sounding different in another room. These are the qualities of Nature.

Ultimately music comes from Nature. To respect the nature (specific essences) of Nature (diverse universe) helps us intuit the nature of music, the sources of expression, and the character of voice. Music can become not just a representation; we can be in Nature.

The art of playing is naturalness. Naturalness comes forward in playing that seems without effort—playing where phrases flow in the way they are spoken with recognizable emotions and empathy yet unafraid to be "outside the box."

Casals frequently commented to cellists playing in his master classes, "It's better to play it this way. It's more *natural*." His playing was sometimes criticized as "taking too many liberties." He would sometimes slightly stretch phrases for certain kinds of emphasis. His playing was direct, and there was never anything nebulous about what he was saying musically, never any doubt about what he meant. He had a freedom—louds could speak out, quiets could be poignant. A listener may not agree with all of his phrasing, but his character was free, and the music spoke simply with energy, assertiveness, dignity, and an enormous loving dedication. It is said that Casals was asked why at ninety-three years old he still practiced cello three hours a day. His reply was,

I'm beginning to notice some improvement.
—Pablo Casals

Wandering or Lost?

IN MY EARLY TWENTIES, I MADE A NUMBER OF VISITS to Tassajara Zen Mountain center. It is where I met my first husband, who was a student of Shunryū Suzuki Roshi, one of the first Japanese Zen masters to teach Zen meditation in the United States. During one visit, I was invited to join other musicians to play for a wedding of two of the practitioners. Normally music was not allowed in the canyon retreat in respect for the quiet meditation practice. Smoking marijuana was also forbidden.

This was a special day of celebration, and at the rehearsal, someone passed a joint. When we were set up on stage and getting ready to play, we decided to warm up with a little freeform. I suppose it could have been called improv, but to me, it was noodling and not necessarily coherent. Then we went on with our rehearsed pieces.

After the wedding, we heard that Roshi had enjoyed the music, especially the first music at the beginning. Perhaps our musical wanderings revealed a kind of American Sui-Zen in a disjointed way.

An Ear toward Self-Censorship

IN OUR PLAYING, WE OFTEN SELF-CENSOR OUR PASSIONS because of the influence of recorded music standards that are actually limitations. We have had these limitations ingrained in our ears. Louds, softs, highs, lows, and contrasts are often mollified in recorded music. The music is homogenized to have an even-keel sound, to produce a standard product that won't jolt anyone when listening in a car or taking a nap.

Long-playing (LP) vinyl recordings from the 1940s and 1950s were much more exciting. Yes, even though they were not as refined in sound engineering, they were exciting. There was power and naturalness in hearing the dynamics and the broader ranges of expression of the musicians. You can feel their presence and the emotional messages more clearly than you can with this era's homogenized recordings. There are great newer recordings of accomplished musicians, but more often than not, a raw and direct recording of expression is toned down and polished. Music that has had all the raw edginess smoothed over loses character.

In contrast to recorded music, live music offers the opportunity to meditate on the music—as opposed to listening while doing something else. It can be a time to make a break, to set aside everything in order to focus on music and those who create it. The audience and performer share a unique magical experience.

I am reminded of a good friend of my family from my grandparents' and parents' era, Dr. Leo Eloesser, whom I got to know in my twenties.[7] "Doc" was an internationally known surgeon based in San Francisco and he was also a violist. In the 1920s and 1930s, he and my grandparents often gathered musician friends to play chamber music. Musicians from the San Francisco Symphony came. It was probably through these circles that my mother became friends with Hephzibah Menuhin,[8] concert pianist and sister of Yehudi Menuhin.[9] In his lifetime, Doc Eloesser refused to listen to recorded music. He called it "canned music."

For a couple of summers in the 1970s, I attended a chamber music workshop at Humboldt University in Arcata, California. The schedule each day assigned each musician to a chamber group—trio, quintet, or octet—with whom to read through a number of pieces. The music came from the collections of the combined music libraries of Humboldt State University and Southern Oregon State University. After reading through the pieces, the group voted on one work or movement to rehearse the rest of the day and perform that evening. The evening performances were excellent. For the final evening performance of the week, eight cellists formed a circle on stage. Anyone from the audience who wanted to could come up and sit on the floor in the center of the circle. They played a Bach chorale. It was more thrilling than surround sound.[10]

Live music needs more sharing. For centuries, European classic music was the privilege of the wealthy. Mozart was one of the first to become a freelance composer and organize his own public concerts. He struggled financially as he had trouble being hired in an official position in a court system, but he paved the way for future composers and performers to find more independence in public concerts. Today, the recording industry allows more music to be heard, but live performances still have the legacy of being restricted to only those who have a better income. Perhaps an enlightened society would ensure people a livable income and would use more of its "commons" through taxes to make live performances available to more people.

Art and Institutions

ART IS SPIRITUAL PRACTICE, BUT ART CAN BE SOUGHT after, bought, and used as manipulation. Religious institutions through history have hired artists, composers, and musicians. Religious stories and myths are conveyed and reinforced by beautiful paintings and oratorios. People who ordinarily have limited access to art in their communities are awed by religious art. They worship and show their reverence while viewing paintings and sculptures, hearing reverent music, and sitting in pews beneath beautifully designed vaulted ceilings.

The institutional church tries to limit and control the spirituality and reverence of artists. Art in churches is used for education and manipulation to make sure that everyone is thinking alike. Thus Leonardo da Vinci was commissioned to do a painting promoting the idea of the Virgin. He and his assistants had trouble negotiating with the demands of the clergy in creating the altarpiece painting *The Virgin of the Rocks*. The clergy stipulated many details about how the painting should look, and the fact that it was painted a second time with gold halos and other gilding may have been at the church request. In any case, there are documents that the payment was poor and slow in coming, eventually ending in lengthy legal disputes.[11]

This is not to say that art in churches and cathedrals is to be viewed with suspicion alone. Profound beauty and excellence can be found, but we must recognize and consider the history, the domination, influence, wealth, and power. Artists were employed with many strings attached, and even as devout as they may have been in various religious institutions, if they had more freedom, they may have expressed their spirituality with more diversity and individuality.

Innocence Issue

Whether sad, playful, happy, or poignant, music is refreshing. Because it can speak so directly to the psyche and soul, it is easily taken for granted. People perceive it as flowing from out of the blue. It surrounds them when they push a button or tap a screen. They feel it as their own private environment talking to them. In a way, this is good—it is a kind of innocence, purely listening to what the music brings across the air.

Rampal spoke of this innocence:

> *Innocent? It is good to be innocent.... Unfortunately, concerning music, we are musicians, and we cannot have the same experience as the public, who is unacquainted with the music. Theirs is a pure experience.... For us, we listen to a concerto, and we know in advance what happens, and since you know, you take the emotion differently. You see, the public takes the complete emotion—like drinking a glass of water.[16]*
> —Jean Pierre Rampal

This is what a musician wants. A musician wants the listener to listen without distraction, wants the magic to take place without awareness of technique.

> *The most perfect technique is that which is not noticed at all.*
> —Pablo Casals

A musician does not have an "innocent" ear. A musician can hear the deliberate efforts others make to convey a piece of music and make it sound one way or another. Maybe that's why a musician can hear manipulation. The music we are listening to at any particular time is what it is, and there is no choice but to accept what is present and what we hear as we listen. On one end of the spectrum, it can be something contrived and artificial like a TV commercial jingle, or it can be playing that is spoken from the heart. As musicians, we need to be discerning in our approach.

In the steps we take in our artistic evolution, we can get comfortable with changing our mind along the path. Even when we are convinced of a best way to play a phrase or a whole piece, incorporating new ideas can expand the art. Perhaps we have thought of a certain piece as being beautifully melancholy, and then we notice that the musical statements can radiate a kind of grandness and noble largess. After years playing it one way, we've found a new approach informed by personal observations and distinctions.

Being Creative

BEING CREATIVE IS KEEPING ALIVE A DEEP INTEREST IN asking ourselves questions and keeping our minds open to finding answers. It is finding knowledge and understanding through experience. We are aligning our life with our commitment to experiencing the nature of Nature, the nature of music.

11

Performance Delight

We each approach the challenges of playing music and performing in individual ways. The ideas and suggestions I put forward here are not meant to crowd a person with information but to allow space and freedom to pick and choose what might apply and to inspire musicians to move forward in their most healthy and natural process.

Words can only point to ideas and experiences. The most interesting part comes when as we practice, we try these approaches. Often it is not the ideas themselves that bring about our next step but how they morph into new ideas while we are bringing the music to life.

When listening to a performance, people can perceive the work being created and sense the approach and presence of the person performing. Someone's unique ways may reveal to listeners approaches other than their own. *She plays that movement thoughtfully, almost a meditation, whereas I've always thought of it as a slow dance.* These perceptions are nonlinear, based in fleeting impressions. They can be direct or indirect. A listener may think, *Oh that's beautiful—the way he played the slow movement, he's not afraid of a depth of intimacy.* A listener at another concert may observe, *She makes this section sound like a wild dance by firelight.* Elsewhere, another impression might be, *I sense a wonderful potential in this person's playing, a calm, like the effect of listening to ocean waves full of powerful energy but calm.* Each musician—the "intimacy" person, the "fire dance" person, and the "calm energy" person—may not have planned for the music to come across in these ways. It may have bubbled forth from their inner nature.

The listeners' individual natures come into play as well. They will find different treasures according to their experiences, influencing how they relate to the music. Perhaps the "depth of intimacy" was experienced by another person in the audience as too dull and unexciting. Perhaps the "fire dance" for someone else was too chaotic. There are many variables, many individual composites of awareness. Unique persons are communicating with each other.

Keeping Your Joy Alive

A flute is more than a fine instrument. It is a transcendent vehicle allowing us to fly, soar, bank, and land. We can explore emotions, send a prayer to the universe, and feel the pulse of oceans. We can align ourselves with beautiful sound, try music of other cultures, sound sweet like a bird, or sound like a cello or a trumpet. We can sing naturally and openly like panpipes or searchingly like a shakuhachi. We can transport ourselves and others. In our musical traveling, we can forget we are playing the flute.

There are accounts of accomplished musicians who have expressed in writings and interviews a longing to feel their original joy in music. It is surprising to hear that their most satisfying performing experiences are often in simpler, unlikely venues.

Violinist Kató Havas, a child prodigy, was born in Hungary in 1920. She was inspired by hearing gypsy violinists with their depth and variety of tone-colors, effervescent enthusiasm, and ease of playing. She has been both a great classical performer and an innovative teacher.[1]

She tells of an unforgettable performance she gave as a teenager. It began when she was delayed in a train in a remote station in Hungary.

> ...it was early in the morning and...in order to while away the time, I thought I would play some Bach—the Chaconne to be exact. Soon, I noticed that some window cleaners and other workmen were gathering in front of my carriage window, signaling to me to let the window down so that they could hear. It was then I first felt that overwhelming necessity to transmit my deep-seated and profound feeling for the Chaconne, without the burden of having to play for approval. And the miracle began to happen. Their immobile silence and the spell of their rapt attention transferred both them and the Chaconne into a blissful unified entity. To equate the limited, harsh reality around them with the limitless, omniscient world of Bach was a very heady experience indeed. That was when I realized that 'giving' the music and not trying to play well was the real secret of performance. But even with that realization, I could never, ever again recapture that first experience. I had many other memorable performances, but they were never quite the same. Also, I never, before or after, had the same marvelous reward as the large hunk of black bread and bacon, sprinkled with paprika, which they produced for me.[2]
>
> —KATÓ HAVAS

Freelance Fun and Heartfelt Listening

IN THE LATE 1970s, WHEN I WAS VISITING Portland, Oregon, through the generosity of owner Goodie Cable, I played in the evenings at the Rimsky-Korsakoffeehouse. It was (and still is) an unusual cafe on the first floor of an elegant, Victorian house in southeast Portland. In those days, the setting was formal. There were tables draped in white tablecloths and an upright piano in one corner. Coffee and tea were served with fine desserts that had been made during the day by bakers in the large kitchen. The hours were unusual—it was open from late afternoon into the late night. The idea was to provide a cafe for people to come to after attending concerts, theater performances, special events, or for an evening out. Some came to hear the musicians featured each evening while enjoying the specialty desserts, coffees, and teas. The atmosphere was cheery and elegant. I played there several nights, playing solo my collection of melodies—Baroque, Celtic, English Country Dance, Swedish fiddle music, South American Indian, Native American, Japanese, and Middle Eastern. I aimed to create variety in my background music program, singular graceful melodies, played more intimately rather than as if on a concert stage.[3]

Through this gig, I was asked if I might play for an upcoming Multnomah County Library book sale. The address I was given lead to a parking garage building. As it turned out, the sale was held under the ground level of a parking building not being used. When I arrived I thought, *Darn! What did I get myself into?* As I began to play, I found the acoustics flattering and fun to work with, so I focused on enjoying the sound.

Out of the corner of my eye, I noticed a man who looked like a homeless person seated slumped against a pillar, his back

Performance Delight 165

toward me, a hat shading his profile. I hoped he was all right, not ill, drunk, hungry, or suffering, although being homeless *is* suffering. Maybe he was asleep.

Although the parking lot was a strange setting, I felt that helping the library was a noble cause, and I put my best energy into playing. I played about an hour and a half while people milled around the tables, selecting and purchasing used books. When I finished and was packing up, the homeless man approached me. His face was beaming as he said, "I have never heard anything like that before." I thanked him and shook his hand. I could tell by his demeanor that he had really been listening, and I felt rewarded to have his direct and heartfelt response.

Another favorite listener was an old woman, a neighbor in the small village of Chauriat, France, where I lived with my artist grandparents for a year and a half. When I was nineteen, I left San Francisco State University and worked for a year. At the invitation of my grandparents, I traveled to France to study music at the Ecole Nationale de Musique et D'Art Dramatique, a branch of the Paris Conservatory, in the city of Clermont-Ferrand (now the Conservatoire Emmanuel-Chabrier). My uncle, John Stackpole, oboist with the Dallas Symphony, had studied there years prior. It was a focused period of my life devoted to music. I was free to study and practice for long hours.

Chauriat is a village with an eleventh-century church at its center and circled by the evident shape of the long-gone Medieval wall of fortification. Our neighbor up the street, Mme Vergnol, was a woman of the land, dressed in a delicately printed black dress like those that most widowed, gray-haired country women wore. She was a bit unkempt but hardworking, and her garden was an immaculate work of art. We were fortunate to buy the freshest and most beautiful vegetables from her.

Mme Vergnol would come to my grandparents' house with a basket of gorgeous produce from her garden. She often came by as I was practicing in the living room and would shyly ask if she could sit awhile and listen. She sat very still, concentrating on what she was hearing. She was a deep listener, and I was amazed to feel her presence. Playing for her felt like a real event; real human communication was happening. Playing for someone who is listening in this way creates a special energy.

When I played a Bach sonata for her, I mentioned that one movement was a bourrée, explaining that it was a dance. She said, "Oui, I know bourrées. We danced bourrées."

Sure enough, on another day, when I went with her to see her beautiful garden and gather vegetables, she was talking about the old Auvergne dances and the bourrée. Her family must have gone far back in the history of the area. She could speak the old patois language of the region. She put her basket down on the garden pathway by the gate and began to dance in intricate energetic footwork. I was delighted to watch her. She said, "It would be better if I had *mes sabots*" (my wooden shoes).[4]

Years later, another situation playing for people gave me great satisfaction. In my search for an informal regular gig, I struck an agreement with the management at Café Express in downtown Boulder, Colorado. The arrangement was that I would play during Sunday brunch in exchange for food—delicious croissant sandwiches and gourmet cafe fare, an arrangement that suited my family and me well.

The ceilings at Café Express were high, so the acoustics carried my sound perfectly. I could play naturally and still be heard and hear myself above the voices and conversations of the diners without invading their sound space. I discovered that regular informal playing in public was of great benefit and offered a pathway to feel less nervous and to take more pleasure in performing. The cafe proved to be a great place to get other gigs. One Sunday, someone asked if I would come that afternoon to play at their wedding party in the mountains. It turned out to be a fun gig, a celebration with mostly philosophy professors and students from the University of Colorado. Informal settings are great opportunities to find joy in performing.

Recording Experience

IN THE LATE 1980S AND 1990S, I HAD THE HONOR of being one of the musicians to play on the albums of Bill Douglas. His music is beautiful and unusual with classical, Celtic, African, and jazz influences. One can hear his brilliant piano work along with diverse instruments as well as choir pieces sung by Ars Nova of Colorado. The albums were produced by the Hearts of Space label.[5]

These days, recording can be done in different technological contexts and with ever-changing types of equipment. There are some important things to keep in mind when playing for a recording. Along with my own quirky approaches, these ideas are presented in the hope that they may be helpful to other flutists or anyone involved in recording.

The biggest objective will be to thoroughly dwell in the music, playing with detailed attention to every note. It is also of great importance, when speaking with sound engineers or fellow musicians, to use precise words. It takes extra focus to communicate clearly when talking about music.

How a composer, engineer, and producer choose to incorporate a flute part into a project is not up to the flutist, but the flutist can and should make suggestions. Pay attention to the qualities in playback. Many people, including sound engineers, have a limited concept about what flute sounds like, and they could be limiting their approach to recording flute. Does the playback capture only the high end of the flute's body of sound? Does it sound one dimensional? Metallic? What qualities in the sound are not being picked up?

Many people don't realize or don't appreciate that flute, when played with body, contains a spectrum of low and high overtones. People tend to conceptualize flute as only a high pitched, one dimensional instrument and may not be aware of the wider aspects of flute tone. Their conception of the sound may be limited by their assumption that flute has merely a shimmery, metallic tone quality rather than the broad and deep, voice-like qualities brought out by the player.

Flute sound is complex. Tiny eddies of air create vibrations that give the tone many harmonics, creating the tone distinctiveness. The physics of how the air moves and causes the vibration of the instrument and produces the sound is not well understood. Scientific photo imagery shows the whorls of air moving in and around the flute as it is played. Yet, unlike the visible vibrations of a violin string, the physics of flute sound is too changeable to detect a completely scientifically definable pattern. It is another beautiful mystery. A flexible approach in recording can work with this mystery. [6]

Flute tone has layers of high and low overtones. It helps to hear flute less like an instrument and more like a voice. For a recording to pick up your broad range of subtleties of "voice," it is your singing quality that will be most important for that "voice" to come across. It has to be there from the beginning, as no subsequent technical electronic adjustments can bring forth those qualities.

Careful placement of the microphones can make an enormous difference. A mic out in the room is okay but can feature too much of the general room sound and make the flute sound too distant and thin. A good balance can be achieved by having a close mic placed five or six inches in front of the forehead and another placed two or three feet in front of the footjoint end of the flute. For guitarists, a mic is often placed near the sound hole because a guitar's sound is relatively quiet, and the qualities of the tone emanate from the resonating box of the instrument. For flutists, it is our body that brings forth depth and resonance.

Another common technical mistake in recording the flute is to squelch the high notes in the mixing. The result is that an ascending line can sound like the energy is cutting out and the musical line is compromised. It is important for the flutist to be very present in singing the high notes as an extended line without punching them (discussed in chapter 8). When those high notes are sung beautifully in the context of the musical line, extensive editing is not necessary.

Too much reverb can deaden some of the natural sparkle in tone. Reverb can also subtly change your approach to phrasing. Most likely, as you play in the recording studio, there will be a bit of reverb in the headphones so that you hear yourself with reverb as you play. When practicing for a recording, it is useful to record yourself at home with a little reverb to get a feel for working with the subtle adjustments that may be necessary.

How do you jump into step to play with previously recorded tracks? Listening through headphones to the musicians you are joining can seem remote. Visualize and feel that you are present with the players. Before your first note, pretend you are already playing along with them while you prepare with your first deep inhalation (as described in chapter 3). Keep a crisp and clear affinity with the beat, almost anticipatory. I find it helpful to imagine that I am sending my sound (extending chi) through the mic and through the wires to play with the other musicians. It is abstract yet real.

Flexibility

WE CAN PUT OUR WHOLE PRESENCE, OUR BODY, IN OUR tone whether we are playing loud or soft. It helps to jump into a piece with a less hesitant attitude. Many people feel a certain amount of shyness by nature, and shyness can be an asset. Being more sensitive to life and perhaps less egotistical (or less obviously so) opens doors to perceiving subtleties. Although we want to cultivate many subtleties in our sound, we do not want to "hide behind it" or play from a reticent or "self-effacing" attitude. Keep a kind of conviction and a fully alive tone quality. Even in playing music that is quiet, mysterious, or questioning, play these qualities with conviction—with body and presence.

We may feel poised and have an exact idea of where we are going with the music, yet small adventures happen. Usually they are rewarding adventures that evolve out of our feelings in the moment and on-the-spot ideas of phrasing. To feel a new possibility and to go there helps our musicality to develop a flexibility. Once we pick up the flute and begin playing, we needn't feel stuck in any rigid approach. If we don't like the way we have begun to play, we can work right away to change what we are doing. There is no need to assume, *Oh well, I started off on a wrong foot and now must see it through to the end as less than ideal.* Try making changes "on the fly."

For example, if you begin playing and your embouchure setting is not in ideal position, preventing you from playing in your desired tone quality, teach yourself to shift as soon as possible at a breathing spot, a rest, or midphrase. The ability to make quick adjustments is worthwhile to practice. By not allowing yourself to stop when things are not ideal, you can find ways to quickly adjust. This helps you cultivate an immediate assessment of your tone quality and know precisely what changes make a difference.

Perhaps as you are playing you discover that the tempo is too slow. You cannot change your tempo just anywhere in the music, but there are ways to subtly speed it up. One way is to push the tempo slightly faster on passages and phrases that compositionally have more energy and excitement; then stay at your desired tempo. This can work only if yours is a solo part and others playing with you have a more accompanying role. When deliberately changing the tempo, it is important to gesture the beat to communicate your speedup to the other musicians. Stay alert to players who have the lead melody and when they signal a deliberate, albeit subtle, tempo change.

In what other aspects of our playing can we practice flexibility and changing on the fly? The following problematic situations may arise in playing and in performance.

- *Dry lips*—We need to find a place in the music to quickly moisten our lips, but what if there is no break in the music? For me, Colorado's semiarid climate made this a frequent dilemma. It helps to apply a light layer of nonflavored lip balm (mint can have a cooling and numbing effect on the lips), but even with this, the lips can become dry while playing. In that case, we must hold out until a rest in the music allows time to moisten the lips. If there are no rests, it is sometimes necessary to leave a note early to create a break in the same way we do to grab a quick breath.

Another possibility, depending on the music, is to tongue some notes with a forward tonguing (the style mentioned earlier as if blowing a seed off of the tip of the tongue). That subtle motion may not completely alleviate the problem but will bring some moisture and make it possible to go on (more on tonguing in chapter 14).

- *Dry mouth*—When the mouth and throat get dry, try to breathe out warm, moist air. This type of exhalation resembles how we blow on our hands in cold weather or fog up glass with our breath. It is important to keep the mouth closed while not playing. By using the nose more for air intake (review Butto's breathing exercises in chapter 3), we can protect the mouth and throat from the irritation of too much dry air. It helps to drink water throughout the day and stay hydrated.

- *Intonation*—Play with a steady airflow, and be constantly ready to adjust. With this steady flow, the notes in each melodic line will be more naturally in tune in relation to each other. The intonation of a note can be technically accurate, measurable by electronic gages, yet there is a subtle range to either side of the mark. Depending on context, tones can sound on the higher or the lower side of the pitch. Whether it seems right is not absolute. Listen carefully. Jazz players play in tune on the lower side of the pitch. Orchestral violinists tend to play in tune on the higher side. Neither one is wrong, as their intonation fits their expression.

When playing with others, the adage "listen and adjust" is important. Being slightly high or low within the pitch can be changed by rolling the flute subtly inward or outward or changing the angle of breath on the embouchure. It helps to cultivate the ability to change as immediately as possible.

I am reminded of the characters performed by comedians Fred Armisen and Kristen Wiig on the show *Saturday Night Live*. They pose as "Garth and Kat," singer-songwriters presenting a new song on TV, usually for a special occasion or holiday. They assure the anchor that they are prepared, but they are not prepared, not having even composed the song. They pretend to know the song and begin singing. What they sing is mostly improvised: Garth begins the phrase, and Kat tries to sing with him by picking up each note and word as instantaneously as possible. It almost works, they almost sing together, but not quite. The degree to which it falls short is hilarious, and the effort is brilliant and terribly funny. Most amazingly, it shows how, with an awake ear, we can "listen and adjust."[7]

- *Lose your place*—Getting lost while playing with a group can be baffling and embarrassing. Quickly finding our place again is made easier by our familiarity with the piece and music in general. If we have never played this particular piece before, it is important to learn it as thoroughly as possible ahead of time. Listen to a recording of it, and pay attention to all the parts, noting the "landmarks"—entrances, what happens during flute rests, changes of key and time signatures, solos, duets, and tutti parts. If we are unable to study the piece ahead of time, we can rely on our general familiarity with how music is constructed to find our place. We can listen for downbeats and the beginnings and endings of phrases. Our best cues might be cadences, new material, repeated parts, first and second endings, patterns of melodies traded by other instrumentalists, and the patterns of progressions of harmonies. These observations can help us find our way. It is our ears that help us.

- *Correcting for someone's mistake*—If someone skips a beat, it is sometimes necessary to leap ahead to join him or her as soon as possible to avoid the "train wreck." We must work with the musician later to ensure that the mistake is corrected. This may involve making an exercise of slowing down the passage with the whole ensemble and perhaps subdividing the downbeats to see and feel exactly how the notes fit together before returning to the natural tempo.

- *Changes of dynamics and tone quality*—As you play, if you are not satisfied with your tone quality, phrasing, or dynamics and hear something better in your imagination, jump or slide right over to playing like you want to hear it. You needn't feel stuck in how you began.

- *Not enough air*—We may have the flexibility to take in very quick, small breaths to get through a passage, but we must be sure to take full advantage of any break that allows a fuller breath. Quick in-breaths through the nose while the lips remain focused for the phrase being played, can give just enough extra air to make it through without running out. Breathing is discussed in more detail in chapter 3.

- *Slippage of embouchure*—This problem frequently happens with a slippery lower lip and chin from sweating. The lip plate and thus the whole embouchure can slip out of position. Tone will suffer unless we adjust its position right away. If you find the embouchure has slipped and is not placed right as you are playing, compensate as best you can with immediate adjustments to intonation, breathflow, and posture, but as soon as possible, in a rest, slide it into the ideal position.

Flutist Murray Panitz used a small piece of paper on the lip plate to prevent it from slipping. I tried using masking tape but did not like cleaning off the sticky part left after removing the tape. An interesting and wiggy historic idea is presented by Baroque flutist and pedagogue Johann Joachim Quantz (1697–1773) in his book, *On Playing the Flute*.

> *In such circumstances, and especially in warm weather, it also may happen that he perspires about the mouth, and the flute in consequence does not remain lying securely at the proper place, but slips downwards, so that the mouth-hole is too much covered, and the tone, if not lacking altogether, is at least too weak. Quickly to remedy this last evil, let the flautist wipe his mouth and the flute clean, then touch his hair or wig and rub the fine powder clinging to his finger upon his mouth. In this way the pores are stopped, and he can continue playing without great hindrance.*[8]
>
> —Johann Joachim Quantz

- *Energy*—If the music begins to sound dull, we can bring energy into our playing by relaxing and changing our stance into a better posture. Offering more life and energy in the music brings less and less distance between feeling and sound, between musician and the music.
- *Stay involved*—Not busy or frantic but simply involved. We can feel eager to learn a piece or to make it perfect quickly. That eagerness is noble, but

it's best to avoid putting too much pressure or too much excitement into the process. It helps to cultivate clearminded engagement. Remaining not overly busy or frantic with over-the-top excitement (although enthusiasm is there), we can calmly engage in what needs to be expressed by putting more energy into our singing of the passages and not "pushing the river."

- *Relax*—We learn best when relaxed. Relaxed means not slouched but having physical and mental balance with a natural attention and alertness. If you feel built-up tensions, ask yourself, *What if I relax my lips, neck, arms, fingers, legs, and feet?* The changes can be made in the middle of a rehearsal, practice session, or performance. No one will notice you lowering your shoulders, widening your stance, or a side-to-side stretch of your head and neck. You will notice a dramatic improvement in sound, making it more warm, open, and centered. The relaxation and improved sound create more energy and inspiration, allowing sincere and natural enthusiasm to unfold.
- *Play for yourself*—To enter the atmosphere of a piece, get inside it. In the moment and over time, live with the piece to feel what is below the surface. There can be continual discoveries and insights bubbling up over a lifetime.

As an artist, you are not afraid to allow yourself to find the expressions that please you most. Of course, there are shapes, forms, and laws of Nature to work with, but being an artist means you work with these in your own way and with your own character. Therefore, being an artist is not something you do by some exterior standard. Honor what is personally right in the moment. Your sound might be a kaleidoscope of possibilities, but it's your own.

Having enough air to allow you to play with a steady flow gives you confidence. You can trust that you have the flexibility to create changes as you play. Need more air? Need to lick your lips? Need to adjust the position of the embouchure? You can do it, because you have practiced handling these situations. Need to energize? To relax or explore more? You can enter each of these the moment you think of them.

Trust Your Ability

Keep reinforcing what you know of your abilities. If you played well once, build on that experience. You may think a kind of magic helped you play so beautifully, and that may have been the case, but it wouldn't have been there if you weren't ready. Repeat the experience including the magic, and likely you'll find even more magic.

Alone to Work and Dream

Although the pressure of an upcoming engagement is great motivation to practice, having no engagement on the horizon gives the time and freedom to explore other music. Alone time is to be treasured, and playing solely for oneself is an important self-communication. This treasured time offers the chance to experiment and expand insights and capabilities.

Some of the time can be used to listen to a variety of recordings. Finding new music to try and further developing favorites are rewarding and pleasurable pursuits. There is time to feel alone with the music and to quiet down enough to find more depths in it.

During this time, you can ask yourself what you long for in music opportunities. What musical setting seems ideal?

What performance situations would you most enjoy? You may not know the answers, but at this point, you have the freedom to imagine.

It might be possible to create performance opportunities for yourself by arranging to play in a setting such as a house concert for invited friends or arranging to play in a public space, perhaps the opening of a show at an art gallery.

There is something serendipitous about doing lots of independent playing and practicing. When you have been playing a great deal without the prospects of an upcoming performance, you are happy when you do get a call to play for an event and can approach it with more energy and confidence.

Performance Delight

IN PERFORMANCE, WE WANT MOST OF ALL TO BE PRESENT.

- Present with ourselves
- Present with the music
- Present with the moment
- Present with the space
- Present with the people listening

All of this can be a delight. We are sharing what we love. We are responsible for manifesting it, for making it happen, but it is not just about us. It is about the place, the time, the people present, the other musicians, the composer, the manifestation of music through history, and the context of our era. We bring our beating heart, our imagination, our courage, to "speak" many facets of the music.

At times, we protect our concentration by blocking out anything that may distract. This may be useful, but sometimes it takes too much energy and becomes a distraction in itself. Being aware and inclusive is more helpful. Inclusiveness includes you, the musician. You can dwell in your private world while playing because you are part of the entirety of the situation. If you shut your eyes as you concentrate, it is not about shutting out but about opening up even more to the music of the moment.

> *Performers...all strive to achieve those, alas, only too rare moments of pure communication, when performer and audience alike are suspended in a transcendental moment of truth.*[9]
> —Kató Havas

In Sickness and Health

WHAT IF AT TIMES YOU ARE NOT FEELING "CHIPPER" yet must practice and perform anyway? This can be a huge problem for a flutist or any wind player. A sore throat, a cough—what do you do?

You must take care of the illness as best you can and be especially careful to stay hydrated (more on healthcare later). It is helpful to look for mild remedies (maybe homeopathic remedies), making sure that they won't dry out the mouth. Some pharmaceuticals have a mouth-drying side effect, which can be devastating for a flutist.

I once played a solo concert I had arranged at a library. Before I was to play, I had an enormous migraine. I took over-the-counter acetaminophen...several...and it took the edge off, but I lapsed into one of the worst migraines I ever had. I played well but suffered later. Sometimes we can feel that we are putting forth our best offering under harsh circumstances, which is as true for musicians as for any other human endeavor.

If we find ourselves not well, temporarily sick but able and determined to continue our practice leading up to the performance, there are many options to practice with kindness-to-self. Short but focused practice sessions are best. To play each work or portions of a piece quietly, *piano* or *pianissimo*, is a helpful approach.

Quiet with Beauty

WHEN PREPARING FOR AN UPCOMING PERFORMANCE, whether sick or not, it is helpful to review all the music by playing it pianissimo or blowing to produce whispering tones. It reminds me of the movie *Amadeus* when Mozart's character, on his deathbed, sings parts of his *Requiem*. He sings *sotto voce*. How beautiful the soft focus on the various lines. Not being on our deathbed, we are very much alive, perhaps only suffering from a cold.[10]

Playing ultraquietly is a valuable tool. It can bring new insights in phrasing and expression. Perhaps in one spot, a single note wants to be brought out and emphasized—more by a singing quality than by an accent. In another place, a pattern may be revealed where the lower notes are more interesting when brought into the foreground. A series of notes might need a clearer declarative feel—another group needs a general calm feeling.

Why would playing quietly bring about so many new ideas in phrasing and expression? Perhaps it is partly because by playing quietly, one feels less "in control." The shape of a melodic line may be freed from our previous conception. When playing quietly, there is no need to manipulate the expression. The lines move along with ghostly potential—a muse whispering in our ear. There is more freedom to observe fresh insights about the direction and expression the music might take.

Sometimes the discovery of an approach will be so inspiring that it is compelling to play "out loud" and to develop this discovery. That's great! Writing these revelations either on the music or in a notebook is useful. Penciling insights as they come can serve as reminders of the discovery, the experience, and the feeling. A noted reminder may turn out to become a direction to continue to build upon, to refute, or to develop into a completely new idea.

Many of the ideas in this book are based on just such notes and reminders. Some pages of my music have peculiar penciled hieroglyphics or a few words to remind myself of a new discovery to consider. If the printed music becomes too congested with markings, a kneaded drawing eraser (from an art supply store) makes erasing easy and thorough, without smudging, digging into the paper, or creating messy tiny rolls of worn-down eraser (which one doesn't want anywhere near the instrument). Kneaded drawing erasers make it possible for the printed music to be marked freely without worry about permanent damage to the pages, and diverse ideas can be noted and revised over the years.

12

Performance Anxiety

*P*laying music takes many kinds of courage. To want to play for others, be it a small group or a large audience, comes from a desire to share and communicate inspiration, beauty, and insight. Approaching a performance engagement can bring on an enormous amount of anxiety.

Pablo Casals, the great cellist and humanitarian, possessed tremendous courage. During the Nazi occupation of France, he faced many dangerous situations, even bravely turning away a couple of Nazi soldiers when they came to his private residence in southern France with a request from Hitler for him to play in Germany. Alone, he firmly but diplomatically declined, not knowing what they might do to him. Casals steadfastly opposed the recognition of Francisco Franco as dictator of Spain, refusing to perform in countries that accepted his brutal dictatorship, including the United States. While displaying great courage in upholding the dignity of humanity and with his long career playing for audiences worldwide, Casals suffered all his life from "stage fright" before performances. As odd as it might sound, some of the finest master musicians who have rigorous careers never lose performance anxiety and go through miseries before each concert, even suffering physical illness.[1]

When we have stage fright (who doesn't?), we must remember not to berate ourselves and add extra dismay or hopelessness to our nerves. To have some degree of performance anxiety is said to be beneficial in keeping alert while performing; it adds an alive edge to our playing. Everyone experiences nervousness. Ours may not be as bad as we think. We can work with it.

We want the confidence to know that when we walk on stage, we will be able to deliver the music, yet the art in playing music is not built on confidence alone. It is an openness and desire to share. We are vulnerable people seeking beauty, enlightenment, connection, communication. To speak from these parts of ourselves is a kind of strength that is broader than the singular desire for confidence. It is a willingness to be honest.

Being involved with creativity and learning is difficult. We have to deal with everything that is human: health, endurance, flexibility, hardship, emotions, praise, and criticism. Being human is lifework and artwork.

Jump In

THE BEST WAY TO JUMP IN IS TO HOLD IN OUR EAR the sounds of the best playing of the music that we can imagine. We can hear in our mind's ear our best performance of a piece, most alive tone qualities, and truest emotional qualities. We can dwell in the "stories" we wish to tell. We stay in love with and dedicated to the music.

In a performance, the first few measures may feel shaky or not "up to par," but soon we gain our footing. Many musicians when listening to each other can recognize these first few moments where everything is in place but not completely "on"—even though one strives to be totally "on" from the onset.

Some ways to begin with "on" energy follow below (discussed in more detail later).

- Take in a slow breath before the first note (discussed in chapter 3).
- Hear your first note and phrase before you begin playing.
- Imagine that you have already been playing and that your first notes are evolving out of a previous phrase.
- Hear in your mind's ear your most beautiful tone qualities.
- Hear the ending of the piece; it sobers you to balance the beginning with where you are going.
- Feel a shape to the composition. You are dwelling in and moving in that shape.

Approaches like these help you adopt specific ways to clarify your artistic direction. These more interesting considerations can replace your less interesting fear and anxiety, which can then recede into the background or disappear altogether.

Guitarist Pepe Romero says that stage fright is in the *conscious* mind, but it is not in the *subconscious* mind. He regards stage fright as illusory—a figment of our imagination. Since we create the "nerves" with our own thought processes, we can make different choices in thought and change our approach. One suggestion he gives guitar performers is to let the eyelids droop a moment or two before playing the first note, to dwell more in the subconscious and enter into the music. He suggests that the best way to sidestep the nerves is to dive into tone and focus on producing our best tone qualities.

When we have prepared for the performance by our weeks, months, or years of practice, we must give ourselves preliminary advantages. If we practice our part 200 percent, we can be confident of playing 98 percent as we would like.

> *We practice for everything we want.*[2]
> —PEPE ROMERO

Looking for Love

ONE EXPERIENCE GAVE ME ONE OF THE WORST cases of performance anxiety I have experienced. It wasn't in performing music but a solo, improvised dance in a contemplative modern dance class at Naropa. I am not a dancer, but I took the class because I felt it related to music and to performance.

From my notes:

> *Today before I stood up to perform my improvised solo, I was so overwhelmed with anticipation I was nearly sick. But I noticed how just getting up and taking the first few steps onto the performance area was such a relief. Standing facing the group, I began to notice that I loved being there although my arms and shoulders were painfully jittery. So I began to move from that jitter. Almost immediately all my sick-feeling symptoms left, and by the time I finished to look back at the audience again, I actually felt good.*

The class comments were appreciative. One of the teachers commented that what is exciting in watching a dance performance is to get a feeling of the nature and character of the person performing.

If you think "no one will be interested in me," you would be wrong. Bring yourself warts and all—in other words, bring your nature to your music. It means you don't have to hide your nature and don't have to manipulate it to try to appear a certain way. The truth is more interesting, intimate, and beautiful.

There is a paradox in this: people are looking for love, but they paint themselves to look different and put on acts to avoid being themselves. Yet it is their real self who longs for love. It is their natural uniqueness that longs for recognition.

Another paradox is that we want freedom but also want confinement. We want to define who we are. We can't stand to live with the mystery.

We want to say definitively:

- I am a man
- I am a woman
- I am a (name of religion)
- I am middle class

None of these defines anything! On the surface, in language, we may fit into one of the categories, but can we describe who we are completely by category? Can we say exactly what it is to be a man? To be a woman? Can we say exactly what our religion is with complete confidence that we understand it? Can we honestly say that we practice that religion or that we can define precisely what the practice should be? Should we put the yolk of the label "middle class" or "lower class" around our own necks? When did we, living in a democratic commonwealth, decide to assign ourselves to a class system and define our freedom-loving selves to a stuck identity in an illusory system? We might be middle income, but the term "middle class" should be meaningless.

Language can define only a generalization (man, woman, etc.), but the reality is that we cannot define ourselves. In being alive, there is moment-to-moment intention, hope, fear, and joy—all in constant movement and change. Words can represent, but they are not who you are.

An Objective Look at Yourself—Your Art

How can we be objective? It is difficult to keep a steady hand on our confidence while attempting to assess our art. Is our playing good?

To a certain extent, critical reflection on the strengths and weaknesses of our performance is useful for advancing our direction. For me, it often generated a state of mind I will call "all or nothing." It comes from the mentality of our culture: "Either you're good or you're not." I told myself, *Either you can do it or you can't and should give up trying.* I eventually found that it didn't matter if I thought I played poorly or thought I played well. Neither thought identified who I was, didn't limit my potential, and needn't have prompted considering quitting playing.

Music meant too much to me for me to quit. Not to play for two or more days made me feel strange, off balance, and as if something were missing. I believe this is true for many musicians and artists. You don't feel wholly yourself when away from your art for too long. Music was keeping me stable through thick and thin. That is another of its beauties and another answer to the question posed in chapter 1: Why do musicians work so hard to play music? You have an enhanced opportunity to look more holistically at your life through music and performance.

The lesson is to differentiate the facets of self-criticism. Worthwhile critiques of our playing—the "good" and the "needs improvement"—must be separated from thoughts that are useless, derogatory demons. It is more rational to trust our ability—past, present, and future—than to have the whole thing laid on the line each performance. We would be much kinder to someone else sorting out these issues. We need to give that compassion to ourselves.

To Face Yourself

THE PROBLEM I DEALT WITH IN PERFORMING WAS thinking I should be able to reproduce my best practice in a performance "package." It would be like carrying onto the stage a decorated cake. By presenting the perfect cake, it would be successful. I already had a fair amount of performance experience and knew that in reality it was never this way, but I was attached to the possibility that it should work.

When I was in my twenties, living in southern Oregon, I became aware of Naropa University in Boulder, Colorado. I was playing chamber music with friends at the home of a dancer who had attended Naropa soon after the school was founded, and she spoke highly of it. Years later, my interest was renewed when I attended a concert of the group Oregon.

The musicians in Oregon come from classical backgrounds, yet their performances are uniquely original. They play original jazz compositions (many composed by their guitarist, Ralph Towner) with imaginative and beautiful improvisation. After the concert, I asked saxophonist and oboist Paul McCandless how a classical musician might approach learning to improvise.[3] He replied that the best teacher in the world was jazz musician, pianist, and composer Art Lande and that Art was going to teach summer classes that year at Naropa University.[4]

To get to Boulder and to be able to afford to go to the summer sessions seemed impossible, but with help from friends, I did get there and was able to attend Lande's class as well as other classes. Two years later, I moved to Boulder to study in Naropa's music department. My aim was to study performance.

Naropa University is a liberal arts school dedicated to a contemplative and compassionate approach in teaching and learning. Originally inspired by Buddhism, the school is non-sectarian, with a unique approach that offers students situations to learn without condemnation, without the pressure of a competitive atmosphere. Bill Douglas, professor and founder of the music department, accepted and worked with music students from a wide diversity of music backgrounds: classical, folk, jazz, and international. The school's focus on being present in the moment, having compassion, and recognizing "basic goodness" allowed me to be free to explore what it is to perform music.

Studying at Naropa was a refreshing approach to learning, but part of the goodness was dealing with the struggle of facing myself. Due to the double-edged sword of sensitivity and shyness, I was hypercritical of myself. The pain of being self-critical can become a block, but it doesn't have to be. We all have limitations. How we work with them helps us evolve.

I found that performance anxiety could get worse knowing that my hypercritical self was waiting at the other end, when the concert was over. It was as if I were telling myself, *I'm so afraid of failure, because then I have to face my harshest self, and everything is at stake.* That was real. Everything was at stake; I was balancing so much in my family life as a single parent while carving out time to pursue music, with nearly impossible pressures.

Even if it takes extraordinary energy, it is possible to include your practice in your busy life. Your practice can offer stability to you and therefore to your family.

I write of this on the chance that it will help another musician get through a similar situation. How strongly would you know something if you hadn't grappled with it? Your criticism that your concert was darned good but not perfect could be an advantage, an avenue to reach greater heights.

We tend to imagine that if we are perfect and do everything right, we will be rewarded with ideal situations in which to work. Neither that kind of perfection nor consistent rewards exist. We may reach a fine level of playing, but the chaos of life around us and the variables of our own art-of-life may not lead to great opportunities. Yet in imperfection, there can be perfection. We can move well in the circles we do have, take stock of our capabilities, and move toward a growing artistic satisfaction.

What are some ways to work through the pains of our hypercritical mind? After a concert, we can have a good cry if we feel like it or sit in meditation. It can help to write down our complaints about ourselves. List the negative ones as well as the constructive ones.

It could look like this:

- I know people heard my flaws.
- I know I have played better and can play better.
- I probably looked nervous onstage.
- At least some of the performance was good, and some really shone.
- Maybe people heard the parts that spoke well.
- Maybe I can take another approach.
- What would I like to feel like when performing?
- What would I like to feel like in general as a musician?
- How would I like to regard myself? Develop this

into specifics: how would I walk, stand, and hear myself play? Imagining these specifics means they are possible, because imagining them is the first step. Your creativity is not only in the music but also in how you dream and imagine conducting your life.

Pianist Seymour Bernstein had a strange surprise after a performance he gave when he was twenty years old. Everything had gone well except for one small mistake in an otherwise expressive and satisfying performance. After playing, he received a harsh critique from his teacher who called into question his ability to have a future concert career in music, all because of this mistake. Bernstein went on to become a concert pianist and a great teacher. In his book, *With Your Own Two Hands: Self-Discovery through Music*, he advises musicians:

> *If you are deeply involved in communicating a musical idea, an occasional deviation from technical perfection does not diminish in the slightest the effectiveness of your performance nor should it be offered as sufficient reason for deterring you from a career in music.*[5]
> —SEYMOUR BERNSTEIN

Work with Distractions and Mistakes

OBSERVE YOUR INNER REACTION TO YOUR MIStakes, be they wrong notes, faltering tone, or any kind of glitch that occurs while playing. How do you handle it in your mind? Do you feel dismayed and demoralized and then try to cover these emotions up? I did, and it made me struggle with the distraction. I would have to push myself beyond the emotional disappointment and go on, scrambling to avoid stopping in the middle of the piece.

We have to train ourselves to go beyond this dilemma by continuing to play when a slip-up occurs. We can accomplish this by developing the habit of substituting feeling bad, shocked, shamed, or guilty with redoubling our focus on tone quality and musicality. Hold onto the reins of musical meaning for yourself and the listener, and a falter will be insignificant.

Often you hear the advice "Just let it go"—let go of your mistake. It is good advice, but it needs more specifics. In dealing with your mind, recognize your ways of reacting, and analyze where your reactions come from. They might be thoughts like *Damn! I went over that part so many times* or *I'm so embarrassed* or *What is wrong with me? Maybe I'm no good,* or any number of other thoughts. Recognize how these reactions do not serve you and cause distraction.

How can we train ourselves to avoid being distracted by our thoughts? How can we stay absorbed in the character of the music? When we practice, we can renew our concentration whenever distracting thoughts arise. Replace reproachful thoughts with a useful thought such as *Let me go deeper into this sound, these phrases.* The potential distraction will instead generate a response of directing our concentration further within the music. Staying inside the music, inside our tone qualities, is a sanctuary.

Soon we can let the occasional mistake go without anguish, because our focus is not shaken, and we can continue playing top quality to finish the entire movement. At another time we can check the area of the mistake for any awkward transitions that need work. We might use the *playful* techniques (mentioned in chapter 4) to help the fingers become happily more accustomed to the pattern.

Practicing the skill and the attitude of not getting flustered at mistakes will lead to making fewer mistakes. They will be rare. Reinforced by our practice of continuing to play and keeping our balance by concentrating on beautiful tone and phrasing, our performance continues smoothly, and we stay in love with the entire process.

Environmental Distractions

SUDDEN, UNEXPECTED NOISES CAN BE DISTRACTING. One way to deal with them is to appreciate them. A sneeze in the audience, a baby crying, a chair scraping, or a door opening—all of these brief noises, although not desired, can actually be considered a relief. In contrast to the noise, the sounds of our beautiful playing become even more wonderful. The noise juxtaposed with our music now aids us in a way. This observation can give encouragement and keep the noise from zapping energy away from the performance. Though we'd rather maintain focus for the music and the audience without interruption, extraneous noises can be accepted as something of a relief, and our music shines brighter above them.

Stage fright can be approached in a similar way. If fear is a distraction, we can pivot on the fact that the music is much more interesting. How much more beautiful is the music than the fear! Realizing this, we now we have a springboard for playing that bypasses the difficulty caused by trying to block out the fear. We can feel an openness, inclusiveness, and acceptance, I call "shakuhachi inclusiveness" (described in chapter 10). The quality of the sound of the shakuhachi flute has an openness to the environment and the present. For any musician, an attitude and a quality of sound that reaches an expansiveness that includes the present moment can transcend fear and distraction.

Internal Distractions

WHAT ABOUT OUR OWN DISTRACTIONS, DAYDREAMS, or disturbing thoughts? How do we grapple with the workings of our mind? Thoughts and impressions will arise. They may seem very important, but no matter what they are, they are simply thoughts, and we can let go of them with practice. It is important to realize that this takes practice; one can't expect to be good at it right away. It takes practice to remember when distracting thoughts arise that we can choose to let go of them.

Instead of thinking, *Well, that thought is depressing*, we could think, *No problem; I'll deal with you later.* As we practice this, we will be able to ignore a distracting thought more quickly, perhaps thinking, *Poof. Gotta soar on this next phrase.* We can take these thoughts less seriously and devote our focus and concentration to the music.

Snags

ONE SNAG TO DEAL WITH AS A PERFORMING ARTIST is self-doubt. We feel that we are supposed to appear confident at all times or people won't engage with us. Inwardly we struggle to have confidence. I was once told that Salvador Dali said, "Never let anyone know you are poor. Always act rich." While you act rich, how do you privately work out your doubts or lack of resources?

One thing that helps in dealing with self-doubts in performance is to make a list of them. This gives us a chance to recognize and examine them. Some of the negative listings will suggest their own solutions as we write them down.

My sample list of self-doubts is random, personal, and uncensored. Please read it with kindness and compassion.

Self-doubts

- Places I worked on in the music will not be "in the fingers" enough
- Mistakes will derail me
- Distractions will overtake me
- Some body part will fail
- I'll have a sore throat
- Muscle tension will present a roadblock
- I'll be too scared to breathe
- People won't like how I appear
- I might stop and be unable to continue
- My knees, hands, or lips might shake too much
- I'll get a headache—a migraine
- My period will start or overflow (remember 51 percent of people in the world deal with this)
- Someone I know and admire will hear my flaws
- Dry mouth from nervousness will compromise tone and articulation
- Clothes will not look right or be ill fitting

When these considerations are listed, they seem less overwhelming. We can look at each one, decide how to deal with it, and write down our solutions.

Not Good Enough

WHEN WE QUESTION WHETHER WE "HAVE WHAT IT TAKES" to play, there are ways to work through this doubt and lighten our load. The phrase "have what it takes" is not legitimate. People approach life in an infinite variety of ways; a life journey can take many different turns. A person could start in music as a child, quit for a period, and come back with great interest and motivation. An individual could discover a desire to learn cello at age forty, as John Holt did and as he eloquently describes in his book, *Never Too Late: My Musical Life Story*.

Many people feel defeated because they did not start to play as a child, or they feel held back by the troubles in their early life. How they dealt with the past and deal with the present are highly individual. If we have nagging doubts that threaten to be roadblocks in our journey, it helps to list them along with why we think they are there. As we list things from our past, it helps to remember that life is rough and is not perfect for anyone. Perpetually thinking *If only things had been different* can be a waste of time. As we list events from the past, we can feel what dragged us down. Memories of the events can paint a picture, but this picture is not the present, not where we are now. What is *now* like? If the present offers an opportunity to do music and music is our love, there is a way forward. Now we "have what it takes."

We can thank the past, because it has led us to the present. Now, being aware and alive, we can grow, knowing who we are and trusting our future. Although we cannot know the future, we can imagine it. When we imagine ourselves playing as we want to, that possibility is made all the more real as we work toward our vision.

Control

IF PERFORMANCE IS PROBLEMATIC BECAUSE OF ANXiety that gets in the way, it helps to look at issues of control.

You thought you had yourself and your playing under control, but anxiety-ridden thoughts bubbled up, even ones you thought you had dealt with. Perhaps the performance was not outwardly terrible but was far from what you know it might have been. This can be crushingly disappointing.

Control is the key here. Such a deceptive concept! The more we hold tightly onto something, the less we have it to enjoy. Like trying to control a person—that person can't be a possession. The concept of control is man-made and not useful. "Work with" would be closer to the truth. (This is also a feminist issue.) In playing music, "work with" means maintaining an openness to allow feeling to come through the caringly trained body and breath. It means staying present in sound and space.

> *Music is a gift which you cannot fully receive until you are giving it away.*[6]
> —Riley Lee

Not a Personal Test but a Delightful Opportunity

When we know we have practiced well and sound pretty darned good (even great), we might still be burdened with anxiety about an upcoming performance. The reasons for "the nerves" can be complex. In performing we are challenging ourselves and accepting great responsibility, yet the weight needn't overshadow the joy of the special opportunity to put forth some of our best playing. We can find within ourselves an increased enthusiasm in approaching the delightful opportunity to play for people in a performance engagement. Even if this attitude is not fully achieved, moving in this direction can lift a good portion of the burden.

Performance Anxiety Suggestions

I AM FAR FROM BEING AN AUTHORITY ON THE ISSUE OF performance anxiety, but I found myself on the edge of great difficulty and had to force my way along. There were often times I asked myself, *This threatens to overwhelm me. What can I do?* I searched for answers. I found that when in the thick of musical preparation, it helped to write a checklist of helpful ideas. While playing in concert, to be able to forget oneself and be completely involved in the music is what we aim for, but it is important to realize that this moment of focus is supported by all the other aspects of life.

The following ideas are my suggestions on ways to take care of yourself and to prepare for the concert. Some of them may seem quirky or silly, but hey, whatever works. Bring your lucky charm to the concert (seriously).

A Few Days before the Performance

OTHER MUSICIANS MAY APPEAR TO TAKE THE anticipation of a performance nonchalantly, but they may be discreetly keeping their feelings out of view. It helps to admit our feelings to ourselves and acknowledge that this is a special time. It is time to take into account our individuality and work with it. It is an inward focus.

- Warn other family members that you need to concentrate.
- Acknowledge that you may be grouchy for this period.
- You may be distracted (a pianist friend once found herself putting a pot on the stove and lighting a different burner).
- Be thankful when the music is running through your head.

- Practice the 200 percent mentioned earlier.
- Set up reasonable rehearsals (scheduling is important).
- Take walks for the rhythm, coordination of body, fresh air, and exercise.
- Forgo dairy products (cheese, milk, cream, ice cream) at least several days in advance; avoid mucous-causing foods that may bring on sinus congestion.
- Create a checklist of what you need to bring (an example of my typical list follows).
- Try on the clothes you will wear. Check that they are in good shape and that you feel all right wearing them. Are they too tight in the sleeves or across the shoulders? Bra too binding? Clothes too warm or cold? Shoes stable and not too tight?
- If possible, go to the hall prior to the performance. What are the acoustics like? Will you be working with an acoustically lively room or a more "dead" room? Will you need to play out? Will you need to play more intimately for a smaller room?
- While practicing at home, imagine that you are in your place on the stage relative to your fellow musicians and the audience.
- Go over the music at slow tempos.
- As the performance date approaches, try playing your program quietly as if whispering it to yourself. It is hard to describe all the ways this has helped me. It calms everything, allows meditation on the music, and gives me the feeling that the music is mine.

The Day of the Performance

What to bring:

- Flute
- Music
- Music reading glasses
- Your other flute in case a major problem occurs with the one you play most
- A long cleaning rod in case there is time in a break to swab flute backstage without taking it apart
- Music stand if necessary
- Bottle of water
- A small handkerchief (this might fit in a pocket)
- Paper or tape for the lip plate if necessary, especially in hot weather
- A comb
- An easily removable jacket, sweater, or shawl to stay warm backstage.
- Good luck charm

Eat a banana during the day. (I don't know why it helps. Some say it's the potassium, though bananas are low on the list of foods that contain potassium. Perhaps it helps because it is sweet without too much sugar and yet gives energy. Perhaps it is because it settles the stomach.) Drink plenty of water in the morning and afternoon to be hydrated but not needing to use the bathroom excessively by evening.

Eat a light dinner. Pasta with veggies works well (perhaps rice pasta) Avoid salt, as it can cause dry mouth. Avoid eating too much. You need plenty of space inside to breathe your best.

Get there early to warm up. You may have a chance to test the acoustics or do a tuning check. You may have space and time to do stretching exercises or your personal meditations.

The Performance

REJOICE THAT YOU MADE IT THERE SAFE AND SOUND and that now is your opportunity to be completely with the music. Meditate on your goals: they might be to listen and respond with others, speak each note, bring forth the character and meaning, keep it alive, keep it continuous (no "holes"), or convey the spirit(s) of the music. If you find that talking with others relaxes you, that's fine. If not, quietly concentrate on the music, maybe imagining the opening lines of each piece. What feels best is an individual matter.

Do mild exercises to relax your body such as swinging the arms gently. Do a few breathing exercises to help with relaxation and awakening your breathing skills. Keep your instrument warm, next to your chest or inside your jacket or vest. Balance yourself in your best posture before walking onstage, anchored on your feet, tall, and lengthened with the shoulder blades down. You might think of how ballet dancers enter the stage. You may not be dancing your entrance, but your motions can embody your musical mood and intention. In the moments before playing, take a few deep breaths through the nose or through nose and mouth.

Before playing the first note, take in a big slow breath while imagining that you are already playing so that when you play, it is an extension of what you are already feeling. This will allow the first note to be present and alive—not coming in new but as a part of the whole. This being said, it can be musically exciting when a first note comes freshly out of silence or perhaps boldly interjects itself into the musical conversation as if to say, "Yes, but did you know…"

Attention to Details: The Nitty Gritty

WE DO WELL TO BRUSH OUR TEETH BEFORE PLAYING. Even if we haven't eaten recently, a quick light brushing will help. Having the teeth clean and smooth and the mouth clear helps in our precision. We might visualize, in a cartoonish way, that the air gets blunted when trying to slide by our mossy teeth. Brushing our teeth means we won't be blowing bad breath around. Rinsing well is important so that the chemicals of the toothpaste don't compromise the pads of the flute's keys or speed corrosion problems.

Avoid foods and beverages that cause dry mouth like coffee, alcohol, or salty foods. Avoid milk, cheese, and ice cream at least a few days before a performance. Dairy products can produce mucous in sinuses and throat and affect the drainage from the middle ear through the Eustachian tubes, compromising our ability to breathe, hear clearly, and play at our optimum.

Stay hydrated by drinking water during the day. At a rehearsal or less formal performance, keep water nearby. To be able to sip from time to time—"wet the whistle"—is especially helpful in dry climates or in winter indoor heating. If sipping is not possible in a formal performance, we can breathe in through our nose more. Close the lips when not playing and let the exhale humidify the back of the throat. We can do this during a rest, a tacet, or whenever we are not playing.

Playing at higher elevations takes a toll on our ability to breathe well. Prepare for it by doing breathing exercises. If playing in Denver (a mile above sea level), the air is thinner, and we need to be conscious of finding ways to take in extra air as we play.

Shun clothing that is heavy on the arms to avoid holding the extra weight while playing. Clothes that have plenty of room around the shoulders are less restricting when holding the flute, especially with the reach necessary for the left arm. My husband laughs at me when I try on clothes, because to check the fit, I hold my arms up as if playing the flute—even for jackets.

If you are a woman and feel that your clothing would look best if you wear a bra, search for bras that are not tight around your rib cage. By cutting and sewing to ease the band around the base, a less punishing fit can be found.

Waistlines and belts for men and women should be scrutinized. A too-tight cinching around the belly could hamper playing or be uncomfortable and distracting. Besides helping you feel freer, more relaxed clothing can help you keep your breathing less noticeable and not distract listeners from the music.

When There's Too Much

WE CAN BECOME OVERLY EXCITED. PERHAPS WE ARE excited about the situation in which we are playing or excited about what we are playing. Being overly excited takes us outside the moment, beyond the task at hand. It is important to come back to the reality that you are shaping the moment and must stay responsible and functional to embody the music without extraneous agitation.

Too much excitement is personified to a painful but humorous degree by comedian Kristen Wiig. Her character "Sue" appears in a series of hilarious sketches on *Saturday*

Night Live. She finds herself in situations where the people she is with are secretly anticipating a celebration, perhaps arranging a surprise birthday party, special announcement, or surprise homecoming. She can't contain her excitement and becomes exceedingly jumpy, making inappropriate exclamations. She fidgets, jumps up and paces, and can barely hold in the secret of the planned surprise. Finally, she is so over the top that she hurls herself out a window. The skit is uncomfortably hilarious.

It is easy to feel the jitters due to excitement, but we need a cool and quietly concentrating head even as our heart conveys the happiness, exuberance, and intensity of the music. We must observe our sensitivities and work with ourselves. This might mean giving ourselves more avenues to find balance. It can be helpful to cultivate contemplative arts such as meditation and tai chi as well as more walking, hiking, and swimming. Arranging our living space can go a long way to supporting our playing. Our personal space needn't be fancy, just include a certain amount of neatness and order with pleasing colors. We might have one or two things of beauty that inspire us displayed where we can appreciate them—maybe a seashell or dried branch. These measures can help us enjoy and support our wholeness.

> *On the night of the concert, the body remembers everything that has happened in the months before, only twenty times stronger. To be able to transmit music with all its meaning and full intensity, musicians need to be whole themselves. This is what Safarova made me aware of. If your hands are trembling onstage, or if your memory is failing you, you have built up blocks somewhere. You can't take these blocks away by focus-*

> *ing on the night of the concert alone. You need to make changes in life generally. For example, be open to experiment with Tai Chi or Qigong. Get some good massages or go to an acupuncturist. Learn to concentrate on your breathing and movement. Try different kinds of mental and physical training. Create a special atmosphere while you're practicing at home. All these things help to create a sense of inner harmony that you bring to the stage.[6]*
>
> —IRINA KULIKOVA

Your Aim

SENSITIVITIES TO NERVOUSNESS VARY. IT HELPS TO realize that you are not alone. In the moment, it can be helpful to admit that you are nervous to someone or just to yourself. Admitting it alleviates some of the sting. Make "friends" with the space, the hall, and the acoustics. Live in the music as an actor embodying a character. Use difficulties, such as a sudden noise during a performance, as turning points to strengthen your musical direction. Find a way to aim your Cupid's arrow for what you desire in your performance.

Pianist Arthur Rubinstein said that he would pick out a person in the audience whom he knew was really listening and play for that person. Perhaps your aim is to transport the listeners. Your aim may be to go beyond the listeners and send messages to the universe.

13

Plays Well with Others

*P*laying with other musicians is complex collaboration. In an atmosphere of respect, everyone can flourish, and each person's best efforts will come forward. Clear communication, verbally and musically, can inspire a group and help it come alive. These occasions are jewels of experiences that have many intricate facets.

Unison and Empathy

IN AN ENSEMBLE, WE OFTEN PLAY IN UNISON WITH another musician, and we may listen carefully to the other person in order to play like he or she does. This can cause problems by compromising our flow and energy. In our efforts to hear the other person, we may feel it necessary to squelch our tone or play in nanosecond delay. These compromises can bring the opposite of the desired close unison. It is better to generate our own playing and trust we will find empathy together. Rather than reflecting someone else, you are one of two people creating something together. Generating your own feel for the music with empathy will result in a better and tighter unison.

On the other hand, being less tight can sound better depending on the intent. Sometimes the slight differences can bring richness to the passage. If a tonal blending of the voices is the desired sound, the players might work to cultivate total agreement in a unison passage. If the aim is to have distinctive voices playing parallel unison, slight natural irregularities may sound better.

When playing chamber music, orchestral music, or duets, how do you play well and remain supportive of the other musicians? One important way is to keep a steady beat underneath their melody line, or if you are playing the melody line, be sure everyone else stays steady. Your melody line will be supported by their steady beat, and they should be careful not to falter when you stretch or come in a nanosecond early. It is your artistic decision to stretch against the beat, which is not necessarily a suggestion for them to slow down or speed up the tempo.

Mozart mentioned the danger of compromising the melody by trying too hard to make a supporting part follow instead of keeping the underlying beat solid. Speaking of his own pianoforte playing, Mozart wrote in a letter to his father,

> *That I always remain strictly in time surprises everyone; they cannot understand that the left hand should not in the least be concerned in a tempo rubato. When they play the left hand always follows.*[1]
> —W. A. MOZART (1777)

His father had written about this in his method book for violin. He condemned accompanists who interfered with a subtle *rubato* a soloist might play, by making too much effort to follow and warping the tempo.

Tuning and Agreeing

ANOTHER WAY TO SUPPORT EVERYONE IN AN ENSEMBLE is to be in tune. Listen to intonation. Sometimes they may be out of tune or pushing the pitch slightly high or low for expression. Our ears must be kept sensitized and our adjustments nimble.

Flutists have in mind the often-repeated adage "listen and adjust." If we hear a discrepancy in intonation in a group, we can instantly meet the intonation of others. Usually it is a note here and there. If the group is seriously out of tune, they must stop and figure out why. The group can tune on several notes, play scales in unison, or play passages slowly to figure out where and why they are out of tune and find a way to correct themselves.

When playing with violinists and other string players, watch out for their escalating reach to be higher and thus sharper in pitch. Flutists often have the same tendency. If you adjust up, they will reach slightly higher still. You adjust higher, and they adjust higher again. Perhaps we all want to hear ourselves distinctly, "above the fray," but this kind of escalation should be avoided.

Two people playing in unison and out of tune is obvious. The buzzing beats of clashing overtones are unpleasant until the musicians close the gap between the pitches and the beats slow until they are gone. The instruments then sound beautifully in tune.

In a summer class at Naropa, Art Lande asked the class to stand in a circle and sing a single pitch. He went to each person and listened closely, advising each individual with hand gestures if she or he needed to raise or lower the pitch to become more perfectly in tune. As we entered a perfect tuning, we heard something extraordinary and otherworldly. We heard bells! It must have been the happy overtones celebrating.[2]

In Balance with Your Group

Establish a democratic process for your group. Find collaborative compromises, and allow room for change. No one person is the leader. An idea can be tried out and assessed by the group. People may agree on decisions and artistic approaches or disagree and find ways to weave it all together. Considering something new can be a catalyst for finding more innovative ways beyond the original issues discussed.

In the late 1970s, I attended a rehearsal of the Orpheus Chamber Orchestra. To watch them in action was mind-bending and their playing beautiful. They famously play without a conductor, working out democratic ways to agree, disagree, and work out the artistic creation of their performances. It was amazing to watch their efficiency. The rehearsal had the feel of one brain working. I loved watching when now and then a musician would hurry to a back seat in the hall to check on the balance of sound as the orchestra played. One time a pointed argument broke out, and a violinist left the stage in anger for a while, returning later. Orpheus has won several Grammy awards.

Listening to different kinds of birds singing at the same time, as might occur in a wooded area, is like hearing an orchestra. Each kind of bird has its own voice range—different distinct levels of pitch, timbre, and texture. Nature evolved this diverse orchestra so that individual birds can hear each other distinctly. With the encroachment of more and louder human-made noise, there is concern that the loudness produced by machines, highways, and construction is making it harder for birds to communicate. Their songs are vital to their being able to function. We know they communicate for territory and for finding mates. Fledglings call to parents, and there are probably countless communications that we have no idea about. More frequently and in more locations, birds can't hear each other over our noise. How obnoxious is that? It is one of many human transgressions against Nature.

We have our own unique "voice" in our tone qualities and how we shape and change qualities to play with others. How do you play with a guitarist, harpist, violinist, pianist, harpsichordist, lutenist, or an orchestra? You don't want to use an "operatic" solo voice or an orchestral sound with a guitarist. Tune into the player and her or his "voice." Too often flutists think they are the star of the show, because they usually have the melodic line. They play in a dominating way as if the more harmonic and rhythmic instrument is only backup or accompaniment. The music is much richer when we feel the deliciousness of the whole. That means that our part is part of the weave, and our quality of voice needs to speak in a relationship with the qualities of the other player. We don't want to sound like a marching band while the other person is humming a lullaby or sound like we are creating a performance in which one person is speaking softly while the other is delivering a loud speech (although that could be funny in a contemporary performance).

In playing flute with a guitarist, depending on the piece, it is usually best to have a singing quality (we know how wonderfully the human voice goes with guitar). Make your flute sound more voice-like. With a more relaxed and open mouth and lips, you can keep more warmth in your tone qualities. When playing with a guitarist, feel the nature of his or her sound, and take up a musical conversation.

Let the guitarist know that you wish to treat the music as a duet with a real exchange and weaving of parts. Ask the guitarist to play naturally, not to feel obligated to be quietly in the background playing only accompaniment. Reach for a real collaboration where each part can be heard—sometimes in the foreground, sometimes in the background, with gradations in between, sometimes humming beautifully in parallel.

Some artistic decisions made by a rehearsing group come naturally; some need thought and experimentation. For instance, in chamber music, the melody usually prevails in the balance, but sometimes it should not. Perhaps the melody has been repeated and is well established. At that point, there may be places where the countermelodies in other parts could be brought to the foreground while the melody supports or quietly weaves underneath them. Patterns of harmony, rhythms, and texture can awaken the ear when brought into the foreground. The melody can still be clearly heard as a theme underlying other beautiful lines or patterns. The counterpoint, parallel melodies, harmonies, or textures can be a great relief to hear and bring fresh interest instead of featuring the predictability of the melody every time.

In quiet passages, it is important to maintain musical intensity and conviction. Even though quiet, your part should be alive and awake in what is being spoken. Many flutists seem to think, *Okay, it says* ***p****, piano, so I will be correct if I lower the volume and recede into the background where I can relax and take a little snooze.* No! We need more energy to play quietly, not less. The composer wants the part to be present or else would have erased or deleted it. A quiet passage needs to be a presence woven into the fabric.

Seriously Classical

I HAD FRIENDS IN THE 1970S WHO PLAYED FOLK music and were beginning to get into Irish music, then becoming increasingly popular in the United States. They told me that they thought classical music is sad music. Sad music!? I was shocked at this perception and wondered how they had come to this conclusion. In the unlimited gamut of classical music, they thought it sad? How could this be? It is true that on an individual level, we can never know how music will affect someone. There is also the factor of developing "ears" for a work that may have been disliked at first and then later loved. For example, it is unbelievable to us now that in his own era, some of Beethoven's works were disliked at first.

It could be that people often miss out on enjoying classical performances because they do not hear them played well. They may not have heard performances that are alive, fresh, or imaginative, played with inner conviction, with a vivid and present perspective. I think many live and recorded performances often fall short. All the notes and rhythms are dutifully there with no enthusiasm.

There are too many performances that lack life, and the reason for this is the trap of assumptions in which people ensnare themselves. One common assumption is that this is "serious" music and must be played with an overall dark sound. They may also assume that there is a standard of style and that they must "toe the mark." They may think that classical music is formal and therefore stiff, and this thought overrides putting life and presence in the music.

If they are listening to orchestral recordings that are "correct" but lifeless, no wonder some people might conclude that the music is sad. Maybe my friends conflated sadness with poignancy. Perhaps they carried the assumption that all classical music is hard-edged and serious. Maybe they were influenced by the painted portraits of composers looking serious. The composers may have smiled a great deal in their lifetimes, but in sitting hours for a portrait, there was no way to maintain a smile.

Could it be that my friends thought the path of a classical musician was sad? There are years of hard work, mastering techniques, fine-tuning coordination, stamina, insights, and understanding. There are struggles, and the self-doubt that can often make it difficult to appreciate one's own progress. Maybe that's why children delight more in the doing. They know they are a "work in progress." Adults suffer because they want to be instantly accomplished.

What is sad? What is happy? I wouldn't call it sadness to experience the relief of hearing the expression of truth even if it is dark, or sad, or poignant. Bach's music is sometimes achingly beautiful and about death. Sheer beauty makes me happy enough to cry. In the same way, I can cry upon seeing beauty in Nature, the ultimate treasure: mountains, deserts, sunrise, underwater reefs. We can strive to reveal this deep beauty in our playing.

Finding People with Whom to Share Music

AS A MUSICIAN, WILL YOU FIND PROFESSIONAL OPPORTUNIties? Will your work be recognized? So much depends on situations exterior to the music. A bigger question is what you want in terms of situation—orchestral, chamber music group, freelance, recording, composing, collaboration with other arts such as theater, dance, or improvisation? What combinations of these?

Along the way, it helps to put yourself in the position of being ready for the best. You can make yourself ready for your dream to come true. While practicing and focusing on the work of the present, you can imagine that you are already in your dream situation, your audience is there, and your colleagues are there.

If your music life seems lonely, you are not alone (pun intended). Many phenomenal musicians express this feeling of disconnect between their interior inspired joy and, on the other hand, a lack of recognition for the art created, a lack of real listening from others. There can be plenty of accolades, but perhaps it is the quality of listening—the participation that is most gratifying.

In addition, there can be the "mundane" attitudes you may encounter in other musicians who regard what they do as just a job. Having reached a level of confidence in playing their parts well can be satisfying enough for them. They may play with beauty, but the personal joy has gone, and the mundane has settled in. Stay with your own original spark. Your playing can bring a quality that buoys the music and all participants.

Dignified Rehearsals

WE MUST BE SURE TO LEARN OUR PARTS AHEAD. THE more we know our parts, the freer we can be to deeply collaborate in the many aspects of balance, exchange, and coherence. To listen to and play along with recordings is one great way to be confident of our part. There is no need to worry that we will end up sounding too much like the recordings. The individuals and the ensemble will naturally find their own phrasing and direction with the piece.

A good rehearsal is one where everyone is kept playing as much as possible. In playing music, we don't know what we can do until we are doing it. You can't learn to twirl plates on poles by talking about it, and the art of the music cannot advance unless we are actually playing.

If playing must stop to discuss making changes in approach, it is best that the discussions are to the point and brief in order to resume playing immediately. Time spent waiting while others talk can be wasted time. Sitting or standing there waiting to play again cools off the emotional connection to the music. Waiting too long can cool off the instrument, potentially presenting an intonation problem when it is lifted to play again. Being annoyed by wasted time and energy can generally cool our enthusiasm for the entire project and even the group. We may feel, *This is not the music I came to play. These people are not motivated.*

Musicians love to talk and tell jokes, but sometimes the talk can rattle the nerves, forcing us to consider things that bring down our mood. We all love humor, but a snarky joke might hurt someone's feelings. "Well, you need to get a thicker hide," some might say. It is a detraction from the inspiration, the reason we got into the art of music in the first place. It is far more respectful to come to a rehearsal with a focus on the music. What gets accomplished in musical collaboration and musical communication is amply more satisfying than "chewing the fat." Stay on task. Stay with the music. Stay with the artistic collaboration. Talking can be arranged for a lunch or in a cafe.

You may need to be a leader in redirecting the group's attention to the music. Getting along with other musicians is important, but even people who don't see eye to eye can collaborate to make beautiful music. Personality clashes can be put aside in the interest of producing art together. Staying focused in the music allows the most rewarding experience.

Bring your best attitude to the group. Be as professional as you can with optimism and respect. An atmosphere of respect and focus helps to quickly build the group's creativity and confidence and will be the foundation for your creative sessions together.

14

Speaking Clearly in Music

We speak with our bodies. What is heard and understood of what we say or what we play is not just the words or notes, but also the qualities of tone and intention. Quality communicates intention. If someone says "I love you" in a flat monotone with a blank expression, you probably won't take it seriously. If the same words are spoken in a focused, tender voice, eyes connecting with yours, eyebrows raised, a slight blush, nervousness based in humility, a certain lowering of shoulders and swelling of chest, tearing up, how rich is that communication from the person's whole being.

Tone quality is key to speaking clearly in music and in communicating the life, energy, and intention that we offer from within. The ardent desire to let the spirit of the music generate through our body and out into the world is the desire that informs our discoveries in our practice.

Artificial Conformity

What happens when technology interferes and, even worse, imposes an artificiality on our playing?

Many sound-engineered effects have too much influence on what we think we should hear *and* how we think we should play. Music recordings of the 1940s and 1950s had more realistic louds and softs, which made for more aliveness and sparkle.

An orchestra could build to a climax that was honestly real. Technologies like Dolby were developed that shaved the louds so that everything sounded more even and homogeneous.[1]

Musicians often unconsciously try to conform to a blander range of expressions. Many flute players feel they should paint only in pastel colors—cool, calm, and even. While it is important to consider proportion in expression appropriate to the composition, it is a shame when people self-censor their vitality. Bold, creative expressions can come forth with passion and excitement when one is freed from the usual recorded soundscape.

Dynamics: Speaking Loudly, Speaking Softly

OFTEN I HEAR FLUTISTS PROJECTING THEIR SOUND well through various dynamic changes, but at a section marked *piano* (*p*), a section to be played more quietly—their line seems to cut out and disappear. It can sound as if they suddenly lost the energy of the music. Playing quietly with a let-down of energy can also make the intonation go flat. The let-down in energy and intonation would not be the flutist's intention, but it can be the result.

It is important to remember that dynamic markings or suggestions are not one dimensional, not simply turning the volume up and down. There are multiple ways to approach areas in the music that are marked with a dynamic indication (*f*, *p*, *mf*, *mp*, etc.) or unmarked passages that seem in their nature to require a certain dynamic level.

Playing quietly doesn't simply mean playing quietly. Consider the context: a part may be marked *piano* (*p*) or *pianissimo* (*pp*), but how it is woven into the tapestry of the lines and harmonies of an orchestral piece, chamber piece, or solo flute is vital. This quiet line may be an important subtle voice weaving around other musical statements. It may offer sparkle, quiet harmony, commentary, or hinted contrast. Perhaps this part is less about volume and more about lightness, prompting us to try variation in tonguing, tone quality, duration of notes, accents, types of vibrato, and intensity of airflow. Perhaps this quiet section is an intense quiet, a relaxed quiet, or some other quality of quietness. The quiet character can be full of energy, alive with plenty of airflow and support.

A quiet vitality can add great energy and depth to the music. Remember, the composer did not write your part so that it would be inaudible. Simply dropping your volume will not give the color desired, and the color need not be "soft focus" and "pastel." A quiet section can speak with clarity using precise tonguing and articulation, yet the clarity is not just in the attack. The initiation of each note must have body. The body of the sound should be present at the precise onset of the tone. This is best accomplished with a steady flow of air with plenty of support and energy.

In the same way, a *forte* (*f*) has little grace if it is simply played loud. Flutists tend to "dig in" too much when playing a *forte* passage, intensifying and thus adding tension to all aspects of their playing. To avoid harsh tone quality in a *forte* section, it helps to relax more and let the power come from chest and belly while supporting a broader, more open tone. The largeness of tone, the openness of sound, carries and projects. We can think of ourselves as somewhere between an opera singer and a panpipe player. Feel that the sound comes from the body, mouth, and lips, not by "pushing" the instrument. We needn't strain to sound big. *Become* big to play big.

Consider that the dynamic of *forte* could be less about volume than about other kinds of expression that are made possible in various ways. Maybe the line can be sung more legato with each note played more broadly to occupy more fully its space within its beat. A *forte* may be achieved by using a different kind of vibrato or by how much it stands in contrast with what comes before or after. Sometimes a crescendo to a climax, with the climax being lyrical and calm, can stand out more than if it is played loudly.

Whether playing solo or with others, every note is important, but we must also evaluate what kind of balance is desired and where our line fits into this balance. Our voice will be at times quietly supportive, at times part of the foreground, and sometimes the leading voice.

All articulations and dynamic levels require a steady flow of air, a steady push with engaged energy. This applies for sustained notes as well as detached, *legato* or *staccato*. A steady flow and pressure are needed for *fortissimo* as well as *pianissimo*. One would think that playing quietly would need less energy and pressure, but it takes a great deal. This enables us to keep the phrase alive and strong. There is strength in quietness, power in gentleness.

"It's all relative," as they say. We ask ourselves, "Should this be a big contrast or a milder one in context? How quiet should *subito piano* (*sp*), get? How strong should a *forte* be?" The answers come as we develop a sense of the entire piece. We cultivate the ability as we play, to have a feeling of place in the whole, and the ability to maintain a sense of direction.

Dynamics can be conveyed by using varied tone qualities as well as textures created by articulations and vibrato. Practice using these different qualities along with or in place of louds and softs. Warmth, largess, and generosity might be the qualities of a *forte*; tenderness, coolness, and starlight, the quality of a *piano*. I sometimes mark the printed music to remind myself of the inspiration for the intended quality (for instance, the word "starlight" above a passage or "redwoods" above another).

Emotions

EMOTION REVEALS CHARACTER. WE EXPERIENCE and study emotion to convey character in music. Emotion is vital to how we relate to the world, how we make sense of what we observe, and what we learn. We respond to everything with emotion: excitement, sadness, joy, or even boredom.

While immersed in the emotion of a piece, beware of exaggeration. Too much excitement can take away from the core of the music. Instead of excessively trying to get our intention across, instead of gripping too tightly, we can search for a more natural way to sing and phrase with an immediate beauty and evolving meaning. We embody the excitement of the music yet also possess an overview, a kind of a broad acceptance, a dignity. If we focus on singing it well, it will come across.

Natural Vibrato

VIBRATO IS A NATURAL WAY TO GIVE ENERGY, EMPHASIS, and a singing quality to a note or group of notes. It can sound unnatural and forced if used too much or in inappropriate places or if it is too fast, slow, shallow, or nervous and shaky.

An appropriate vibrato is a matter of taste and intuition, and it is discovered and developed as we practice and work. One great way to check our vibrato, as well as all aspects of our playing, is to record ourselves. In listening, it may help to write notes about what we hear and what we would like to change.

Mozart wrote about the subject of vibrato in a letter to his father in 1778:

> The human voice vibrates naturally—but in its own way—and only to such a degree that the effect is beautiful. Such is the nature of the voice; and people imitate it not only on wind instruments, but on stringed instruments too and even on the clavier. But the moment the proper limit is overstepped, it is no longer beautiful—because it is contrary to nature.[3]
> —W. A. Mozart

For vibrato to sound natural, don't *apply* it—*be* it. Don't think of vibrato as an add-on effect to a note but rather the nature of the note. Vibrato should be sung as part of the tone quality. If you think this way, you will play vibrato not as decoration but will play notes that have shape, richness, and tone color.

"Why Be Normal" Vibrato

A predictable, even vibrato seems standard, seems correct, seems acceptable, but it is limited in what it can express. A way to expand the range of expression is what I call "why be normal" vibrato. I find that more life can be present in a note or notes if the vibrato is subtly uneven.

Excitement doesn't come from mechanical "correctness." Mechanical repetitive perfection is boring. Looking at perfectly spaced stripes is annoying to the eye. There is nothing of note, nothing interesting, unless there is an "imperfection." Attention isn't awakened by predictability. Not being perfect is more perfect than perfection.

Irregularities create interest. If you draw freehand a straight line across a page, it will have some mark of your life in it. It will have the vibration of your heart and nervous system and your eye-hand coordination present in minute imperfections. It is imperfect, and as such, it catches your eye. It is interesting to look at. It has a vibration of aliveness. If you draw a straight line using a straight-edge or ruler, your eye skims over it long enough to affirm that, yes, it is perfectly straight, but your eye does not linger to study it, because there is nothing alive about it.

Subtle variations of the speed and style of vibrato can enhance dynamics and direction. They can expand your options in expression, creating variety in dynamics beyond degrees of louder or quieter. A widening and slowing vibrato can convey a quieter realm without being very quiet, perhaps allowing a flute part in a *diminuendo* not to get lost or covered up. A faster, more intense vibrato could be used for a *forte* that doesn't necessarily have to be loud.

A single, poignant, longer note can be kept more alive by subtly varying the speed of the vibrato at various times through its duration. We can dwell within the note rather than considering our vibrato as merely ornamental. This can be used to provide shape and color and a more alive accompaniment to other voices who have the moving parts. You are subtly adding to the vitality of their melodic lines.

Uneven vibrato can convey a movement of emotion in a single note or a group of notes. It can give life to a fast passage or add excitement to a run by bringing out underlying colors and singing qualities. It can sculpt a run or a passage that might otherwise sound like just a collection of fast notes. It takes experimentation and opens up an avenue of freedom in playing and interpretation.

Explore uneven vibrato. It may be subtle or wild and outrageous. Decide where you might like it faster or slower. At the beginning or end of a note? Oscillating throughout?

Vibrato can be part of a sense of direction in the music. One note or phrase building into another can intensify by using a quickening vibrato. You can taper the intensity from one phrase into another phrase, perhaps a cadence or ending, by slowing the vibrato. There are infinite possibilities and subtleties to work with.

Notes played completely without vibrato can have expression. It can be expressive to play some notes without any vibrato to convey a purity, a bleakness, or other emotions within the context. Celtic music singers often sing without vibrato. Many Baroque musicians insist that the music of that era should be played without any vibrato at all. Some use it sparingly. Careful listening will inform you as to when and how you feel it is appropriate and how you want to use it.

We tend to think that there is only one best way to play a piece and all we need to do is to meet that standard, but this isn't necessarily true. There is infinite room for discovery. Discovery is the basis of creativity, the most thrilling part of playing.

Runs and Fast Passages

TO PRACTICE RUNS, TAKE A MORE FUN APPROACH: play with them. Rather than trying to conquer them to prove technical prowess, let them become creative, lively flourishes.

There are helpful ways to get the run "in your fingers" in the first place. Using the *long-short, short-long* technique mentioned in chapter 4 is a good start, but consider searching for a more subtle musical phrasing. Often the beat is suspended for the run, which invites the musician to have a certain freedom in how he or she plays it. The context of what came before and what comes after will be part of what informs the musician in matters of style, proportion, and how fast she or he wants the run to be.

The notes of a run can be felt in subtle groups with certain notes brought out that are not necessarily the downbeats. If there is a fifteen-note run, you can focus on what it wants to do musically, and based on that feeling for the phrasing, find its landmark notes to create secret subdivisions. Perhaps the fifteen-note run can be divided into a pattern—4, 4, 7 or 6, 6, 3 or 5, 5, 5 or 8, 4, 3 (or another)—played more or less evenly. These divisions are your secret conceptual grouping and not necessarily obvious to the listener. The run can sound even and smooth with no accents, but the secret subdivisions known only to the musician help give it shape.

In 4/4 time where there are four sixteenth notes to a beat, a lengthy passage of steady sixteenth notes can be played more gracefully by thinking of them in different groupings rather than the often-choppy 1234, 1234. Instead of hammering away in groups of four and feeling the 1 (one) as the starting point, vary the starting point of your conception. The passage can be played smoothly without any emphasized downbeats or with certain chosen notes for emphasis. After playing the initial note or notes, the passage can be secretly conceived of in different ways. It could be 2341-2341, or 3412-3412, or 4123-4123, or combinations of these. Different groupings can be used in any passage that has patterns of four. Whether the passage is fast or slow, changing your conception of how the notes move opens the possibility for more grace in your phrasing. You can do away with choppiness. You are freer to sing each note—each one a voice in space without the punch from the tyranny of the often-overemphasized downbeats. It keeps the overall feel of evenness—each note singing smoothly into the next. This can also apply for groups of six or other groups of notes. Successive groups of six might be felt as 234561-234561 or 456123-456123.

Runs of eight or twelve notes can be more graceful when conceived as groups. A run of eight notes can be felt as 123-12345, a group of twelve notes as 123-12345-1234, or any other combinations that make the movement of notes speak naturally with life in them. Experimenting with groupings to find the best one can greatly ease difficulties in playing fast passages or runs. Sometimes runs can be felt in a solid sweep, an ability that might come more easily from having practiced them with groupings.

Although each note should be clear in a run, you can also be playing shapes, gestures, and "sweeps." Playing the Khachaturian *Violin Concerto* transcribed for flute, I was searching for a way to make a rapid passage sweep up to the high notes in one broad gesture instead of a lot of fast notes. I found myself thinking that I needed to let go, which occurred as relaxing everything and letting the breath flow from lower belly and chest. I also needed a certain element of a cool and quietly concentrating brain, so that I could be the architect of the passion rather than be lost in the excitement. It worked, forming a strong arc in the musical architecture.[4]

Odd-metered passages can make more sense with different groupings. For instance, a measure of eighth notes in 5/8 time can be felt in steady eighth note values divided into unequal beats: 12-123 or 123-12, in 7/8, as 123-1234 or 1234-123 or 12-12-123. The groupings needn't be obvious to the ear unless you want them to be. They are only a helpful way to conceive of the steady and even movement of the notes. In the mid-1970s I took some lessons with bassoonist Les Weil who published an excellent progressive method book, *Odd Meter Studies*, which offers exercises and melodic etudes that help develop the ability to play in odd meters using unequal beats.[5]

Composer Bill Douglas has published a series of rhythmic etudes, *Vocal Rhythm Etudes*,[6] to help musicians learn a broad variety of complex jazz, rock, contemporary, and world rhythms while using spoken syllables—much like percussionists and other musicians from India perform and study rhythms. Clapping, tapping, jumping, and hopping, while vocalizing these rhythms, becomes so fun and energizing that only later does one realize that these complex rhythmic patterns, regarded by many musicians as very challenging, are now ingrained in the body and musical mind. One becomes fearless in future encounters with these unusual rhythms. Lively performances of some of the *Vocal Rhythm Etudes* can be seen on YouTube.

Tempo, Tempi

BE CAREFUL NOT TO CONFUSE LIVELINESS WITH speed. Each note has a place in space. It is important to know the difference between rushing in an effort to give the music energy versus giving it liveliness in a more natural tempo. The tendency to set tempos that are too fast seems contagious in our speedy culture. Even playing slightly too fast can make the content and substance of the phrases and statements seem glib, shallow, and "tossed off." It is like thinking that by singing the lullaby faster, the child will fall asleep sooner.

Music can be lively without rushing. We could think of liveliness as if kicking up our heels in an energetic dance, not as if we are running to catch a train. If we keep our energy up and our sense of direction activated, excessive speed will be unnecessary.

How do we remember our ideal tempo? When we have chosen and have been practicing in our best tempo, we may feel confident that we will automatically remember it in a performance situation. We probably will, but if there is any doubt, it helps to select a place in the music that is particularly sensitive to tempo, perhaps a fast passage that won't work if it is played too fast or too slow. We might select a slower passage as a reference. Just before beginning to play the piece, we can mentally review that reference passage in our mind's ear. Mentally hearing it in the tempo that seems most natural, we have a basis to begin the piece with our ideal tempo.

Tonguing

SINGLE TONGUING CAN BE ARTICULATED IN GRADAtions from soft focus to clear focus to full attack. In most cases the airflow is a constant stream, while the tongue gives the "pronunciation" by articulating a syllable behind the upper teeth as if you are whispering "Doo, doo, doo."

Here are three ways to think of tonguing; subtleties can be found in gradations of these approaches:

- To tongue softly for quiet passages or for more *legato* yet detached passages, use "doo" with the front edge of the tongue lightly hitting the gums above the back of the front teeth.

- For a more clear and emphasized articulation, "doo" can be used with the tongue slightly more forward, touching the back of the front teeth.

- To sharply emphasize an articulation, allow the tongue to momentarily block the air at the back of the lips like spitting a seed off the tip of the tongue. Listen carefully, as this technique can exaggerate the intention or can be a strong and fitting emphasis of a note or group of notes.

Articulation

IN PASSAGES THAT ARE WRITTEN DETACHED SO that each note is to be articulated, it shouldn't be assumed that every note is necessarily short or percussive. Often they are played to their best expressive advantage by playing them closer to a *legato*—not slurred but with delicate tonguing that barely breaks the even, steady flow of sound from one note to the next. There could be minute breaks, allowing a little more daylight between notes. Detached passages can be interpreted in many ways, and we need not assume there is a standard way to articulate them.

If percussive staccato seems appropriate, be sure that although the notes may be ultrashort and light—they must still have "juice." They are generated from the strength of a steady flow of air and a steady singing voice. Think of Mozart's "Queen of the Night" solo. The soloist must have a steady strength of breath support to sing those sparkling, melodic, high staccato notes.

In detached, articulated passages, it may seem like accuracy is all that is required, but don't let down or abandon the life implied in these passages. People sometimes use aggressiveness in playing articulated notes as if saying, "Now I get to be a spitfire." Musically, it may be humor or happiness that is the intention of the passage, and it can be sculpted with light touches. The notes are not representational—they are the shaped existence of the music.

When playing or practicing, we can monitor ourselves for "ugly notes" that seem blaring or one dimensional or "instrumental" rather than like a voice. It may seem counterintuitive, but a good place to turn our attention is to those areas of a piece where we feel we do fine and there's no problem. These are the places we normally "breeze through." Give them more scrutiny. The things to listen for are intonation problems or a dull, lackluster tone on certain notes. We may notice a glib quality, being too weak or mechanical, or some quality that falls short of what we want to say. It could be that we have withdrawn our energy on these phrases, because we dismissed them as easy. Recording ourselves can help locate these areas where we are falling short of how we think we sound. We can give these passages the life we want to actually be there.

Phrasing

Every note is important and grows out of what preceded it and gives energy to what follows. Slow down the passage. Try playing the subdivisions of the phrases.

Musical phrases can be like those spoken in a description. For example, we can hear the following little story (I made up) musically:

> *She rode at a gallop through the frosty field, slowing to a canter along the sandy path by the creek. Icy branches on either side shone pink, sending tiny reflective beams of light to pierce the quiet morning air. Her gentle horse moved elegantly alongside the water, where flowing and bubbling voices chanted that the freezing season would not last forever. Finally reaching the old barn, they stood still, their breathing appearing in transient white clouds. She peeled herself to the ground, hugged Shadow's neck, and led the sleek, dappled gray back to the stables.*

By separating each phrase, we can sense many things. What needs connection and continuity? What needs delineation, a sharp contrast or emphasis? What do we want to be the high point, and what is its quality? Some notes are pivots, and some are part of an arc. Some notes serve as endings and simultaneous beginnings.

Slowing at the end of a cadence can be lovely at times, but a steady diet of slowing at cadences can become excessive and ultimately distracting or boring. I've heard musicians slow down on far too many small endings and interfere with the energy, momentum, and message of the piece. By not slowing but instead going on, it is possible to convey an ending to the cadence and make it be a part of a continuing. Whether brief and continuing or slowing to a stop, endings should be sung with plenty of life no matter if they are quiet or loud.

If the top note of a phrase is a high note, it can be sung as much or more than others. High notes don't need to be held back as we often hear them in recordings, smoothed out by engineered mixing techniques. We are playing live, and we are allowed to sing out. The key is to *sing* the high notes rather than "punch" them (playing high notes is discussed in chapter 8).

Issues of Accents

THERE ARE MANY DIFFERENT APPROACHES TO ACCENTS. A note need not be poked at or played suddenly loud to emphasize it. It can be made to stand out by being strident or soft, lengthened or shortened, or brought out by understatement. Feel what the accented note means in its context. Is it assertive or sparkling? In a series of accented notes to introduce a waltz or to outline a march, a clarity can come by making the first note of each phrase speak with more richness. A single note of poignancy in a soul-searching line can be emphasized by vibrato, how it is articulated, or its placement within the beat.

There are many ways to emphasize notes:

- Accent
- Richer tone

- Vibrato
- Suddenly singing more quietly
- Playing more legato as a contrast
- Sparkle (a more sparkling quality achieved by perhaps a quicker vibrato, a more clearly spoken staccato, or a feeling of a lighter touch)
- Unequal vibrato (described above)
- Placement of a note in time (pushing or pulling, a little ahead or behind the beat)
- A little swing—equal notes in time, subtly played unequally

The first note of a piece sets the mood and direction. A first note that is played with intention helps orient the listener to the tonality, key, and attitude, and it conveys confidence and a sense of inevitability in the music. Embodying the meaning and intent of the piece, a first note might say, "Did you know?" "From the depths of darkness," "She arrives on wings," "All is peaceful," or "Get ready to dance."

When playing in a group, play parts that may be inner melodies or supportive phrases by making them sing and have their own progression and development. Being "second fiddle" is by no means secondary to the tapestry. When you are playing musically, you inspire the person who has the lead melodic line. You are playing in complementary and harmonious colors; your accents, dynamics, timing, and phrasing are important and add vitality.

Breathing to Phrase

We develop our stamina in breathing to play longer musical sentences. In these sentences, there are often natural places to take a breath. Wherever possible, play a passage on a single breath between these natural breathing places. However, sometimes there are not enough natural places to breathe, and we need to listen carefully to find where to take quick breaths that don't interrupt the flow of the phrases. It helps to mark with pencil on the printed music the obviously natural places as well as where to take quick breaths.

A quick breath can be hidden by leaving a note slightly early, breathing in just enough and landing on the next note right on time with a continuous feel for the direction of the phrase. It helps to play the note previous to the quick breath with conviction and send the tone out into the air to "hover" while taking the hidden breath underneath.

The skill of the short breath needs to be practiced. If it is taken without changing the formation of the lips and mouth, the notes that follow will be stable. Breathe in through the nose and mouth together. Take in just enough air. Often a little air is all that is needed to complete the phrase and make it to the next big breathing spot.

A big, slow breath before the first note of a piece gives time to pretend you have already been playing. The first note and phrase will be an extension of the expression you are feeling. (See the comments on breathing in chapter 3.)

The Direction of the Piece

PHRASES RELATE TO ONE ANOTHER WITH DIRECtion and design. Sometimes the progression of phrases can be like a conversation. Each speaker, each phrase, can have a different mood—sometimes searching, sometimes awakening, perhaps humor or anger.

Here's a line of three phrases:

Although frost gathered on the window pane, the fire inside was like a piece of sunshine, and in his imagination, he visualized the garden in spring.

The words evoke images, sounds, smells, and feelings. How would you play these phrases? Subdivisions of the phrases could be as follows:

Frost gathered: Delicate, spontaneous patterns

Window pane: Lonely, barrier, or expansive (window on the world)

Fire: Peaceful energy, or crackling brilliance

Sunshine: Brilliant energy, contentment

Visualized: Fantasy

Garden: Color, variety, earthiness

In spring: Hopeful

In practicing phrases or lines by themselves, we can explore what the expression could be as an actor might rehearse a line, phrase, or word to bring it life and be true to the character. As actors or musicians, we want a heart-connected voice instead of assuming that that character is one dimensional. In music, we can rehearse ways of playing that allow us to more closely be the music. We can *be* the character and *become* the music.

Internationally famous Egyptian singer, songwriter, and actress Umm Kulthum (c. 1904–1975) was the most popular and respected singer in the Middle East and the Arab-speaking world. Great poets wrote the poems for her songs, and great composers wrote music for her. She composed music herself and sang with orchestras of virtuoso musicians. Audiences sighed and swooned during her concerts. She was more popular than Elvis Presley was in the West. Workplaces shut down for whole afternoons to allow people to listen to the radio broadcasts of her concerts.

Listening to Kulthum, we can hear that as she sings she dwells in the weight and meaning of the poetry. She sings the phrases, and now and then she stops to repeat a phrase or a portion of the phrase to savor, to explore, to discover different facets. She improvises, varying the tone colors on certain words. Her singing was responsive to the emotions of the audience in a kind of ecstatic communication. This ecstasy charged the air and traveled over the airways. When she died, four million people were present when her cortege passed through Cairo.[7]

In working on how we want to express a note, a phrase, or a passage, we are free to try wilder ideas. It is interesting to try the opposite of what we think should happen—*legato* instead of detached, light instead of dark, loud instead of quiet. We might use exaggeration in places to offer clarity.

I once tried to copy a drawing of a woman's face by Leonardo da Vinci. The more I observed, the more I saw exaggeration and "imperfections" that were perfect. I found in Leonardo's drawing examples of the opposite of what one might think, such as an impossibly deep and dark shadow, unnaturally large eyes, or a chin too pointed. When looking at the drawing as a whole, it had tremendous life and a recognizable feeling of reality. That was a profound artistic lesson. Intentional imperfection for the sake of expression can be more perfect than perfection and feel more correct than correctness. Conveying a strong impression can seem more real and alive than a more technically accurate representation.

The exercise of copying in any art can bring countless lessons and revelations. Trying to copy the work of a master can be eye-opening or musically ear-opening. Artistic exaggerations, contrasts, and "perfect imperfections" have a place in playing music.

Echoes

THE OFTEN-ASSUMED STYLE IN BAROQUE AND EARLY CLASsical music is for a repeated phrase to be a quiet "echo" the second time it is spoken. I doubt it was *always* done this way. Why not try a variety of approaches to bring more life into it? I like the effect of switching it around and playing the second "echo" stronger, especially if it leads to an ending or wants to continue the thread into another strong area. You can lighten up on the second repeated phrase by playing shorter note durations (within their beats), or singing it sweeter, or by playing with a little vibrato where there hadn't been much the first time. Whatever contrast in the phrases you desire, you can use it to help create a bridge to what comes next. This way a repeated phrase is more than a repetition, it is developing a melodic idea.

The Thrill in the Trill

WHEN PLAYING A TRILL IT IS IMPORTANT TO KEEP the singing quality for both the principal note and the trill note. Avoid thinking of the trill as simply the tapping of the key. Keep the voice, the tone quality, throughout the whole body of the trilled note.

Within the standard ways to play trills, there are ways to push and pull on the speed of the alternations to make them calm or busy, expansive, shimmery, or more singing. This can add life—more "thrill" in the trill—so that the trilled note has movement, emotion, and direction. A subtle push to quicken or a pull to slow a trill brings a slight asymmetry, which can reveal shape and varied emotive qualities. The trilled note will have more of a directional feel. It will sound more alive and active than the more static sound of an evenly trilled, ornamented note.

Dusty and Old

PEOPLE HAVE PERPETUATED A MISTAKEN IDEA about music of the Baroque era. I wish listeners could be warned—*You will hear much more in the music if you hear it performed by aware, awake performers rather than those who play in a mechanistic way.* Playing mechanically can be a problem even for professional ensembles, and this is why people disparage Baroque music as being "sewing machine" music.

Unfortunately, we have no recordings to hear how Bach's music was played in his time, but I doubt he would have accepted the mechanical and "punchy" way it is often played in the modern era. Many have an idea of Bach as a scowling mathematical genius, that his music came out of calculation and intellect, and that everything he wrote followed prefigured, academic rules of harmony and theory.

Another way in which I believe people fall short in performing Baroque music is playing with a mental fixation that it is "old" and therefore played through a veil of antiquity as if imagining being back in time conjures visions of dusty, half-lit corners. The playing tends to be slightly flat with weak endings in phrases and rigidly articulated notes with no legato. The music rattles on like an old train on a track. It can sound good mostly because the original compositions are excellent, not because the musician has insight. Bach will sound good in any setting, even on the kazoo, because of the excellence of his compositions. What

I call the "dusty corner" interpretation makes the false assumption, *These quaint people were not like us. They were slower and didn't have our advancements.* True, they didn't have today's machines and electronic gadgets, but I believe they were more alive, active, and dynamic than we are now, partly because they were familiar with fresh air and Nature. We have become "shut-ins" from industrialization, concrete, asphalt, TVs, computers, and pollution.

The wrong-headed assumptions we have about the people and animals with whom we share the Earth, and about whom we have written deceptive histories, block our joy and creativity.

Keep the Beat

WHERE NOTES BEGIN AND END WITHIN THEIR TIME FRAME in a beat depends many times on finger synchronization. We can start slightly before the beat for excitement or slightly late to play broadly or to calm things down. We can push or draw out a few notes of a single run or other series of notes or make the transition from one note to the next as smooth as possible for a singing quality. There are many more possibilities. These many ways to find expression can be done only when we keep a solid pulse—in other words, "keep the beat." When we know where the beat is, we can shape it in subtle ways.

Fingers can move from pitch to pitch as smoothly as our voice can go from one note to another when we sing. When singing, vocal chords make smooth shifts while the flow of air on the exhale generates the sound. The exhale in playing flute is also the generator. The quickness or slowness of a lift or fall of each finger in sync with breath flow can make infinite subtleties in expression.

Speaking Clearly

Music helps us to think. It is not only the structure of the music that informs us; the messages put forth on those black-and-white pages can come across only by how they are played, how they are stated. Everything depends on the musician's experienced intuition, discovery and decisions in finding what needs to be brought out and in what colors. At various points the music might need to be intimate, lingering, moving ahead, light, heavy, anticipating, or laid back. The flutist's approach might be to play in ways that are clear, misty, reflective, happy, bouncy, operatic, folky, plain, pure, or ornate.

In the study of elocution—the art of verbally speaking clearly—phrasing and timing are important. For singers, musical phrasing is linked with the words and meanings of the poetry, libretto, or lyrics. As instrumentalists, in an infinite variety of ways, we create musical thought by the way we "speak" the music.

15

Don't Let Them Tell You

*D*on't let anyone tell you that you are one thing or another. Within yourself, you are infinite possibilities.

- *You are capable of discovery, innovation.*
- *You are capable of experimentation.*
- *You are capable of finding more creative freedom.*
- *You are capable of singing the way you want to sing.*

Attitudes in Our Culture

Our culture takes the existence of music for granted. Music is a readily available commodity—just push a button, tap a screen, and plug it into your ears.

What musicians do, is not generally understood. The cultural bias in the United States implies that music and art are frivolous and that unless we are famous, there is no point to our efforts, our work. The path of learning is not respected, not supported. There is the mistaken attitude that playing music is not real work but something non-essential. In war and famine, the arts suffer setbacks. Music and the arts might seem non-essential when starving and impoverished people struggle to survive, but impoverishment and deprivation are the suppression of *all* human capabilities, including the arts.

There is the theory that in bad times people don't do art, so it is not a necessity. This is not true historically. In times of tragedy, of war, people crave music. They do their best to protect visual works of art. Many great composers and fine musicians have experienced times of bleakness due to political and cultural dictates and whims. Many artists have continued to work under oppressive environments of war and political strife. If you are starving or being bombed, your first need may not be art. However, there are many stories of dangerous war-torn areas where concerts given, often under great risk, were considered essential in restoring a sense of human decency.

Artists are dedicated to their work even under harsh conditions in their lives. The expression "starving artist" is used to describe the sacrifices artists commonly make to pursue their field. What high value is art! Creativity! Art brings observation, discovery, and evolution. Participation in the arts uplifts giver and receiver.

Where do so many negative views about musicians and artists come from? We are imbued with the so-called "work ethic," which claims we are not really working unless we have disdain for what we are doing. "Real work" is a drudgery job that "you're damned lucky to have." Many musicians *also* have a day job, which means they work doubly hard, yet the work and devotion to music is seen as play. People who truly love their work are happy to put as much energy into it as they can muster. There is never a desire to retire from music. It is important to recognize and to protect the sparks that are the origin and continuation of our art.

Talent

TO SAY THAT A MUSICIAN IS LUCKY TO BE TALENTED is often a kind of dismissal in an odd belief that it only takes talent and that some people have it and some don't. The experience of playing is 1 percent talent and 99 percent work. Our music comes from years of honing skills and developing more aware levels of artistic perception. Much so-called "talent" comes out of loving music, wanting to do it, and working on it with dedication for years.

"It's so great you can just sit down and play that piece" is a comment that concert pianist Kimball Gallagher often hears. He laughs as he relates his dismay and how he addresses it in concert:

> *You can't just sit down and play it. It's thousands and thousands of hours of practice....I try to actually educate people and recently when I've been playing Chopin Etudes, I'll actually play it slowly first, and demonstrate what it's like to practice at a slow tempo. I tell people, "This is what goes on for months and months."* [1]
> —KIMBALL GALLAGHER

Then he plays the entire piece at tempo and continues with the concert.

People may assume that in performing we must be simply having fun. Yes, there is fun, a thrill, and artistic satisfaction. There is also the work, the discipline to know our stuff. We accept the challenge and risk-taking in preparing a performance. Once a concert is scheduled, there is no backing out except in dire situations, so we are holding a significant responsibility. There is the sense of holding in our heart something of great value and offering it for an honorable and valiant cause.

> *One of the attractions of art is the possibility it affords of opening the heart, of being exposed to a level of in-*

spiration not usually experienced. It excites and delights. People all over the world have sought this experience in many ways.[2]

—Kenny Werner

Speak to Me!

Our culture is full of cynical attitudes, focused on a product mentality, looking at music mainly for commercial value. Product mentality is manipulative and formulaic, interested only in what sells. This deadens and discourages creativity. Many people are content with the commercial bestsellers: the words, pitches, rhythms are there, but it's all gloss and no communication, no engagement. It *seems* to be something, but it isn't. The gloss is there, the music is represented, but the content has no substance. It is artificial.

You are not artificial. You can let go of the cultural insults. Your exploration and experimentation will yield new insights about the depths of the phrases, the colors of different notes, the architecture of the composition, and the many different qualities of sound that allow the music to soar. You are alone and having a great time. *You* play an instrument, and you can fly!

Your own natural insight is your teacher. Insights can come from any aspect of your thinking and reflection or chance associations. You may be watching a bird sing and decide to direct your sound as birds do. Hearing someone sigh in midsentence may help you understand a musical quality you are looking for in a lament. It could be anything. The pure joy in watching baby goats prancing, kicking up their hind legs in play and abandon, was the inspiration I used for the second movement of the *Flute Sonata, Op. 94* by Sergei Prokofiev. Music seems built upon Nature, thought, and speech.[3]

People's Attitudes and How to Deal with Them

WE ALL LIKE TO BE COMPLIMENTED ON OUR GOOD work. It can be human recognition at its best, yet words can be hard for any of us to find when trying to express deep feelings of recognition and appreciation for music performed. A person's attitude and sincerity convey more meaning than the actual words, and the words themselves may not be the important part. Happy stuttering can be good communication when it is heartfelt and the shared joy is appreciated.

Glowing accolades or deflating negative comments, if we take them as definitions of ourselves, can perpetuate false thinking. These comments are not who we are. Buddhist thought warns against taking too much stock in compliments as well as in derogatory remarks. Believing either of these false notions can inflate or deflate an already untrue sense of self. Whether our idea of ourselves looks grand or meager, neither one is our true self.

Positive or negative feedback can be used as worthy adversaries. Feedback helps us reflect upon important questions and find answers, adding greater stability and confidence in our own choices of direction. If someone says to you (as was said to me) "You don't have enough stage presence, you don't move around enough," you may ask yourself, *Where do I want to focus? Am I presenting the music or a visual show?* Examine the stage presence of musicians you admire with this question in mind.

Hearing guitarist Raphaella Smits perform the Bach *Chaconne* is a profound and multidimensional experience. Seeing her play is watching someone in meditation, opening the space for listeners to meditate as well. Listening to the depths she reaches in the music is an expansive, all-consuming experience. If she did anything more, it would be a distraction.[4]

People's comments can be hurtful. Music and the arts are about communication. To be misunderstood brings about a kind of loneliness. I don't have any perfect answers to this, only ideas that may help. Situations and feelings are highly unique and individual. Talking with other musicians might be of help but could well be the opposite. There is no guarantee you will find great communication with someone (including other musicians).

What to do about the loneliness? Stay with your connection, relationship, and evolving understanding of the music. Music is itself your friend. The composers, speaking to you from their art, are your collaborators. Finding another musician with whom you are artistically compatible is a thing of great luck, a great fortune. Keep practicing and growing in all aspects of your playing, and if you are prepared, you will recognize fortune and luck when they come your way.

Why Aren't You Doing Something Else?

AT THE MEMORIAL FOR MY LATE BROTHER, SOMEONE whom I didn't know said to me in a derogatory way, "Oh, you're the one who plays all that 'la, la, la' music." He had heard the lyrical, often Celtic-sounding music I played on the albums of Bill Douglas. I knew it was a put-down. I was grieving and couldn't deal with it—I said, "Yes, I do" and walked away. His was a laughable mistake, because he obviously could not hear what was there and was not broadminded enough to recognize artistry in all kinds of music, even music he might not be drawn to.

As "classical" musicians, we may hear the comment, "You play only classical pieces. You only read what is written. Improvising is where it's at." The implication is, "You aren't very cool or creative." We may fret, thinking, *I love playing Baroque music, but I should be studying more modern works.* If we are immersed in working on certain music devoting all our attention and creative energy to it, there should be no guilt for not doing another style of music. We needn't berate ourselves or feel we that we ought to drop what we love doing. Where we put our energy is enough, and there's nothing wrong in staying with it.

If to be working on something different is our sincere desire, we can make conscious decisions about the directions we want to go and what we want to include at any point along the way.

Listening to diverse genres of music brings us worlds of musical perspective. Any music we study can inform other genres of music in our focus. If we move from playing classical to playing jazz, our classical background may bring more interesting, nuanced dimensions to playing jazz. If we move from jazz to classical, we may find that our background gives us extra confidence and fresh innovation. What we have played in the past can inform our present endeavor.

Paul O'Dette was originally a rock musician. Now a lutenist, he plays Elizabethan, Renaissance, and Baroque music. His playing is direct and bold yet with extreme sensitivity, and he has the most purely natural and graceful phrasing I have ever heard. He is a star in his field and a sought-after teacher.[5]

Honor Being a Musician

THE ROAD TO DEVELOPING AS A MUSICIAN IS ROUGH in this country. The prevailing attitude is that a musician is a slouch, whittling away hours in unimportant activity. Some people assume he or she doesn't have talent because there doesn't seem to be money or fame involved. To them, the player's prospects appear dim. They might even complain about the practicing—so much repetition.

As a beginning, intermediate, or advanced player, hearing negative reactions can be confusing at best or become roadblocks at worst. We can try to please the person grumbling outside our practice room door, and we can try to prove to others we are better than the derogatory remarks, but this effort divides our energy and creates a torn feeling.

It is often said, "You need to have thick skin," but how do we grow it? Our love for music and our ambition for progress may be strong, but ignorant attitudes and remarks can add a burden of unnecessary feelings of inadequacy and self-doubt. Thick skin or not, it helps to double down our focus on the music, find our own approaches to working, find our musical ideas, and seek the musical directions we want to take. We are developing our art.

If there is a way to adjust the situation—practice elsewhere, or practice when individuals with derogatory attitudes are not in the vicinity—we have a better chance of feeling unfettered. We can also sort out the remarks and realize their mistaken perceptions. Realize that those remarks took a little destructive effort, while the hours of our practice are a much larger, long-term offering that we make to ourselves and to the world.

Things change, and people can sometimes change. The person making the remark is not necessarily our adversary, but the *attitude* is, and to engage in that fight is useful. We can freely be angry about the attitude, and it will bring realizations:

- Ha! I am not obligated to entertain anyone in my practice sessions.

- Music is my personal path in life, my spiritual path.
- A year from now, I will be able to play five (or more) new pieces...a worthwhile goal.
- I'm playing to the stars alone.

None of this is easy. Remarks are not easy to sort out. A young person needs at least one advocate. My mother was my advocate, and she persevered in taking me to lessons even when family demands made it difficult. She was a painter and one of the artists of the Works Progress Administration (WPA) era in San Francisco. She played flute and double bass in her youth.

The attitudes that prevail in this country are toxic to an artist-musician. In India, a musician is an honored person, and the practice is respected. People stop and listen to a musician practicing. They know that for a classical player, the training is rigorous and involves developing ever finer sensibilities over a lifetime. All is learned by rote memorization and sophisticated skills of improvisation.

In the 1960s, Indian sarod master Ali Akbar Khan (1922–2009) was teaching at Mills College in Oakland, California. Some friends were studying with him. They would gather for a weekend in a house in Canyon, a small community in the then-wild and unspoiled Contra Costa hills east of Oakland. They would hold a marathon of Indian music, playing throughout the day and night. Neighbors in the area supported the musicians by bringing them meals, while the music wove ethereal pathways through the beautiful oak, madrone, and chaparral hillsides.[6]

Indian classical music is aligned with Nature. I once heard a story that as part of their training, advanced singers were required to go alone before dawn, stand in a river, and sing as the sun came up. What awareness, sensitivity, and insight such a memorable experience would bring! It would be humbling and rejoicing at the same time. What soft little beings we are in this vast universe, yet our capacity to experience and express can be noble.

Foolishness

DEALING WITH INSTANCES OF "DON'T LET THEM TELL YOU" can come about in bizarre ways. Some of my experience with ridicule and degradation has been humorous. "You play such a phallic instrument." This was said to me in front of some musicians I respected and who I hoped would respect me. I was shocked because I hadn't thought of the flute like that and because I was shy. Not that I didn't laugh easily at dirty jokes or that I was unfamiliar with lustiness, but this comment was out of the blue and seemed to be aimed at denigrating my relationship to music.

I am not quick with come-back remarks. Anything I said would have made me seem a "prude" or a "whore" and entangled me in useless thoughts. I was embarrassed and crestfallen. (I might add it was an arrogant male who made the remark.) It was a slap in the face that rattled me until I began thinking seriously of the reality of the flute, this beautiful instrument, this vehicle that transcends itself in sound and in melody, and that can sing with poise and meaning.

I had to laugh when I realized that the opposite was true. The flute is a *tubular* instrument. Isn't that far more feminine? Besides being tubular, it is a womanly instrument with a womanly range of voice. If one wants to get sexier about it, one can note that to play flute, you blow across a hole against an accurate edge, and it is an open system (not closed). It is the interior construction through which the sound moves and is born. Ha! The flute gives birth.

What I should have said to my arrogant co-musician is "Some men are so preoccupied with their penises!"

Verbal self-defense is not one of my strengths. When insulted, I tend to leave, but looking back, I could have used some practice in defending myself. People can be mindless and hurtful. No matter our character or our ability to react in such circumstances, we need to hold our practice of music high overhead as we slog through the cultural mud.

Don't Let Them Tell You

When young, we find many of our contemporaries attracted to pop music. We too may like certain songs. However, in the pathways we choose playing flute, we need not feel conflicted, as I did, by judgments and put-downs. While working on a Bach piece (Bach—the epitome of innovation and creativity in music), if we are criticized for being a prude and told that we should play with a backbeat or get hooked up to an electric amplifier, it would be time to let their comments pass like clouds.

There may not be much we can do to turn them on to the music we love. Whatever conversation takes place, we must spare ourselves the inward conflict. Separate out the hurt. Feeling left out of the "cool" world is an illusion. What remains? Consider what is artistically satisfying. Trying out other kinds of music might contribute new inspiration to our main focus—folk, pop, ethnic folk, world-classical, and more—but so-called "cool" choices by someone else's standards will not support our individuality or our love for music.

Exploring the music of other cultures can open up our creativity. Other kinds of music I played and what they revealed to me were the following:

- Indian (briefly): Ragas, call and response, micro tones
- Middle Eastern: Beautiful melodies, dance rhythms, improvised call and response, micro tones
- Native American Indian: Simplicity, respect for Nature, steadiness, purity, imitating the sound of a Native American flute
- Japanese Shakuhachi: Introspective yet broad and inclusive
- Celtic: Irish and Scottish, clear melodies, dances, ocean air, wooden flute sound
- South American Indian: Sweet melodies from vast landscapes, dancing rhythms, panpipe, and kena sounds
- Scandinavian: Fiddle tunes with unusual turns in melodic direction
- English Country Dance: fun melodies, some Elizabethan sounding, played for dancers

Don't Let Them Drag You Down

Using voice inflections in downward spirals, people like to complain and moan and groan. I know I do it. Life can seem mostly about complaint, but if our circumstances are relatively mild and we are not being bombed, fleeing a violent country, or languishing in a concentration camp, detention center, prison, or refugee camp (as so many people are), our options are open. We must be mindful of the gigantic fact that if one person is not free, no one is free. We are fortunate in the moment to be free enough to search and find joy in music.

Every field in music has its pluses and minuses. Professional orchestral musicians complain of competition in sections, disliked conductors who make degrading remarks, and warhorse music played season after season. Such accounts might seem likely to create barriers to artistic satisfaction, but an orchestra is a complex system, and despite difficulties, playing in an orchestra can encompass much artistic fulfillment.

It is best to stay with our own energy in music. While others around us may seem to be dulling the glow, don't let that be discouraging. If playing makes our hearts burst with the beauty of the music and a person next to us approaches it as a more mundane task, we must ignore the let-down and stay with our joy. Our joy may just rub off on and inspire others. It's better to fly than to fit in.

Realms

AT THE AGE OF TWELVE, CHILD PRODIGY, SINGER, and cellist Bejun Mehta was a soloist in a series of performances of Handel's *Messiah*. With the thrill of singing this beautiful music, he was in an ecstatic state. When there was a break in the performance, he asked the singer next to him how she was doing. She snarled an off-hand negative statement about her voice. He described how it brought him down:

> *Never before had I been ripped quite as unceremoniously from the precious world of my imagination, a world where Handel was miraculous, and where we might all be lifted up with joy and thanksgiving at being part of such an event.*[7]
>
> —BEJUN MEHTA

Slowly he was able to gain back his equilibrium and joy for the remainder of the performance.

Music and art need human beings to encourage each other. Vincent van Gogh received little encouragement and recognition for his art in his short lifetime. In descriptions of his artistic discoveries in letters to his brother Theo, he spoke of hoping that his work would be helpful to artists and human beings of the future. He longed to encourage others.

Even a tiny comment of encouragement or acknowledgment can bring renewal of energy, validation to go on, or a feeling of connection. Why the tight-lipped lack of enthusiasm we know today? Why be dour? It seems people think they won't be taken seriously unless they keep a scowl. They fear that they will be taken advantage of unless they look mean. Being nonresponsive is cool. Some men believe that being expressionless is more professional. Many women have figured out that in our male-driven culture, they are damned if they do, damned if they don't. Smile, and you are too open and wishy-washy; frown and you are too bitchy and domineering.

Let us lift up the value of each other's insights. Open-minded recognition and responsiveness can be hopeful, fresh, and helpful. Children in particular have unique observations and ideas. Their fresh insights and expressions vitalize our lives and remind us to keep our perceptions open. The insights of elders based on their life experiences can shed light on what is important. Their perspectives may encourage a person of any age.

Do Let Them Tell You

ALL MUSICIANS WORK HARD. WHAT IT TAKES TO learn a piece is highly individual but always involves work. A genius may pick it up quickly, but even then, there's room for development. This work is always evolving. To play a sonata or an entire concert all the way through with confidence, with our best art, may take months or years.

We need to learn to be honest with ourselves while preparing a piece for performance. On one occasion, I had to seriously reassess myself. When rehearsing the Beethoven trio for flute, violin, and viola, I thought I was progressing well, but one member of the trio complained that I was not taking it seriously enough. I felt crushed but had to take a good hard look at myself. It was true that I had an overly optimistic, "can do" attitude. She was right; I was not progressing fast enough. When I taught lessons, I advised my students that one should learn a piece 200 percent in order to perform it 98 percent, and it was time to follow my own advice. I doubled my efforts, and the piece was successful. It was filmed for the local community TV and aired often. This was a case of "*Do* let them tell you."

Lightweight

Insults can force us to consider and strengthen our appreciation of the truth. At an outdoor harvest party, someone introduced me to a woman who was a cellist. I told her that I loved cello and that being a wind player, I envied the wonderful string repertoire, especially the string quartets. She said, "Flute is such a simple instrument. All you do is blow and depress buttons." As the shock hit me, I searched her face to see if she was joking. She was serious! I didn't know what to say. Perhaps she was having a bad day. I politely excused myself and left to enjoy other festivities of the event, but I've thought of the insult ever since. I was stunned by her lack of realistic perception of what fellow musicians do and what it takes to play an instrument.

Early in my music education, I was taught that every instrument is complex to play well, including the triangle. It is miraculous that each person brings his or her unique spirit into playing music. There is no need to be disrespectful. How much more creative and realistic it is to lift each other in encouragement.

The question remained: Why would the flute be perceived as a simple instrument that is easy to play? Perhaps it is because while watching someone play, it doesn't appear as physically involving as a string instrument and doesn't seem as loud as other woodwinds or brass instruments.

Yet the physical effort is immense! The flute is the only instrument that requires blowing against an open edge. All other wind instruments have mouthpieces that offer resistance that, in various ways, guide the flow of the breath. With the flute, the musician does the guiding. Long and complete exhales are needed to speak the beautiful musical passages.

To play a long phrase, a flutist must maximize intake of breath. In contrast, an oboist must budget the breath, because the opening he or she is blowing through is small. Too much air intake can back up in the lungs, trapping carbon dioxide and causing toxicity that can bring on dizziness and loss of concentration. An oboist, and also a bassoonist, must sometimes give a quick exhale before taking in a breath while playing—one of the many aspects that makes the oboe and bassoon difficult instruments.

It would be silly to pit instruments against each other to decide which one is the most difficult, because to play any instrument well is not easy. For some reason, the flute gets labeled as easy and simple. I believe it comes from how flute music is perceived by listeners. The music is often regarded as light, airy, cheerful, flowery, and shimmery—the icing on the cake or "lightweight music." People tend to think of the effect it has on them and are oblivious to the work of the art and background of the artist.

It is like the way comedians are taken for granted. They are funny and make you laugh. They seem like happy jesters, yet they have worked hard to develop their skills in speaking, acting, timing, quick thinking, imitation, imagination, insight, and worldview. Their speaking is honed and, as in music, delivered with skilled phrasing to make their intention and meaning clear. They are often individuals who have experienced trauma or tragedy in their lives. Some suffer from depression. As they offer the world levity, lifting off the heavy weight, they use tremendous skill and creativity.

It is the same mistake in our culture that many people make about women. Women are perceived as lightweights. Nothing could be further from the truth. Women are heavy-duty and bear many burdens. Not that men don't bear weights, but they don't get labeled as passive, pretty decorations, fluffs, or incapable of doing anything significant. Where does that come from?

No matter the physical capabilities with which she is endowed (which are also heavy-duty), a woman is a thinking human being who takes on the cares and concerns of humanity as much or more than a man might. A woman has at the helm the intelligence of the person she is and her guiding wisdom.

Then she slipped into my pocket with my car keys. She said you've taken me for granted because I please you.[8]
—Paul Simon

Preserving versus Sharing Tradition

In 1978, I attended a weekend workshop given by the group, Boys of the Lough sponsored by the music shop, Lark in the Morning in Mendocino, California.[9] Celtic music was beginning to catch on in the United States, though it was not as wildly popular as it soon became. For the occasion, I learned five tunes from a recording of the great Irish flutist, Matt Malloy, and I played them well; I could imitate the wooden flute tone qualities, the slides, and even the subtle "cranning." I was not a stranger to the music of the British Isles, having played for some years English Country Dance music and Scottish Strathspeys, playing in ensembles for dancers and at grand dance balls. These balls were attended by dancers who also participated in the Shakespeare Festival's "Green Show," Elizabethan and Renaissance dancing and music performed before each Shakespeare play at the Chautauqua in Ashland, Oregon.

When I went to play for the first session led by Irish flutist Cathal McConnell, one of the founders of Boys of the Lough, they didn't want to hear me. They wouldn't let me play! They lectured me about how an orchestral modern flute shouldn't be playing Irish music. My flute wasn't authentic. They played Baroque-style wooden flutes, penny whistles, and fifes. They didn't want Irish music bastardized by other cultures. For better or for worse, Celtic music can now be heard everywhere, played by many different kinds of instruments.

I was crushed by the rejection. I had paid their fee (which we could ill afford at the time) and made arrangements with my family of two young children to make it possible to attend the workshop. My abilities to play and my interest in learning Celtic music were rejected. I went alone deep into the woods and sobbed for a while as I questioned the entirety of what I was doing in music. Why was I there? What was I thinking to want to attend this workshop? What was my intention in playing music at all?

I thought of leaving. In walking out of the woods, as I approached the buildings, I heard a lone concertina outside, played by Dave Richardson. I stopped to listen. Next, I listened to a presentation by fiddle player Aly Bain from the Shetland Islands, north of Scotland, and he played beautifully. He explained that Shetland style was unique. Some of his music made you feel that you were there on a windswept island. I decided to listen, observe, and take notes.

I understood that in guarding their music in its original sound, Boys of the Lough wanted to preserve the deep nature of the culture as it had evolved over time. Today they are appreciated for keeping the traditional sound in their music for fifty years. Cultures *should* preserve their treasures. Then again, different cultures influence each other with their music and art. The global reality is that there is cultural dilution and also evolution. South American composers of the 16th century added a new flair to European Baroque music. Today's Baroque musicians argue about a more pure style versus a more open approach. A fusion of cultural influences is not necessarily disrespectful. Over the years, I went on to play a great deal of Irish, Scottish, and English Country Dance music, including the Celtic-African-Jazz-Classical fusion of Bill Douglas on his albums recorded for the Hearts of Space label.

Great Musician—Not a Great Teacher

A GREAT MUSICIAN MAY NOT NECESSARILY BE A great teacher or the best teacher for your individual direction. If possible, arrange a first lesson. Honestly speak with the musician about your interests and the direction you want to aim for musically. She or he will be as interested as you are in a good working rapport between student and teacher.

We may find teachers where we may not have thought to look. We may find a wonderful teacher who plays a different instrument or who sings. The arts inform each other, and the insights of people working in painting, sculpture, dance, theater and other arts are often outstanding sources of insights that also apply to our own work.

Human beings are capable of handling many different concepts, and we enjoy constantly refreshing ourselves with discovery. As artists, we can nurture our far-flung imaginations. Nature is our best teacher. It is enlightening to study Nature and to perceive many awe-inspiring connections. We seek the truth in what is natural.

Creative versus Re-Creative

"You're just reading notes." Some people have the idea that musicians are not creative if they only play written works. We may be criticized for not playing *original* music that we have improvised or written ourselves. The act of composing is deemed "creative," whereas the musician performing that composition is only "re-creative."

Pianist and teacher Seymour Bernstein states that musicians are not "creative," they are "re-creative," because they are interpreting the composer's work.[10] Violinist Isaac Stern said the same thing.[11] He said that theater acting and performing music are "interpretative arts." He claimed that a writer, painter, playwright, or composer will always be more important than an actor or performer. He acknowledged that for the performer, the parameters may be at times wider or narrower. By this logic, when we set out to play a written composition, we are "re-creative." I strongly disagree.

Composition. Improvisation. Performance. These arts are complete worlds in themselves. Can their differences support the idea that two are creative and the third is re-creative? We can work in all three, but the merits of one should not disparage another.

The work of composing calls heavily upon skills, knowledge, and creativity. It is a superlative experience to create something where there had been nothing. All arts do this. To have written the music that others will play and know can be superbly gratifying. However, the other side of composing is the work of finding capable musicians to play the piece, and finding a venue, a way to have it heard and "get it out there."

To improvise and spontaneously compose as you play can be a wondrous art, involving practice, imagination, and sensitivity. It comes out of a background that includes the cultural history of music, kinds of harmonies, familiar turns of phrases, developed skills, and an aware ear. Supreme familiarity and mastery of the instrument are needed. Invention is to be truly admired, but often it isn't invention but a recycling of familiar patterns. A musician improvising often relies on characteristic patterns that can be played artfully or not.

Some performances of classical music can sound like a rehash that lacks life, color, and originality. There are also musicians who are supremely inventive and spontaneous in performing classic works; their playing sounds freshly created and original. There are many stories of a composer being grateful to a musician for bringing out aspects of the composition he or she hadn't considered, thus elevating the work with the musician's insightful playing.

Playing music is discovery and a never-ending quest. We don't learn to play a piece and then duplicate it the same way every time. Each time we play, we hold something that lives and evolves. Skill and innovative ideas are constantly at work, myriad details are organized and reorganized, and subtle emotional qualities are explored to produce each harmony, melody, and rhythm at the height of our honesty and conviction. Since the work of an individual artist is not static but always searching for truth and essence, should this work still be considered merely "re-creative?"

The word "re-creative" seems wrong and inaccurate when describing a performer. The art of playing encompasses a broad spectrum full of freedom of decision, infinite subtlety, and room to roam. Each time we play a composition, it will be played anew, and each musician will play it differently. The playing of a piece can evolve and change profoundly over a lifetime. Guitarist Raphaella Smits playing the Bach *Chaconne* offers deep insight that can only have evolved from her life experience and wisdom as well as her having considered and discovered countless approaches to playing the piece over many years.

In the Romantic era, musicians were valued as artists, free to assert their individual artistry when playing, but it has been less the case since the 1900s.

> …the late twentieth century, [was] a period in which subjective expression and imagination in musical performance in general flattened out and shed the remaining vestiges of Romantic performance practice. This is a complex subject with myriad causes, but the idea of the performer as a co-creator with the composer was gradually replaced by a pernicious objectivity.[12]
> —CHRISTOPHER BERG

Composers such as Bach, Mozart, Beethoven, and probably many more composed with certain individual musicians in mind. Their music was often built with a desire to feature the mastery, musicality, sensitivities, and inventiveness of that individual. Mozart in particular wrote for the instrumentalists and singers whose artistry he admired.

Musicians are sometimes surprised when listening to a composer play his or her own composition—surprised that it's not played particularly well. In the hands of another musician, the music lives and breathes. At times composers may consider a composition to be not their best, to later discover that, when played by a fine musician, it is elevated to unimagined heights.

If the real creativity is accomplished only with the composition, what would be the point of the musician's efforts? A computer could play back the data from the black-and-white written notes, and that would make audible the complete and accurate form of the composition. It might be thrilling to hear the form and design, but it would be only the potential of what a live performance can be. The human performance reaches into the diversity of living experiences, the miraculous brain and heart, feelings for the land, the Earth, sunshine, rain, mysteries of planets, stars—all these are far outside the limitations of a computer. We communicate, touch each other, learn, and evolve profoundly from listening to each other create music.

Landscape painters haven't created the landscapes they paint. Their painting might be more representational, more abstract, wild and loud, quiet and subtle—the possibilities are unlimited. In a similar way, in music, we can see what's there, but it's up to us to paint it. Our painting, our performance, reveals a way of seeing that conveys meaning to our eyes, ears, and minds.

The "tree" of a music composition is invisible and inaudible until you paint it. The tree comes to you in black-and-white symbols. You may take that page of paper and ask yourself, *How do I make this branch reach tall and that supporting branch have strength and balance? How do I create lovely curves for the leaf shapes, the angular twigs, the glow of delicate buds, and the subtle colors of the tender blossoms? How do I convey...* and so on. The degree of artistic insight to bring the music to life and light can take the utmost of a person's abilities.

Painting a landscape involves innovation, imagination, and interpretation. Is a landscape painter "re-creative?" You might paint a tree, and it could be a good likeness, a very good likeness, but it could be uninteresting because it lacks myriad aspects of observation and emotional and spiritual connection. Vincent van Gogh wrote that he approached painting a tree as he approached painting a human figure, full of character and nuance, embodying respect and curiosity for the nature of Nature.

> ...*in all of nature, in trees for instance,
> I see expression and a soul.*[13]
> —VINCENT VAN GOGH

Consider the first four and the second four notes of Beethoven's *Fifth Symphony*—the proverbial "knock at the door of fate." No two orchestras play them the same way. Under the conductor's direction as well as the musicians' presence, skill, and sensitivity, some orchestras play these eight notes in a manner that is agitated, ominous, noble, anticipatory, aggressive, or thunderous. They may be played quietly natural, like a woodpecker drumming in the woods, or rattled off like someone signing initials. They may be played with slow deliberation, setting the stage for something monumental, with terrifying ferocity, or with other emotional expressions. Some orchestras play them dully and with disengagement, because the piece is an old "warhorse" that they have played hundreds of times. Listeners know that they have just heard the *Fifth Symphony*, but did it shake their psyches, touch their souls, enrich their consciousness, or give them new insights? Is a performance that stirs up one's life "re-creative" or "creative"?

When we view a printed composition, we know the parchment contains something miraculous, great, and powerful. We can hear it in our mind's ear, but the performers manifest the work of art. Are they merely coloring in the outlines? The outlines are concepts through which the musician dives deeper into subtleties, making wild and divergent creative choices. The performance is a shaping that could be compared to a sculpture on an armature. Imagine the armature posed as a human figure standing with one arm raised. Will this figure be compassionate or uncaring, intelligent or dull, imaginative or bland? Will the music coming from the structure of the composition be simply robotic, industrial Muzak? Or will this performance lift us off our seat, transport us out of time, and allow us to fly? That depends on the creativity of the musician.

16

Capable and Legitimate

We are born artists. Every child has an individual spark. Children run, dance, sing, draw, act, and verbally express their ideas in fresh ways. They wield crayons and paintbrushes with their own individual flare. They sing or hum, skip and leap, and tell stories with toy characters, dolls, rocks, sticks, or pine cones. They take great joy in their imaginations, pretending to be a character, a superhero, an animal, a teacher, or a doctor. They are keen observers. They tune in to the nature of things. As infants, they are sensitive to the way they are held and the vibrations in the atmosphere, be it stress or harmony in the people around them. Often the best way to calm a crying baby, when all requirements for food, cleanliness, and physical comfort have been met, is to relax and calm your own being.

As soon as babies can hold an object, that object is brought to their mouth for examination. This is not a babyish habit but a vital scientific method of learning important perceptions of what's what. What is the nature of this object? Is it angular, textured, rounded, large, small, from nature or man-made? Is there a taste to it? Each subtle attribute is an important scientific lesson.

Babies bang objects against the floor or against other objects, listening intently to the effect. They are often wide eyed as they create variations in loudness. Children are thrilled to be given a percussion instrument such as a tambourine, drum, triangle, box, kitchen pan, or wooden spoon.

I will never forget my kindergarten teacher, Ms. Pratt, who always had the class doing interesting activities. A favorite activity was having the children march or walk in line around the classroom each playing a small percussion instrument along with a recording of a classical march or dance. We were free to play along, and at times she called out for certain instruments to play. "All triangles play. Now just the drums. Now the shakers and cymbals."

Experiences like these are priceless for children. They encourage self-confidence:

I can do this

I am doing this

I like this sound and want to hear more of it

These sounds have strength and influence

I am a capable person

What I do is significant in the whole

I can collaborate

All these insights open doors throughout a person's life. The feelings can be accessed in adulthood to apply to music and all areas of life.

Helen Lanfer was a pianist who taught music to dancers at The Julliard School in New York. She played for the internationally famous, award-winning dancer and choreographer Martha Graham (1894–1991) and her dance company. Lanfer developed a way to teach music that was inclusive and inventive. She was invited to give workshops and classes at universities and institutions including the Massachusetts Institute of Technology. Working with both children and adults, she found ways to encourage people to trust their creativity. She taught that anyone can participate in the creation of music and even compose music. A class might begin with asking students to discover individually how many sounds they can make with their hands, then asking each student to pick three favorite sounds and create a sequence with them. She might ask them to locate interesting sounds around the room—a book set down, a door knob turned, a cupboard opened and closed, a pencil tapping on a window—and to collaborate with others in small groups to organize and perform their work. Compositions would be written, drawn, or diagrammed in students' invented notation. Musical instruments would later be used, making possible a large variety of experiences and explorations, evolving into organizing and composing music. A natural introduction to Western notation would eventually come forward. She led her classes with quiet and genuine respect for the individuality of each student and with patience to allow natural creativity to blossom. She wrote a short book (recently republished) about her teachings, *Music Within Us: An Exploration in Creative Music Education*.[1] Based on the teachings of Helen Lanfer, I taught a series of music sessions at the small grammar school that my children attended. The responses were creative, fun, and joyful. The insights of Helen Lanfer are of inestimable value. Her book reveals a treasury of pathways to how we naturally learn and create and the potential for teachers to help people find joy and creative fulfillment in their lives.

Doors Opened, Doors Shut

WHERE AND HOW DO PEOPLE'S DOORS GET SHUT? What causes people to feel incapable and say belittling things about themselves like the following? (Rebuttals are also listed.)

- "I'm no artist; I can't draw a straight line." (If we can write, we can draw. We improve each time we try.)
- "I don't have the talent to play music; I am tone deaf." (One note at a time, we can train ourselves to sing pitches.)[2]
- "I can't write; I don't have anything interesting to say." (Everyone has unique experiences and unique stories to tell.)
- "I'm so clumsy; I can't dance." (If we can dance clumsily, from there it is possible to find all sorts of ways to dance.)
- "I love plays and movies, but I can't act." (We are acting and interacting all the time and constantly observing our own and others' behavior.)

Who or what has shut us down? Society has accepted and institutionalized an assumption of what people "should be doing" to "succeed" in life. The pursuit of art, music, dance, theater, and poetry: how many ways are these fields quashed by well-meaning but shortsighted adults? The arts are crushed by a culture that negates such endeavors as frivolous and does not recognize the enormous gateway to learning they provide. The arts are the first to disappear in schools when there are budget losses. Classes in the arts are wiped out by organizations and schools that demand conformity. Vital, creative activities are not seen as "real" learning that conforming, corporate tyrannies believe occurs only behind a desk or in organized sports.

We might be shut down for other reasons. I knew a brilliant reference librarian who wanted to write, but because so many books were already out there, she said, "What's the use? What could I add?" I protested that she as an individual has her own insights. Even if some insights might have been written previously, an idea or imaginative story expressed in her unique way could take on meaning for someone as never before.

A fresh expression may be a catalyst that opens the way for someone—including the writer—to go further. Let us value our own and each others' insights.

Practice Schedule

TO KEEP A DAILY PRACTICE SCHEDULE IS VITAL BUT not always easy. The following practice options may help. These could be a morning time or an evening time, using both on some days. If on some days it looks hopeless for having any time at all, squeeze in a ten-, fifteen-, or twenty-minute session to play intervals, long tones, scales, arpeggios, or excerpts of a work. Being focused on tone quality, smoothness, and musicality, even if briefly, can create a worthwhile practice session that enhances abilities in full-session work on other days.

We must work with not only our *time* but our *energy*. Despite being tired at day's end, if we push through our fatigue and begin a practice session, we may happily find that playing revives us. Energy begets energy. To some extent, the more energy used, the more we have. To occasionally find a more ideal time when we are fresh, clearheaded, and at our best (perhaps early in the day) allows us to more energetically meet with our miraculous art and realize our extraordinary capabilities.

Tell People You Need the Time and Why

I STRUGGLED WITH FEELING THAT I WAS STEALING time for practicing, especially after becoming a mother. It was not only the "woman in her place" cultural trap, but the general cultural failure to recognize music as valid, important, and requiring real work. It was not recognized as a "practice."

To the extent I kept up my practice through thick and thin, I believe it strengthened the children, offered harmony in family life, and helped them find some of the insights and appreciation they now enjoy in adulthood. However, the feeling of stealing remained ingrained in me. On one hand, the mischief of being a social rebel by delving into music was invigorating. On the other hand, it was hard to feel legitimate. *When can I call myself a musician?* Wisdom should have advised me to find a way to tell people around me, and fully admit to myself, what music meant to me.

To avoid this trap, it is important to find precise words to convey the necessity of making time to develop our art. People should respect us and respect that this is our practice—in a large sense, our spiritual practice. For people who see nothing practical about music and don't understand our love and pursuit of it, more communication is necessary. How to communicate well depends on the individuals involved. Maybe the other person will understand better if he or she is included in the joy we find in music in general, perhaps by attending concerts together or inviting other musicians over for rehearsals. If nothing helps, finding a space to practice away from the household may work.

If our practice schedule gets compromised too much and too often by outside circumstances, it can be reestablished with calm and assertive discussion. We must talk with ourselves and people in our lives with an approach of mutual respect. "How can we find a way?"

Love and Self-Criticism

LOVE FOR MUSIC, AND THE SPIRITUAL ASPECTS OF the practice of music, can be stymied by harsh self-criticism. We can berate ourselves and cleave to an impression that we don't "make the grade." We may be especially self-critical when we have been rejected for employment, a position, or another opportunity. It is helpful to remember these facts:

- It is common for everyone to experience many bumps in the road.
- In seeking an orchestral position, remember that there are many flutists and not enough positions. Many musicians may be great candidates for the position, but the fact remains that only one can be selected. Not being chosen doesn't mean you don't play well.
- Sometimes one opportunity that "falls through" makes space for an even better opportunity, and when we look back, the failure becomes a "blessing in disguise."
- Congratulate yourself for trying. Don't be embarrassed that you did not win. The fact is *you* play music. It is a noble human activity. You are not bad and not incompetent.
- Perhaps you know you did not play your best. Reassure yourself that you will be able to try again, perhaps in other circumstances when you have had time to further your capabilities. Pick yourself up, and keep working.

Disappointment with oneself can seem acute at times. Disappointment shows that there is a fine awareness in you that serves you well for a panorama of possibilities that includes the potential for letdown as well as joyful achievement. Take the self-criticism, feeling of failure or inadequacy, and loneliness and consider them profound teachers. They may seem like adversaries, but they can be used like springboards. Even if you are angry, the anger can be used as energy for breakthroughs in your approach and abilities in music. You might even have a feisty attitude: *I'll show them what I can do,* which is saying *I'll show myself.*

I once heard Sam Bush, master bluegrass mandolin and fiddle player, playing at a record shop in Boulder, Colorado. He was in town on a CD release concert tour. He played alone, and it was "knock your socks off" alive and creative. After he played, he answered questions from the audience crowded around him. Someone asked, "What inspires or motivates your playing?" His reply was surprising: "Anger." That's all he said. Was his anger political? Personal? That was his business. Whether he was serious or joking, his reply was eye opening for me. The music had been leaping, dancing, joyous, and intricate, a flexible variety of multifaceted beauty—none of which sounded angry. I began to think anger could motivate a real outlook in music. What do we do with our anger about the ugly, violent, ignorant, money-grubbing tragedies in the world? We can transform the anger by sending forth the best we can reach. As musicians, as artists, we are doing our part to bend collective consciousness toward truth, beauty, and joy.[3]

When feeling depressed, we can reach the bottom, and it can be like jumping into a pool: when our feet touch bottom, we can spring off and launch ourselves to soar to the top. Feeling that we are at "rock bottom" can be where we find a springboard.

In his autobiography, pianist Arthur Rubinstein tells the story of his serious depression. In his early twenties, finding himself alone in Paris and in debt with hardly the means to survive, he attempted to take his life by hanging. Breaking down in a torrent of tears, he found great solace in playing his piano.

After he revived, he realized how hungry he was (he had been living on little money and little to eat). He went out to walk to a restaurant, deciding to budget for a better meal. Once he stepped outside, he experienced a series of life-changing realizations and "I fell in love with life."

> *Out in the street, however, a sudden impulse made me stop. Something strange came over me, call it a revelation or a vision...I looked at everything around me with new eyes, as if I had never seen any of it before... I suddenly started to think. The life I had been leading consisted of a series of events for which I had no responsibility; I acted entirely by instinct, following blindly the road drawn out for me by circumstances; I never tried to analyze anything. Well, on that night, right there in the street, on my way to Aschinger's for my dinner de luxe, my brain was full of philosophical thoughts, and it resulted in a new conception of life and a new criterion of values, all for my private use. The eternal, unsolved question—What gave birth to the universe? What is the reason for its existence?—would involve a long dissertation. Let me say only that in this chaos of thoughts I discovered the secret of happiness and I still cherish it: Love life for better or for worse, without conditions.*[4]
>
> —ARTHUR RUBINSTEIN

The reasons we get down in the dumps are varied. If the burden seems too heavy, it may help to seek someone who can truly listen. If there is no one, we can write the worst points and study them. We can consider a problem a worthy adversary, a good match for our potential to dispel difficulties with insight and understanding. Recognizing the conflicts can bring forth the strength to deal with them.

Criticizing ourselves, or criticism from the outside, might be beneficial. As painful as our anger, frustration, and hurt are, those emotions might be useful to generate more energy in our work. This energy can enable us to push through and beyond what we think is our shortcoming. If we remember that everything can change and is constantly changing, we can feel less stuck. Our current status or state of mind is not "concrete," because nothing is "concrete"—not even concrete. Nothing is permanent.

I talk with plants. When alone, I have walked in the woods, stopping now and then to talk with a fern, a wild rose, or a tree, and although it sounds eccentric, I have found real answers to the questions I pose. I consider and try to recognize the presence of the plant's life that I am standing near, and also acknowledge that it is a mystery. I cannot know its exact nature, consciousness and sensitivity, yet being receptive to its form, beauty, and presence goes a long way to inform me of its reality. Michael Pollan, bestselling author who wrote *The Botany of Desire: A Plant's–Eye View of the World*, writes about new research in plant sensory perception—akin to neurobiology. He describes how plants, which have many more sense perceptions than humans, react to the environment. Plants form 99 percent of life on the planet.[5]

Ask the plant a clear singular question, not necessarily expecting an answer but in any case appreciating the beauty of the being that shares space with you in the moment. Maybe no answer will come. Maybe a piece of an answer will occur to you. I have been astonished more than once how immediately a wise and freshly insightful reply will occur to me. Is it from me? Is it from the plant? The replies from plants come much faster than replies I have sought by sitting in a chair trying to concentrate. This may seem eccentric, but perhaps there is some element of normal in "paranormal."

Original Instruments and Coffee

IN USING OUR CREATIVITY AND IMAGINATION IN working on a piece, it is helpful to study writings, comments, critique, and advice in pedagogy books, history books, and surviving personal accounts of the era of the composer. The letters of Mozart are revealing about musicians of his time and his performing style. To know the instruments of the era, their attributes and qualities of sound, can reveal that the music Mozart wrote must have been played with certain approaches befitting each instrument. The construction of all orchestral instruments (except for the trombone) has changed since Mozart's time.

Pianist Andras Schiff speaks of the earlier keyboard instruments of Bach's time: the clavichord, with its intimate sound (even capable of vibrato by vertical movement of fingers), and the harpsichord, which contributed a more brilliant sound for concertos. He credits harpsichordist George Malcolm with making him aware of how clavichord and harpsichord music was written and how to adapt it to the modern concert grand piano.[6]

The flute of Mozart's era was still the Baroque flute made of wood with its more earthy sound. (Boehm system metal flutes were invented in the 1840s.) Mozart wrote parts for his favorite instrumentalists as well as for favorite singers in his operas. His opera *Idomeneo, re di Creta* has beautiful musical parts that he wrote for his friends including flutist Johan Baptist Wendling and his wife Dorothea Wendling, an accomplished opera singer. At age twenty, Mozart first met the flutist in Mannheim where he spoke of the orchestra in that city with especially high regard.[7] Playing on modern instruments, we would do well to study the qualities of the earlier flutes and gain insight into the music written for them.

The study of music history and styles is important, but in the end, the most important thing is the underlying humanity and individuality of the musician. Would Bach have played everything with a scowl and mathematical, mechanical exactitude? It can't be that music of such variety of mood and spirit was played only in a cool and calculating way. There must have been plenty of passion and emotion in his playing—not with cloying sentimentality but the kind of frankness and openness that seems inherent. Surely his children loved his music, and three of them became great composers in their own right: Carl Philipp Emanuel Bach, Johann Christian Bach (friend of Mozart), and Wilhelm Friedemann Bach. We have to wonder if there were any composing daughters, but their efforts would have been sublimated and lost to history, as in Bach's time "women were allowed no public role in creating or performing music."[8]

J. S. Bach's daughter, Elizabeth Juliana, married one of her father's students. It is suggested she may have been the daughter who J. S. Bach worried was drinking too much coffee. Coffee, relatively new in Germany, was becoming the new popular beverage in Europe. Cafes were opening even as coffee drinking was still controversial in the 1730s. Bach may have been thinking of his daughter when he composed the "Coffee Cantata."

Schweigt stille, plaudert nicht ("Be still, stop chattering"), also called the "Coffee Cantata," is a comic, mini opera about a teenage daughter who sings the praises of coffee and argues with her disapproving father who tries to bribe her to give it up. The voice of the daughter, named Leischen, is accompanied by an energetic and beautiful flute obbligato. A portion of the libretto, sung by Leischen, is translated:

> **Ei! wie schmeckt der Coffee süße,**
> *Ah! how sweet coffee tastes!*
>
> **Lieblicher als tausend Küsse,**
> *Lovelier than a thousand kisses,*
>
> **Milder als Muskatenwein.**
> *smoother than muscatel wine.*
>
> **Coffee, Coffee muss ich haben,**
> *Coffee, I must have coffee,*
>
> **Und wenn jemand mich will laben,**
> *and if anyone wants to give me a treat,*
>
> **Ach, so schenkt mir Coffee ein!**
> *ah!, just give me some coffee!* [9]

When we study music of different eras, we can consider the people, the homes, the community, the individuals, the hardships, and tragedies that occurred in the lives of composers and musicians. Their experiences would likely have intensified their approaches to playing music—not necessarily in the direction of sounding dour. Joy and humor would have even more importance. The importance of musical expression included release, pathos, meditation, humor, equilibrium, searching, and faith—all the more reason to approach music as human communication rather than as if we are making a series of calculations.

Subjective and Emotional

A PROFOUND TRUTH OFTEN COMES TO US EXPRESSED in utter simplicity and simple language. "Do unto others as ye would have them do unto you" is simple and profound.

In literature, a story where two people begin to fall in love can be movingly described in their courage to touch each other's hands for the first time. That simple gesture can be infinitely more profound, meaningful, moving, and sensually exciting than describing the characters as immediately jumping into the sack and rolling around.

The words *sensitivity* and *sensibility* express truth better than the heavily laden words *emotion* and *reason*. *Emotion* is associated with weakness and almost considered a bad word, often used for female degradation. "Don't pay any attention to her. She's just emotional." *Reason* is associated with sanity and logic and superior male thinking. This is a faulty dichotomy and a manipulative way of thinking.

We needn't be afraid of emotion in music. In fact, emotion is the key factor. As a foundation of our lives, emotion is what impresses us, gives us "gut feelings," and influences us in choosing our direction. Musically, we can express emotion with an overview. As we play, a certain amount of objectivity needs to be there—an outlook, a view—a vista of what is coming out in the sound waves. Our emotional content is subjective, yet we have the capacity to assess the qualities of our output.

When my grandson was about six years old, we talked on the phone. He had been studying famous artists at school, and he asked, "As an artist, how do you know if you are good or not? Van Gogh didn't know he was good. Do you only know if you are good if people tell you that you are good?"

My heart melted that such a young child was concerned about such a broad and deep question. Then honestly I didn't know the answer. Even though I said, "You must know yourself," I personally hadn't resolved this completely.

Dear Theo: *The Autobiography of Vincent van Gogh* (edited by Irving Stone) is a compilation of Vincent's letters to his brother. It is evident that Vincent suffered for lack of recognition, but he exalted in his love for his art, his explorations in light, color, and design, and his glorious discoveries. He knew what was good. He created and saw what was good, yet with so little recognition, he suffered incredible loneliness. We must find our confidence in knowing and finding our own way.[10]

What makes a person a legitimate musician to herself or himself and to others? That will be elusive. Along the way, we deal with sensitivities and fear of criticism. We can't pretend that we are impervious to criticism, nor would it be to our advantage to ignore it. We can find ways to consider the messages, learn from them, or let them go.

To let go is often the most logical thing to do, because people hear differently. What they bring of themselves to the experience of listening influences what they perceive. One person's perceptions are different from another's. Although we may feel we are sending a clear message through our music, we can't be responsible for how it resonates with another person.

Spontaneity

"Play as if you are improvising" is a valuable suggestion we sometimes hear. This is a wonderful approach and can bring much freshness to our playing.

What does it entail for a "classical" musician to play as if improvising? It involves playing as if each note, each direction, and intention is our decision, as if the composition is our original design. For example, a piece might have a spiritual feeling. By internalizing the spirituality over time, the music has the potential to be expressed as our own meditation, open to new pathways of thought. While fully respecting and executing the compositional content and the design, we can include our imagination and spirit. Even though the piece is familiar, it is possible to explore creative, inventive insights and make each note arise as if it has never been played before.

Don't Fence Yourself In

WE ARE MUSICIANS FIRST AND INSTRUMENTALISTS second, just as one is a human being first and a man or woman second. Being a human being and being a musician brings huge, open-ended questions. What is it to be a musician? What is it to be human?

To be a musician is to become broad and expansive, not narrow and confined to a corner of society. Society mistakenly portrays a musician as the geeky person practicing in a small room: self-centered and wasting time that could be more profitably spent. People may cling to categorization and identify themselves with false standards, allowing joy, discovery, and invention to be suppressed by these false assumptions. We needn't let them fence us in.

Many people give up any notion of bringing music or art as a practice into their lives. They give up before they try, because they claim they have no talent or don't see a practical way to begin. They know their own situation best, and their judgment may be "spot on." Perhaps their life situation does not allow the time, or the desire to play music is not strong. However, many people long to pursue their inspiration but don't because they hold onto societal deceptions.

There is the deception that the musician plays from an original gift from birth and that one must be lucky enough to have this talent. That deception would be dissolved by observing the work that goes on behind the scenes—the patient *try* and *try again*, the perseverance that brings step-by-step progress.

How does art in general, music, visual art, dance, or theater relate to humanity? "Artists express themselves" doesn't cover the range of what the arts mean to humanity. The magnificent masterworks of Beethoven, Leonardo da Vinci, Shakespeare, Picasso, Georgia O'Keeffe, and Martha Graham have informed humanity in some of the deepest ways—informing us of our nature, our core, our capabilities, and our direction.

Music is ephemeral; it happens in the moment, but it can change our chemistry and bring us awe, tenderness, ferocity, love, and healing. It can bring realization beyond words. With a shiver of recognition or a warm embrace, the experience of music can lead us to recognize our human self in the cosmos.

17

One Half of Humanity

The question that is the "elephant in the room" is how do you manage in music, in the arts, in the world, if you are a woman? Women often don't want to talk about it almost as if it's bad luck, saying defensively, "I've never encountered any problems. I've always been able to do exactly what I wanted to do." Perhaps things are better these days, but roadblocks for women are still everywhere.

There are more women in previously all-male lines of work, but the jobs pay women terribly. Currently she earns an average of seventy cents to every dollar a man makes. In some states, it is as low as fifty-five cents. It is a system whereby corporations profit (or steal) off the backs of women. People who earn less than the cost of living are mostly women, most often single women who are supporting their families. She may be working two or three jobs. Like many people, she has no paid vacations or sick day leave. Society relies on her service and her work yet abandons her and her children.

Recognition of women as full human beings, and as half of humanity, seems a long way off. In many cultures, especially those under the domination of major religions, a woman is a possession, kept as a servant, and not allowed to be an autonomous human being. She is denied education and gainful work and, in some countries, unable to walk outdoors in her community without a male escort. Beyond these basic transgressions are many more sickening and heinous violent violations and abuses that keep women injured and isolated mentally and physically.

In the United States, a commercial focus on *woman as product* puts everything she might be interested in out of reach. In the male-driven culture, women are stuck in the role of being supportive of men and gaining a dubious recognition only if they meet standards of fashion in hair, makeup, and dress. In Hollywood style, a woman is commercialized to be a commodity.

When Pablo Casals was beginning to go bald, he was asked to wear a wig on stage to improve his appearance.[1] He would hear nothing of it. Women are pressured to be alluring, glamorous eye-candy on stage. *Show your skin, your flesh. We've got to see your arms, back, and shoulders, maybe a bit of cleavage. You must be amiable, light, and smiling, never feeling the gravity of anything. Never as strong as a man.* Corsets, girdles, makeup, colored eyelids, hair gel, bras, pantyhose, high heels, all the rigging...and...what? Casals wouldn't wear a wig to improve his appearance on stage.

We need to stand firm to be who we are. Musicians—female or male—need to be free to not conform to imposed standards and to wear what allows them to feel their own beauty, dignity, and comfort.

Brilliant Careers

WOMEN HAVE BEEN CAREER ARTISTS IN MUSIC FOR centuries, yet we don't hear about them because the male point of view in historical records excludes interest in women's accomplishments and experiences. British conductor, musician, and scholar Jane Glover wrote an enlightening book about the people who were among Mozart's family and friends and for whom he wrote much of his music. *Mozart's Women: His Family, His Friends, His Music* tells the amazing histories of the women opera singers who created the roles in Mozart's operas as well as some who were top fortepiano and clavier performers. With her important research and deep musical insight, Glover describes the strengths of the individual musicians for whom Mozart designed his music—strengths evidenced by the music. We can almost hear them singing or playing as we read of their lives. Glover shows that these women had long, brilliant careers in which they provided all or part of the income for their families. Their extensive careers were interwoven with many tough circumstances, spousal abuse, pregnancies, and the deaths of babies and young sons and daughters, yet these women persevered to become masterful musicians and to create outstanding performances widely acclaimed throughout Europe.[2]

A History with No History

Music history hardly mentions women. The authors may have had every intention of representing the history of Western music accurately, yet it is almost entirely a male story, in a male language, and from a male viewpoint.

The History of Western Music by Donald J. Grout is a standard text used in college music history classes. It has been reprinted many times over many years. My first encounter with the book was the 1960 edition. There was a twenty-one-page chronology of music history from 800 BCE to CE 1955 that listed important music events and composers, notable accomplishments in other arts, and world historical events.

Spanning 2,755 years, the list contains *no* mention of women musicians or composers. In fact, the chronology hardly mentions women at all. The only mentions of women are the following, none of them related to music or composing:

1431 Jeanne d'Arc executed

1692 Salem witchcraft trials

1702 Queen Anne of England crowned

1902 Discovery of radium by Pierre and Marie Curie

1911 Edith Wharton, author of *Ethan Frome*

1918 Willa Cather, author of *My Antonia*

1927 Virginia Woolf, author *To the Lighthouse*

1932 Gertrude Stein, author of *Matisse, Picasso and Gertrude Stein*

What was a student, male or female, to think? *The History of Western Music* has been one of the most respected texts for the study of music history in colleges and universities for decades.

If that history were to be believed, all composers and professional performers were men. I *believed* exactly that for most of my life. I believed that there were hardly any women composers. I thought it was because women were held back in education and confined to domestic work. As I was growing up in the 1950s and 1960s, there were few women musicians in symphony orchestras. How the absence of women's names, lack of information about them, and bleak silence in place of recognition of women composers and musicians affects a girl (and a boy) is profoundly disturbing. It is robbery. It internalizes a belief that as a girl or a woman, you are not as capable, and a woman is not a full human being. The deceit is horrific.

In music history, as in all history, women are not heard, not acknowledged, not recorded. Women made tremendous accomplishments and contributions in recent times and in antiquity. Nevertheless, even today, standard accounts persist in hardly mentioning women at all. What are the reasons for the exclusion of women in the history of Western music?

Restriction and Standardization

The history of Western art music properly begins with the music of the Christian Church.[3]
—Donald J. Grout

The term "Western art music" refers to the styles of music that have been culturally accepted in Europe and the Americas since the dominance of Christianity in the Middle Ages. This period of time is said to have contained the origin of the wealth of Western classical music beginning with the Christian church and Gregorian chant.

> *The Church was the chrysalis out of which our Western society emerged. Its germ of creative power in the realm of music was embodied in the Gregorian Chant…one of the seeds from which in the fullness of time our Western music developed.*[4]
> —Arnold Toynbee (1889–1975)

After Christianity was legalized in the fourth century, women were banned from participating in music and even verbal communication in church. Music of the Church was music fashioned in the effort to set absolute standards and push away unwanted aspects. Women were explicitly excluded. Secular music was silenced. The Church ruled and strictly enforced what was and was not permitted. Intervals of octaves, fourths, and fifths were considered mathematically consonant, and only these intervals, sung in simple parallel lines in chants by men and boys, were deemed pure and devoid of any temptation to corrupt the listener with emotion or sensuality. After the Church set up its sanctioned institutional music, change in music was exceedingly slow, often with great internal conflict through centuries of domination and limitation.

Music history is presented as if simple plainsong chants were a foundation that gradually gave way to more complex harmonies. The slow-moving parallel octaves, fifths, and fourths were the church standard, gradually giving way to other intervals and eventually polyphony. When he appeared on TV in the 1950s, in one of his lecture series, Leonard Bernstein (1918–1990) went to the piano and demonstrated in five minutes the evolution of harmony in the history of Western music. Starting with claiming that cave men, women, and children would have naturally sung in parallel octaves, he demonstrated the slow evolution to adopt harmonies in fourths and fifths, then thirds and sixths, then harmonies based on the relationships of the circle of fifths. The problem is that it is described through a narrow lens.[5]

Western music history focuses myopically on the condensed, restricted music of the Christian church. It is presented as a pure, primal origin of music, when in reality it was a death of sorts. After missions of destruction, conquest, and expansion, the Christian church used institutional enforcement to control the vanquished and to reduce music to tight restrictions. Prior to the era of "Gregorian" plainchant, there were centuries of diverse and highly developed music in

Europe and the Middle East with cross-cultural influences extending to and from India and the Far East. The overland "Silk Road" as well as some of the sailing routes were a deep source of cultural exchange for Europe, China, Korea, Japan, India, Persia, the Horn of Africa, and Arabia from two centuries BCE to several centuries into the Common Era. Pre-Christian Greece and Rome enjoyed enormously popular music festivals and competitions. Music was composed for plays and poetry, and music schools were established. These rich and diverse cultural mainstays were forums for music innovation and development.

Gregorian chant is said to have brought about the first *notation* in what became Western music's system of notation, the organized written music on five-line staves. Just as it is deceptive to say that Gregorian chant was the beginning of Western music, it cannot be said that it was the first European system of music notation. Fragments of ancient Greek notation and earlier forms of notation exist. Terpander (c. 680 BCE, poet and legendary kithara player) founded a music school in Sparta and is sometimes credited with having invented notation.[6]

Destruction

ARCHAEOLOGICAL EVIDENCE INDICATES THAT early civilizations were societies where women owned land, kept order in their communities and cities, were innovators and inventors, worked in art and architecture, held festivals with music, and worshiped the divine Creatress. There were viable matriarchal societies as late as the time of classical Greece. Archaeological finds and research have revealed that Goddesses were a center of spirituality. For thousands of years and in large areas of Europe and the Middle East, women had influence and respect in civil organization, laws and morals, spiritual realms, and the arts.

The feminine was of great importance in the spiritual consciousness of these cultures. The Egyptian goddess Maat (earliest record 2375 BCE), symbolized by a classically rendered female figure wearing the ostrich feather of truth or the kneeling Goddess with wings extended, expresses all notions of equilibrium and poise. Maat represents accuracy, honesty, fairness, faithfulness, and rectitude. Maat is also the symbol of harmony in accurate tones and perfect musical accords. In the New Kingdom (after 1567 BCE), harps are often decorated with a figurine of Maat.

> *This profound awareness of equilibrium and harmony gave the Egyptian people and their leaders a wholesome and pure moral sense, as the early visitors to Egypt attested. This same awareness is the sole explanation of the marvels of their craftsmanship, indisputable records of a need for perfection, a taste and refinement that remained undiminished over nearly three thousand years.*[7]
> —Lucy Lamy

Recorded in the Bible and known from history, the great antagonism of Judaism, Christianity, and later Islam toward all manifestations of religions that preceded them caused the savage destruction of ancient writing, statuary, sacred artifacts, works of art, people, and towns. Following the command by Yahweh in the Bible:

> *You must completely destroy all the places where the nations you dispossess have served their gods, on high*

mountains, on hills, under any spreading tree; you must tear down their altars, smash their pillars, cut down their sacred poles, set fire to the carved images of their gods and wipe out their name from that place.

DEUT. 12: 2–3

What were these places really like, and what were the beliefs before the bloody conquests of the Hebrews, Christians, and Muslims? We are told that the preceding communities of people were primitive "pagans," dismissed as not conscious. They were lowly "heathens," the word suggesting they were godless, impure, and unholy. Derogatory names are an age-old military technique. Brainwashing makes it easier to kill people and destroy their lands. Calling them "chinks," "nips," "gooks," "hooches," or "towel heads" eliminates any need to think of them as human beings.

At the end of World War II, my mother traveled by train in California to meet my father. He was returning from Saipan where, as a photojournalist, he had been a war correspondent for *Life* magazine. She was surprised to see that many of the returning US sailors who were crowded in the train were wearing necklaces of teeth. When she asked one sailor about the necklaces, she was told that they were teeth from dead Japanese. Appalled, she asked how he could stand to wear other people's teeth. The reply was, "Oh, they're not human." That is the brainwashing of war and conquest.

For the early Jews, Christians, and Muslims, the words "pagan," "heathen," and "witch" had a purpose: conquest and subjugation. "*They* are not human, they are not like us; therefore, we are right in destroying them." It is a karmic irony and extremely tragic human failure that those who label others *barbaric* and *inhuman*, themselves perform the most heinous, barbaric, inhumane acts.

In later periods Christians were known throughout the world for their destruction of sacred icons and literature belonging to the so-called 'pagan' or 'heathen' religions… it may well have been the evident female attributes of nearly all of these statues that irked the advocates of the male deity.[8]

—MERLIN STONE

In the Judeo-Christian Bible, the sexual identity of the deity is referred to in the Old Testament as Elohim (masculine gender), translated as God. The Koran of the Muslims states, "Allah will not tolerate idolatry…The pagans pray to females: They pray to a rebellious Satan." (Sura 4:117)[9]

The destruction of "idols," sculptures, art, literature, temples, and altars expressing spirituality in which depictions of Goddesses were common was the beginning of the subjugation of women, which continues to hold humanity back. The consciousness of humanity is diminished when respect for the intelligence, experience, social participation, and spirituality of half of humanity is denied.

Earlier Cultures and Consciousness

DATING AS FAR BACK AS 25,000 BCE, NUMEROUS SMALL sculptures of female figures made of stone, bone, and clay have been found in sites in Spain, France, Germany, Austria, Czechoslovakia, and Russia. The oldest "Venus" sculpture found in southwest Germany dates from 35,000–40,000 years ago. Archaeological diggings in the Near East and Egypt have discovered similar figurines dating from the later Neolithic cultures (early agricultural).

James Mellaart, renowned British archaeologist, discovered forty shrines, dating from 6500 BCE onward, created by a culture that existed in the Cilician plains near Konya, in present-day Turkey.

> *Art makes its appearance in the form of animal carvings and statuettes of the supreme deity, the Mother Goddess…The statues allow us to recognize the main deities worshiped by Neolithic people at Catal Huyuk. The principal deity was a goddess,…shown in her three aspects, as a young woman, a mother giving birth, or as an old woman.*[10]
>
> —James Mellaart

Human creativity, consciousness, and spirituality are the important dimensions revealed by relics and works of art discovered by archaeological digs and research. They reveal human aspiration. Built into our quest for more accurate history is (or should be) the quest to understand human consciousness. We need an expansion of consciousness that places all creative insights on the table in order to move beyond the narrow rigidity and shortsightedness of our self-destructive era.

Archaeologists recently convened a conference near the site of Çatal Hüyük in Turkey.[11] The title of the conference was Consciousness and Creativity at the Dawn of Settled Life. Independent curator and writer Nazli Gürlek included in her review of the conference a profound statement:

> *After all, it can be no coincidence that this inter-disciplinary conference on the topic of consciousness and creativity in the context of a Neolithic site was organized at this precise time in history. Consciousness is not a hot topic today in a globally entangled world…and it is no less than common knowledge that we need to be*

highly creative and imaginative in this precise moment in history in order to build a future for ourselves in this world. It is also obvious that we need to understand the past in order to create a future for ourselves. Perhaps the question this conference made most evident is, are we ready to see this? [12]

—Nazli Gürlek

Some of the most sophisticated cultures studied by archaeologists are the Halaf cultures along the northern end of the Tigris River, where digs have unearthed small towns with cobbled streets dating from 5000 BCE. Metal was in use.

It is probably from the Halaf period that the invention of wheeled vehicles date.[13]

—Professor H. W. F. Saggs

Oddly, our modern suppressed minds assume that wheeled vehicles were invented by men, whereas it is possible that necessity was truly the *mother* of invention. Goddess figurines have been found at all the Halaf sites. In 4000 BCE, Goddess figures appeared at Ur and Uruk on the southern end of the Euphrates River in present-day Iraq.[14]

The earliest examples of written language appear at the temple of the Queen of Heaven in Uruk in Sumer just before 3000 BCE. The Sumerian (Mesopotamia) people developed writing with a sharp stylus on wet clay. These are the first pictorial signs that we know of whose symbols represent combinations of consonants and primary vowels as syllables. With the invention of writing, history emerged in Sumer and Egypt.[15]

In these early historic times, in every area of the Near and Middle East, the goddess was known. Through the centuries, the religions transformed in many ways, but the worship of the female deity survived into the classical periods of Greece and Rome.

> *It was not totally suppressed until the time of the Christian emperors of Rome and Byzantium, who closed down the last Goddess temples in about 500 AD.*[16]
> —MERLIN STONE

Women were important singers in the congregations and choirs until the early fourth century. After the legalization of Christianity in the Roman Empire, congregational singing was abandoned, and women were officially silenced in the church. "All musical portions were entrusted to professional choirs of men and boys."[17]

It is at this point that the history of Western music is said to have begun, but a long and violent transition was going on. The previous art, culture, and religions in Europe and Asia Minor were being destroyed and replaced with what fit the ideology of the Christian Church. Why was the exclusion of women from music so important in the Christian Church? What effect did it have on the accepted history of Western music?

What glimpses do we have of the lives of women and men before these restrictions and exclusions? There are some accounts of early Christian music, and from them, it is possible to get an idea of the ethos of religious music before the fourth century. One account by Philo Judaeus (c. 10 BCE–c. CE 50) describes the participation of women singers among the Therapeutae, a partially Christianized community of Jews in Egypt in the first century:

> *…the chorus of the male and female Therapeutae afforded a most perfect resemblance with its variant and*

concordant melodies; and the sharp searching tone of the women together with the baritone sound of the men effected a harmony both symphonious and altogether musical. Perfectly beautiful are their motions, perfectly beautiful their discourse; grave and solemn are these carolers; and the final aim of their motions, their discourse and their choral dances is piety.[18]

—Pilo Judaeus

In his time, the first century, women were musicians of sacred and secular music. The great music festivals in the Roman Empire included women. In Greek and Roman art of this time, depictions of both women and men musicians can be seen in fresco paintings, mosaics, bas relief sculptures, and designs on vases and urns.

Three champion athletes who were sisters, Hedea, Tryphosa, and Dionysia, from Tralles, won many running races and even chariot races in various major competitions around the Roman Empire in the middle of the first century CE. They were made honorary citizens of a number of cities. Hedea was not only a great athlete but also a musician who won music competitions playing lyre and singing. The sisters traveled thousands of miles to participate in major competitions. Sometimes these competitions were open to both young men and young women, and it is possible but unknown if any of the three sisters competed with males. Hedea, clad in armor, raced war chariots. There is an honorary dedication for the three athletes in Delphi. Delphi was the most important spiritual center and "the International Hall of Fame for great athletes, musicians, intellectuals and other famous people." Therc, in addition to the inscribed tribute that still exists, there had been statues of the sisters that are now gone.[19]

Early Influences

IN THE OLDEST FOUND TREATISE ON GREEK MUSIC spanning several centuries before the Christian era, there is some indication of what music may have been like. Aristoxenus (c. 330 BCE) presents in his treatise, *Harmonic Elements*, a highly developed melodic system organized of tetrachords of three types: enharmonic, chromatic, and diatonic. He describes certain specific "shades" of the tetrachord (a four-note figure) created by locating the two inner notes at various pitches within the two outer notes that form the interval of a perfect fourth. He wrote that theoretically the possibilities of "shades" (in the two inner notes) are infinite and that the true way of determining intervals is by the ear, not by mathematical calculation. The method of measurement was not by proportions but by a fractional system.[20]

> *We can infer from Aristoxenus' descriptions and from accounts by later theorists that the ancient Greeks, like most Eastern peoples to the present day, were able to sing (or play) and hear a great variety of micro-intervals that have no place in our Western scales and like people in today's Middle East and India, they commonly made use of such intervals in their music. Obviously such distinctions would make possible certain qualities in a melody of which we can hardly form a clear idea, and which must have had an effect in determining the ethos of a particular composition.*[21]
> —HISTORY OF WESTERN MUSIC (VOL. 7)

Aristotle (384–322 BCE) spoke of the various and powerful effects of modes. The word "modes" is our modern term. "Harmoniai" refers to the modes of Aristotle's era, encompassing something related to but different from what we hear today:

> ...the harmoniai have quite distinct natures from one another, so that those who hear them are differently affected and do not respond in the same way to each. To some, such as the one called Mixolydian, they respond with more grief and anxiety, to others, such as the relaxed harmoniai, with more mellowness of mind, and to one another with a special degree of moderation and firmness, Dorian being apparently the only one of the harmoniai to have this effect, while Phrygian creates ecstatic excitement.[22]
>
> —ARISTOTLE

Theorists are not sure what the modes of Aristotle's time were. *Harmonia* was not a technical musical term but a general word indicating a style that included certain pitches, rhythms, and ethnic backgrounds. It is possible that these "modes" were complex rhythmic and melodic patterns similar to the *ragas* played in India that use microtones (as do Middle Eastern *maqams*).[23]

The names of Greek modes come from ethnic groups in wide-ranging geographical regions of ancient Greece. *Dorian* comes from a group located in several regions, prominently in Corinth, a major trade port (and mentioned in Homer's *Odyssey,* in the eighth or seventh century BCE). *Locrian* corresponds to the region of Locris, and *Lydian* and *Phrygian* are from neighboring regions of non-Greek people from Asia Minor. *Aeolian* comes from regions that spoke Aeolic dialects such as the island of Lesbos. Aeolian dialects were spoken and written by poets such as Sappho (630–570 BCE), the most revered female poet of ancient Greece. From these examples, we can see that Greek music enjoyed many cross-cultural influences.

Early Greek descriptions of the harmoniais reveal the excitement, diversity, and cultural inclusiveness of music in those times. Unfortunately, the only sources of information about what pre-Christian, Greek music sounded like are twenty treatises (most fragments), dating from 350 BCE to CE 350, and sixty-one written pieces of music, all fragments except for the Seikilos Pillar on which an entire musical text is carved.[24] It is impossible to know how this music was played, but some ideas of the ethos may be formed by looking at the arts and mythologies of different eras and the neighboring cultures. It may be that expression in the other arts paralleled musical expression just as Romantic and Impressionistic artistic styles in later Western culture paralleled the music styles of the period.

The early Greek dramas might give us a clue. One of the fragments of early Greek music is seven lines written on papyrus in 408 BCE for the play *Orestes* by Euripides. It is thought that Euripides composed the music himself. It would have been sung by a chorus of women in the "orchestra," a half-circle section in front of the stage. It is a dark and deep fragment that expresses the madness of Orestes after he has killed his mother, Clytemnestra. This is serious "art music" way before Christianity.

After the economic decline of the Roman Empire in the third and fourth centuries, music—previously enjoyed widely in grand festivals and contests—was no longer celebrated on such a large scale. After the fifth century CE, there is practically no recorded trace of secular music. The mathematical and philosophical works of Pythagoras (570–495 BCE), Plato (c.

428–348 BCE), and Aristotle (384–322 BCE) were filtered through the Christian church, and ideas on the meaning of music from these three were interpreted hundreds of years later by the Neo-Platonists whose major Christian promulgator was St. Augustine (354–430 CE). Christians from the fifth century wrote treatises on the role of music, based with a narrow lens, on views of Plato. Most influential among them was a five-volume compendium, *De Institutione Musica*, by Boethius (480–524 CE), written eight hundred years after Plato. The theories of Boethius set the foundation for music theory throughout the Middle Ages and Renaissance.

Purely Numbers, the Power of the Church

THE BASIS OF BOETHIUS' PHILOSOPHY OF MUSIC IS that music is *number* made audible. He purported that all things that are beautiful are subject to the power of numbers and can be explained by them. He divided music into three levels:

- *Musica instrumentalis* (Vocal or instrumental music, where the ratios of intervals could be measured in physical distances; octave, fifth, and fourth, which were labeled "consonances," and all others were considered "dissonances")
- *Musica humana* (The harmony of body and soul)
- *Musica mundane*: (Harmony standing as the foundation for all existence, "the music of the spheres")

Boethius regarded the musician who understood the science and ratios of music structure as more worthy of respect than the composer and much more worthy than the musicians who performed the music, calling them merely servants.

To Boethius and men of his era, it was necessary that the "practical applications of music be capable of philosophic explanation." They wanted music to be explainable with an intellectual conformity. The Church molded these theories to become conflated with a pure link to God and a way to avoid being seduced by any kind of sensuality. Music was to be built on the so-called "consonances" in order to quell the passions and to have only "pure" experiences.

In a written confession, St. Augustine wrote:

> …I am moved, not with the singing, but with the things sung, when they are sung with a clear voice and modulation most suitable, I acknowledge the great use of this institution. Thus I fluctuate between peril of pleasure and approved wholesomeness; inclined the rather (though not as pronouncing an irrevocable opinion) to approve of the usage of singing in the church; that so by the delight of the ears, the weaker minds may rise to the feeling of devotion. Yet when it befalls me to be more moved with the voice than the words sung, I confess to have sinned penally, and then had rather not hear music. See now my state; weep with me, and weep for me, ye, who so regulate your feelings within, as that good action ensues.[25]
>
> —St. Augustine

From the third and fourth centuries, the Christian church made great efforts to standardize the liturgical patterns. The enforcement of the rules for all music performed in churches throughout Europe met with resistance and was made difficult by lack of communication and the growth of individual traditions, but the Church persevered. Unification of the

Church under the Bishop of Rome was directed at eradicating divergences in liturgical practice, the goal being conformity to Roman procedures. It was accomplished by the eleventh century in basic outline, and any variations of choice of text and in the music were eradicated by the sixteenth century.

What of Women?

THE PAULINE INJUNCTION OF THE FOURTH CENTURY stated "Mulier in ecclesia taceat" (Let women keep silent in church). This was the first obstacle to women as professional or even acknowledged musicians. It was possible to make music only in separate women's convents, which meant they were heard on a far smaller scope than male musicians in the church at large. In the beginning of the Middle Ages, the church destroyed all music associated with social occasions and pagan religious exercises. Meanwhile, the common woman experienced the rapid and increasing denial of her basic human rights by the dominance of Christianity, as the church held fast to its goals of maintaining a male-dominated society. Using the Eden-Paradise myth as "proof," women were regarded as mindless, carnal creatures, while men were identified with the male-deity and considered direct messengers of the Lord.

> *For the husband is the head of the wife even as Christ is the head of the Church...Therefore as the Church is subject unto Christ, so let the wives be to their own husbands in everything.*[26]

> *Let the woman learn in silence with all subjection. But I suffer not a woman to teach, nor to usurp authority over the men, but to be in silence. For Adam was first*

formed and then Eve and Adam was not deceived, but the woman being deceived was in the transgression.[27]

—Timothy 2:14

The sixteenth-century Swiss reformer Jon Calvin spoke against political equality for women as "deviation from the original and proper order of nature." The imposed suppression would now be identified as the *natural* order! [28]

How has this oppressive history been assimilated into our society today? What toxicity has been entrenched in our consciousness, and what effect does it have on women and men? What have women been able to do to bring back their basic human rights and live free, full lives as spiritual human beings and artists?

In the realm of music, the history of women has been full of barriers. The castrati provided the female voice ranges used in the service of music for the church and nobility. The castrati were male singers who had been castrated in prepuberty so that their voices remained higher. They were a great public attraction and were honored by the church and nobility. In the mid-1500s, many castrati were in the employ of the Sistine Chapel choir. From the earliest operas (Monteverdi), castrati took the female roles. Trained, educated, and well paid, some became as famous as rock stars today. Poor families would sacrifice a son to this abusive disfigurement in the hope that his service as a singer in the church, royal court, or theater would help the family climb out of economic misery. In the late eighteenth century, with the decline of the use of castrati, women found their place in opera, but it was not until the nineteenth century and in some cases the twentieth century that women could participate in choruses and church choirs.

It took another century for a female musician to be hired to play professionally as part of a symphony orchestra. Doriot

Anthony Dwyer, principal flutist of the Boston Symphony Orchestra from 1952–1990, is recorded as the "first woman principal player of an American major orchestra."[29] Prior to that in 1941, Helen Kotas was appointed to the position of principal horn, making her the first woman to hold a rostered position in the Chicago Symphony Orchestra.[30] In 1934, cellist Elsa Hilger was the first woman, aside from harpists, to become a permanent member of a major symphony orchestra, the Philadelphia Orchestra, where she played for thirty-five years.[31] Before the mid-1900s, it is fair to say that there were no women performers in the major symphony orchestras. Female harpists were hired but faced harsh challenges. Harpist Edna Phillips was hired by Leopold Stokowski to play for the Philadelphia Orchestra in 1930.[32] She was regarded with resentment by many of the male musicians. Alice Chalifoux, principal harpist of the Cleveland Orchestra from 1931–1974, also faced challenges.[33]

> *The Vienna Philharmonic, founded in 1842, did not allow women as full members until 1997. Anna Lelkes, a harpist, became the first woman member that same year. Prior to that, she was a regular but unofficial part of the orchestra. Her name was never listed on the program.*[34]
> —Cynthia Collins

Because of nonobservation, nonrecognition, nonappreciation, and silencing for hundreds of years, one half of humanity is held back, humiliated, made to feel inferior, denied creative outlet, and denied relevance. The ramifications are dire. Our sick culture needs to heal.

Men lose out as well. They have been taught that they are the only "movers and shakers." They are made to believe they

One Half of Humanity

are the only active actors on the planet, which leaves them lonely and resentful because of their inability to see or recognize the contributions and work of women in all aspects of life as well as the arts. Women are portrayed as the nonactive, noneffective, nonindividual blankets of comfort and docile domestic servants that God provided to men. They do not realize that there can be no realistic and satisfying relationship between two people when one person is regarded as owned and subordinate. When she is free to be herself—free to develop her life as a self-realized human being—the more she can proclaim and bestow her full love for life and for another individual. Because women are kept socially invisible and regarded as ineffectual, no one would want to be like them. We make the mistake of defining ourselves by accepted cultural standards: *I must be a man, defined as such because I am not a woman. Being in any way womanly would diminish me as a man.* This disavowal ignores the fact that both genders are full human beings. They share the same hormonal construction in different and varied proportions. With this recognition, they could be sharing in what makes humanity humane.

Only recently is the reality of women's contributions in the arts being slowly revealed. There are now books about women composers and musicians. There is an excellent list on Wikipedia called *List of female composers by birth date*;[35] when I saw it, I was overwhelmed with tears of joy, dismay, and anger. It is a list of female composers from before the sixteenth century to the 2000s. Over a thousand notable women composers are listed, but I never heard of almost all of them. Only now are people catching up in creating performances and recordings of this music, and maybe some of these artists will, at long last, be heard.

Lully, Rameau, and Couperin of the early 1700s are household names among musicians and listeners in "classical" circles, but who has heard of Elisabeth Jacquet de la Guerre? French composer Jacquet de La Guerre (1665–1729) was a child prodigy. She received her musical training from her father. She performed on the harpsichord before King Louis XIV, and she was accepted into the French court where she stayed until age nineteen when the court moved to Versailles. She was one of the well-known composers in her time. She composed in a variety of musical forms including opera and the new sonata form. Thankfully, today there is a resurgence of interest in her music.

Women are routinely spoken of as a minority in the United States. The list goes "Blacks, Hispanics, Asians, and women." Technically, the word "minority" refers to representation in government, and minorities are labeled as such because they are underrepresented in the very government that is supposed to be a democracy. That makes it even worse. It should be remembered that globally, people of color and women are hardly minorities. Skin color worldwide is mostly variations of brown pigment, and women comprise over half of the world population.

In many places around the world, there is the fight to suppress women by holding onto the perception "'twas always thus." Women are inferior and weak and therefore will *always* be kept in "their place." We know it was not "always thus," and strength is a relative term. There are many forms of strength available to both women and men.

To recognize an accomplished woman as an exception is another way to not recognize her at all. Calling attention to the rarity of her accomplishment as a female and extolling that rarity as more remarkable than her actual art and achievement results in nothing but distraction. Nadia Boulanger was the first woman to conduct world-class symphony orchestras.

When she was invited to conduct the Boston symphony, she was asked by a reporter how she felt about being the first woman to do so.

> *I've been a woman for a little over fifty years, and have gotten over my initial astonishment.*[36]
> —NADIA BOULANGER

It is important to remember the power of words in history. The prevalent terminology of our culture—in psychology, religion, history, and sociology—is masculine. We tend to define ourselves individually or collectively by an accepted, narrow range of experiences. Women's ideology, their voices, and their stories are beginning to resurface in Western culture and in the world.

Sara Þórdardóttir Oskarsson, cofounder of the Jæja Group and member of Parliament in Iceland, is pushing for gender equity in representation as well as pay. She is also a painter whose work is regularly exhibited in Europe. In an interview on the news channel France 24, she spoke standing next to one of her fluid and forceful paintings:

> *I wouldn't have painted this like this, if what was happening in the politics wasn't happening. I would have done some other type of painting. And also this is going to be in my mind when I speak in the podium next week—this image —this is the effect I want. I'm going to be angry.*[37]
> —SARA ÞÓRDARDÓTTIR OSKARSSON

Art influences the development of our understanding and our effectiveness. Creative inspiration becomes culture-making when it is heard and people recognize and grow from it. Art feeds the soul, and art comes forth from the soul. The *sacred well of the soul* is the origin of a limitless spectrum of human experience and fresh creativity. The voices, the ideas, and the artistic works of women need to be heard. This alive, vibrant, and productive half of humanity can enrich us all enormously and infuse culture with consciousness that could rescue the world from its downward spiral.

18

Art, Life, and the Dark Side

Art is everywhere and a part of everyone. Art is:
How we fit our life, our being, into the world
How we "paint our picture" each moment
in the present
How we "paint our picture"
of the past and the future
How deeply we observe everything
How much we explore
How we show our love for others
How much we appreciate,
value anything and everything
How much reality we are willing
to see and hear

Art expands perceptions. We learn and know through our perceptions. When there seem to be limits in what we can know, we can expand our perception through art and imagination. Leonardo da Vinci recommended that through art, valuable scientific insights can be found. In certain notebooks that he intended to later become treatises on art and painting, he wrote about the act of drawing as being an ideal way to observe and discover.[1] He often used the art and practice of drawing to understand such things as:

- How plants grow

- How the eye sees
- How animal and human anatomy work
- How a bird flies
- How to use mechanical engineering
- How water flows
- How light and shadow affect what we see
- How to understand rules of perspective
- How to design useful canals and harbors
- How to design a city for commerce and protection
- How to look down from a mountain and draw the landscape's great distances in realistic perspective

Drawing can become a source of great discovery. Imagination and observation can push through the limits of understanding. Science and art use the same procedures: imagination, experimentation, observation, theorization, testing, conclusion, and implementation.

Philosophy is an art. Philosophy asks imaginative questions and uses observation, theorization, testing, conclusion, and documentation. As in art, there is a push to go beyond limitations:

- Is this true relative to that?
- Is it true relative to something else?
- What if it is true?
- What if it is not true?
- What if it's partially true?
- What if the truth is completely different from all these considerations?

The human-made environment we live in and create for each other is art. City planning, architecture, and the designs of structures are art, for better or for worse:

Art, Life, and the Dark Side

- The sink faucet
- The McDonald's arches
- Suspension bridges
- The office chair
- The Taj Mahal
- Shopping centers
- The shirt you wear

Human minds came up with these designs whether ugly and depressing or beautiful and inspiring. It comes from more than marketing and money; it's the art of our times. It is where we dwell. The human-made environment is the art in which we live during our finite time, our sojourn on Earth.

The Dark Side

TRAGICALLY, ART CAN BE USED AS MANIPULATION, power, abuse, and even torture. Americans tortured prisoners in Afghanistan by shackling them and making them stand for hours as they were forced to hear heavy metal music played at horribly loud volumes.[2] "Metal" music was also used to stimulate US combatants in Iraq to kill people.

Sound has become a weapon that is given to police in the United States, funded and supplied by the military industrial complex. In some cities, as a brutal form of "crowd control," police arsenal now includes devices that emit sound at an extreme loud decibel volume to hurt and even to damage people's ears. Police protection? Protection for whom?

It doesn't help us to deny or ignore the horrible things people do. Human beings are capable of horrendous torturous acts. We are like the paintings of Hieronymus Bosh: landscapes populated with people who stab and gut each other and poke out eyes. Today we have the shame of Abu Ghraib, Guantanamo, and secret Black Sites for torture. On US soil, we kidnap refugee children and hold them in pens in foul, life-threatening conditions.

As human beings, we can recognize our dark side and choose better directions. It comes from a conscious commitment to not impose suffering, misery, and pain on others. It comes from refusing to blindly follow those who, with ulterior motives of power and money, persuade young people to perform despicable acts.

> *I would no more teach children military training than teach them arson, robbery or assassination.*[3]
> —Eugene V. Debs

Anything built can be destroyed. What has been discovered, built, and created—nurtured over lifetimes, centuries, or eons—can be destroyed in an instant. An elephant, a redwood tree, or a human being took eons to evolve and an instant to destroy. The mentality of destruction is everywhere. It wants a quick answer to everything. "Bang bang shoot shoot."[4]

The model of killing to solve problems is pervasive in our culture. Killing is convenient. Each spring brings the awe-inspiring miracle of life emerging. After the long, gray winter, people generally respond with great joy and fresh wonderment to see buds, flowers, leaves, baby birds and mammals spring forth, a resurgence of life!—yet many eagerly go out into their gardens to kill. Lacking the understanding of balance in the insect world, and lacking the will to find healthy alternatives, they spray herbicides and pesticides. Instant death serves as instant convenience. They wonder why their dogs and cats get cancer and why they get ailments such as Parkinson's disease, which has been documented as linked to herbicide and pesticide use.[5]

The refrain "Death's alright with me when it's on TV" in the song by the 1980s punk rock group The Dead Milkmen points to the American fascination with death—on TV.[6] It has become acceptable for TV and movies to frequently and flippantly show the ending of life. In spy stories, war stories, Westerns, murder mysteries, sci-fi, and historical dramatizations, blowing out brains or blood-spattering blasts to the torso are a matter of course. The broader truth is conveniently ignored. No need to watch the agony. No need to clean up the mess, to find a proper place for the body. No need to think of the life of the victim from his or her childhood, the individual who came from a lineage of ancestors. No need to think of the family members who may almost die of grief when their loved one is murdered. On TV, it appears to be a simple game where someone takes a shot and someone falls. The game is won. Whether the good guy or the bad guy, the killer is considered the strong one, a winner.

They know not what they do.[7]
—LUKE 23:34

Ideas on the Table

BENJAMIN BRITTEN (1913–1976) COMPOSED HIS *War Requiem, Op. 66* for two orchestras (one full and one a chamber orchestra), three soloists, a boys' choir, and organ. Completed in 1962, it was performed in the new Coventry Cathedral (built after the fourteenth-century cathedral was destroyed in a World War II bombing raid). The vocal parts include the poetry of Wilfred Owen who, during World War

I, wrote of the "shame of war." One of his poems, "Anthem for Doomed Youth," begins:

> *What passing-bells for these who die as cattle?*
> *Only the monstrous anger of the guns.*
> *Only the stuttering rifles' rapid rattle*
> *Can patter out their hasty orisons.*[8]
>
> —Wilfred Owen

The most despicable actions humans can do—murder, pillage, rape, torture, kill children—are the common actions of war. The young men (and some women) who perform these acts under the sanction of the government-military-industrial powers must deal with what they have done for the rest of their lives. Some cannot endure their deep depression from post-traumatic stress disorder (PTSD). Many cannot face themselves or feel they cannot trust themselves to keep loved ones safe from their rage, shame, and confusion. Many take their own lives (an average of twenty veteran suicides per day in the United States in 2014). Some find rehabilitation.

Peace seems more out of reach than ever with the continued killing, maiming, and destruction of cities and countries and unending wars. The United States has been involved directly or indirectly in war activities in Afghanistan, Iraq, Syria, Libya, Palestine, Lebanon, and Yemen. Our tax dollars support untold depths of human suffering. Those in power do their best to silence people who object to the wars. It seems mostly beyond our capacity to change it—or is it? Maybe one beautiful musical phrase we play will turn on a light for someone who inspires others consciously or unconsciously. One or two of those people, in their own way, might lift more people.

We try to conduct our lives bravely and without evil, yet evil is everywhere. Some evil is born out of hatred based on false assumptions such as *women are weak and inferior*. If "hatred" is the only thing on the table to explain it, a whole lot is not being examined. Why? Why? Why? Why did he beat his wife to death? Each "why" should go deeper. The first "why" would be the immediate situation: *there was a terrible argument*. The second "why" could be the larger cultural situation: *the objectification of women*. The third "why" could be the world situation: *the assumed ownership of women by men*. Asking these questions is not to excuse the crime but to understand it—to find and make improvements in human consciousness, change false perceptions, inspire society to get away from institutionalized ideas, and inform each other of a better outlook on life.

Music by The Beatles, so popular around the world, was banned in the Soviet Union of the 1960s. Young people in Russia took extreme risks to make bootleg recordings of Beatles songs. If caught with Beatles albums, they could be thrown into jail, yet they continued to illegally share recordings. They discovered a variety of ways to copy recordings, even inventing a way to use a stylus to cut them into the film of medical x-ray negatives! What was it about Beatles songs?

The documentary movie *Paul McCartney in Red Square* records the first time a member of The Beatles was permitted to perform in concert in Russia—about forty years after the rest of the world had hailed The Beatles as the international top artists of popular music. In May 2003, Paul McCartney and his band traveled to Russia to participate in a cultural exchange and to perform concerts in Red Square in Moscow and in St. Petersburg. In other countries, it was mostly people in their sixties or older who nostalgically remembered The Beatles from their teens and twenties. In 2003, in Russia, children, teens, and middle-aged and old people attending a live Beatles concert for the first time could be seen singing along in English, with precision, the words in McCartney's performances.[10]

The documentary shows interviews with Russian people who had been part of the era of the ban on The Beatles. The surprising thing was that many people who were interviewed gave credit to The Beatles music as *causing* the fall of the repressive Communist regime. The period from 1986–1991, known as Glasnost, ushered in the end of the system of the USSR and most of the censorship of music from the West. Even more surprising was that this quiet revolution was described as having taken place because so many people no longer believed in and were no longer intimidated by the bullying restrictions of the totalitarian regime. Regime change was instituted without bloodshed; people no longer believed in it. Historians and politicians, including Presidents Gorbachev and Putin, acknowledged that the music of The Beatles played a great role in changing the consciousness of the people.

What was it about the music of The Beatles? How was it able to change consciousness? I believe that a more worldly attitude and respect for women were among the most important elements. Women are addressed as autonomous, self-directing people ("She's Got a Ticket to Ride" and "Norwegian Wood"). It's not the one-dimensional, one-sided "I want you, babe, because you're mine" way of relating to a woman. The love songs speak of relationships that consist of the evolving admiration of two conscious and independent individuals. Their music includes an awareness of human beings as being normal people around the world ("Back in the USSR"). Some songs point out with compassion the absurdities of people and their consequent loneliness ("Eleanor Rigby"). They speak of spiritual quests that include wisdom from other cultures ("Within You and Without You"). They embody a freedom in all kinds of abstract and imaginative ways and poke fun at institutionalized media's ways of addressing celebrity ("Baby You Can Drive My Car" and "A Day in the Life"). They explore the individuality of the nonconformist ("Fool on the Hill").

The sheer variety of topics, arrangements, and sounds created something worldly and inclusive in The Beatles' recordings. The sound of an Indian sitar, using three pianos of different qualities, or using a string quartet or symphony orchestra were and still are unusual innovations in popular music.

Creative recording techniques were implemented producing a clarity and richness of sound. There was none of the static electric buzz that seems requisite today, rendering voices and words barely discernible. The Beatles' songs brought quality sound, fresh air, and new possibilities to a world that was stuck in stiff, competitive, hostile, money-grubbing, corporate gloom. Then as today, the world was stuck in the "war between the sexes" and nuclear brinkmanship. The Beatles revealed that we could approach our lives in more enlightened ways with more respect, love, joy, innovation and peace ("Imagine").

Leonardo da Vinci was appalled at people's lack of imagination and poor skills of observation. He used art for studying, for observing, and shunned the common practice among intellectuals to consider themselves learned if they could only memorize and repeat quotes from classic Greek and Roman philosophers. In his notes, he talks about these so-called great minds who never engaged in experiential learning, direct observation, and discovery. His inventive ideas showed that people could be learning and doing things in different and more enlightened ways.[11]

The world needs ideas of this kind—more ideas on the table. People can sense through your art, your being, and your presence that you have an understanding and creativity, and they find encouragement for their own explorations and ideas. Being a person who embodies another way is vital. You show different possibilities through your art, your music, your individuality.

Hold the Plastic Talk

Music that comes from a person's heart and soul is music that can speak to other hearts and souls.

When we communicate with each other without the shiny, plastic commercial talk, we speak through music, or any art, from the presence of our humanity, our honest and deep understandings and feelings.

The corporate, cheap, plastic, product mentality creates a depressed society. It is tyranny installed by corporate institutions creating a high potential for oppression—under the boot. Fossil fuel corporations hold destruction and ruin over everyone, especially young people and children. Their future is likely to be dark, polluted, and full of life-threatening climate disasters unless alternative energy practices are implemented immediately. Earth Guardians, a movement of and by children and youths, is suing the government for failing to protect them and future generations and to act on climate crisis.[12]

The Earth cannot be a home with continual abuse. Our individual lifetimes are fleeting. What good does it do us to create environmental and human disasters that will destroy many lives? Is this destruction coming from greed, depression? Is it the lack of understanding that comes to each individual through true perceptions and observation? Artists lift humanity and show each other possibilities of new perspectives. We help each other become better human beings.

Paradoxes

"Superheroes," constantly promoted in popular movies, are boring. They are portrayed with unfailing, supernatural strength and ability to conquer any adversary. Impervious to ordinary reality, they are better than any mortal. The fantasy may be intoxicating, but the paradox is that this mythology does not demonstrate real courage or strength. Automatons preprogramed to fight and always win are formulaic, predictable, and boring. There is no courage in a "superhero" who slays all problems through death and destruction.

Real courage is the courage to be vulnerable. Real courage is accepting being human. Moment by moment, we have a great number of dependencies and vital needs. We must drink water, find, prepare, and eat food, take shelter from heat and cold, sleep, eliminate, blow our noses, be loved, be touched, avoid dangers, negotiate intricate social situations, find employment, search for love, find a partner, work out problems, menstruate, have a healthy pregnancy, give birth, nourish and guard children, be sick, accept becoming aged, and die. All of these endeavors involve courage, and the sweep of being alive is epic. It takes courage to live a mortal life, seeking truth in nature and the human condition. We need courage to face our fallibility and transience. This is real courage.

The courage to be vulnerable is the same in music. It is a strength in performer and listener to be moved emotionally and spiritually. To express ourselves truthfully and directly includes allowing and understanding our vulnerability in the human condition. It is knowing that there is more strength and power in tenderness, more courage in speaking to our inmost feelings. It is knowing that love is stronger than hate and that we can reflect upon and change our responses to life.

There is strength even in uncertainty, because uncertainty is open to discovery and change. There was a point in my life when I made a big move to Colorado from the West Coast, where I had lived for more than twenty years. I felt uprooted. I felt I had one foot in each place and had lost my identity. Someone said, "Well, loss of footing is a great state to be in. It means you can be flexible, open for anything. You can go in any direction. You are not stuck." Realizing this, allowed me to be who I was: someone in transition with room for possibilities.

When we feel uprooted or vulnerable, we need not be stuck. Courage can be found in viewing these feelings as strengths rather than weaknesses.

Religious Experience

RELIGIONS COULD NOT PROMOTE THEIR IDEAS without art. Architects, sculptors, painters, composers, and musicians were hired to impress members of the general public who were often illiterate. Cathedrals and temples, with their wealth, architectural grandeur, lavish artwork, riches of gold, and beautiful music, brought people to a prepared location to receive a certain message. These churches harnessed people's natural reverence for life in one place. They tried hard—even by killing and war—to make sure everyone was on the same page. They wanted everyone to believe the same thing, worship at the same church, accept the words of the same priests, bow to the same church-ordained kings, and pay fees to the same. This ensured the wealth and domination of the church.

The Christian church in Spain in the fifteenth century commissioned Hieronymus Bosch to paint human sin and illustrate the terror of hell and the glory of heaven. They got more than they bargained for. In addition to painting beautifully, Bosch was, in my opinion, a great comedian who laughed about the foibles of the human condition including the church. People in his art, clergy included, are shown in sinful acts. Today, Bosch would have many more examples to paint.

Spiritual Experiences

BEING EPHEMERAL, MUSIC HAPPENS IN THE MOMENT. Within a moment, we can play or hear something so beautiful that it can bring tears. The experience gives us a realization beyond words. It reveals possibilities we can know beyond our searching.

In working with music, we work with ourselves. No matter what the nature of the musical statement, there is something urging us to be honest in how we play—to touch a "chord" in order to communicate with existence. Actively playing music is a mystery and a ministry.

> *Musicians are priests...Music is a priesthood...When you listen to a song you love, it can almost make the world stand still...It's like everything's black and white except there's this line of colour between you and whatever it is the music's come from.*[13]
> —SINÉAD O'CONNOR

19

Looking Back, Looking Forward

How can anyone write about music? Music cannot be represented in words. How can words adequately represent anything?

A peach?
Your hand?
An animal?
A person?
A rock?

Everything has a history, a transience, an individuality and a complex path in the universe. What is the history of that boulder, that rock, or this pebble? On what hillside in sunlight, moonlight, rain and wind, grew the tree that became this chair I sit on? In the future, what will become of this chair?

Can we know a mountain? I heard about a Native American tribe that believed that we should never point at a mountain. It shows great disrespect. A mountain is so immense and complex that we cannot possibly know what we are pointing at.

Attempting to write about music may be like pointing at a mountain. The intention of this book is to put into words some approaches to the art of playing music, but the words themselves are nothing. We have many choices in seeking new and better ways to grow in our art and our humanity. Finding pathways that help us understand the intricacies in music and life involves being ourselves and inspiring those around us to be themselves. This is the essence of what we share when we are touched by music.

There are many designs in Nature that we have not understood, yet they capture our imaginations. We search within ourselves, feeling that *we*, being a part of the natural world, should be able to recognize natural patterns. How we recognize them goes beyond examining and measuring. Our engagement in finding things out has a lot more to do with creativity than calculation. Calculation *is* creativity.

It is the *qualities* that are meaningful to us: rhythms and colors, a heavenly snowflake, a lonely wind, rustling leaves. A purple flower makes us feel differently than a white flower. How to see, draw, and paint different kinds of atmosphere, hazy or clear, morning or evening light, were considerations that led to some of Leonardo da Vinci's scientific observations Everything is imbued with our subjective perception of qualities. What is subjective? What is subjectivity?

Borrowing from Webster's Dictionary, we could say that subjectivity is reality as perceived rather than as independent of mind. Subjective knowledge is defined as experience conditioned by personal mental characteristics or states.

Even empirical knowledge and "objective observations" do not have meaning unless they spark feelings, allowing for impressions of qualities. Numbers can be used to prove facts, but the impact, importance, and meaning comes from qualities we perceive through experience and imagination.

It is an empirical fact that a duck can fly 65.2 miles per hour. We might say to ourselves, "Wow. Those placid creatures who waddle as they walk and serenely float on the water can fly that fast!?" Our retention of the information comes with our subjective impression of the qualities of a duck.

If you have held a duck—felt its weight, smooth chest, neat wings tucked back, cool webbed feet, if you have watched its tilting head as it looks up at you, felt the rounded bill as it nibbles wet duckweed floating in a pool in your cupped hand—the figure 65.2 becomes more impressive. When I was a child, we raised three newly hatched mallard ducks that we found in an abandoned nest by a roadway. When they were full grown, we returned them to the nearby river where they continued to thrive.

Although a duck's flight numbers in miles per hour are impressive and add to our amazement, it is the subjective feeling and experience that acquaints us with the reality and brings about our caring involvement. We might wonder, *How can you fly that fast, you wondrous and sweet creature whom I know?* We won't forget the amazing 65.2 miles per hour figure. We can empathize with the wonderful creature even though its life is a mystery. We can't assume we know what it's like to be a duck and are advised to avoid being anthropomorphic, but as living creatures, we can empathize. To empathize is to imagine putting yourself in someone else's place. Many animal behaviors are a part of our experience of living: eating, resting, and playing. We are related. What is objective?

Being a fellow creature with a beating heart, circulation system, and certain patterns of behavior, we can fully enjoy that we are not alone on the planet. Sadly, nonobservant attitudes about animals cause people to overlook the obvious fellowship. The assumption of dominion over Nature is false. We curse our lives with hollow and unnecessary loneliness.

Crows in cities can remember individual people they have seen, but people mostly ignore individual crows.[1] Crows, ravens, magpies, and jays have intelligence on par with the great apes. They can use tools, solve problems, and memorize large numbers of places where they have stored food. Dogs have hearing that is many times more sensitive than people have, yet people yell at their dogs. Plants create repelling chemicals in their systems when they sense that an insect is biting their leaves.

> *In a recent experiment, Heidi Appel, a chemical ecologist at the University of Missouri, found that, when she played a recording of a caterpillar chomping a leaf for a plant that hadn't been touched, the sound primed the plant's genetic machinery to produce defense chemicals.*[2]
> —Michael Pollan

There is precise sensitivity, awareness, consciousness, and intelligence in living beings all around us. Music helps human beings to think and perceive qualities of being, qualities of nature. Music is sometimes used to restore a degree of normal movement to people with Parkinson's disease. It miraculously brings back some memories for dementia patients. Brain imaging shows that people who play music are quicker to recognize patterns in language.[3] Music influences thought patterns, and thought patterns influence musicality.

Ancient people in caves played the earliest music, probably singing, clapping, and using percussion and flute. The acoustics in caves must have been awesome, far richer and more alive than the artificially created "space" of electronic reverb. Their music must have influenced and inspired people as it does today. Music allowed time for contemplation that brought encouragement for the daily work of survival. The performance of daily activities was likely enhanced by musically inspired, graceful rhythmic coordination. As it does today, music may have been playing internally, in their imaginations, as they dug up roots, picked leaves, or stealthily crept up on animals. The music of early humans evoked visions, experiences, emotions, and dreams, and it was an important building block in the development of language—and thus social organization, discovery, and invention.

We have such a cynical outlook about ourselves as a species. Many people assume that in our prehistoric stage, we were rough, grunting, empty-headed versions of ourselves, whereas the opposite had to have been true. "Early man" survived by using finely tuned perceptions and by having great physical endurance. "Modern man" lacks sensitivity to the environment, has poor health and weakened stamina, and has lost knowledge and abilities to survive outdoors. Our pollution threatens our survival. It is *we* who have become dim-witted and backward.

In his stunning, award-winning documentary *Cave of Forgotten Dreams*, Werner Herzog reveals the earliest known cave paintings, discovered in 1994. The cave artists of thirty-six thousand years ago depicted animals of the European Ice Age: lions, rhinos, bears, insects, eagles, bison, reindeer, ibexes, and horses, rendered with exquisitely graceful lines and deep regard for and knowledge of the subjects. Herzog points out that the paintings in the Chauvet Cave (more than two times older than the paintings at Lascaux in southwestern France) are as accomplished and masterful and as fine or finer than any art in all of human history. These people were not clumsy, bumbling oafs! Seeing their art, we are tremendously moved by a glimpse into the intelligence and consciousness they possessed in their lives.[4]

For these early people, their relationship to nature was familiar, intimate, knowledgeable, and creative. They were highly observant of the ways of nature, the characteristics and behavior of animals, locations of edible and medicinal plants, and the changes of atmosphere. Their art reveals how fine their perceptions of detailed qualities were and how they appreciated grace and beauty. They felt Nature intimately, all of their senses open and receptive.

Prehistoric flutes were found in other caves of the region, one made from the wing bone of a vulture. For early people, the value of music was immediate. Music then, as today, offered reflection, a deepening dive into understanding Nature, human nature, and human creativity in learning. Music must have supported a creativity that nourished the ability to dream, think, and develop and act on these thoughts and dreams. Acting on inspiration, dreams, and thoughts is the basis of shaping new knowledge and invention. Music honed their skills in communication, language, physical grace, and spiritual sense of existence, all vital survival skills. *Their* survival skills created *our* survival.

Recognizing the brilliance of our ancestors is a stepping stone for freer thought. The fine artists who painted the masterpieces in the caves of Chauvet and Lascaux, tens of thousands of years ago, likely experienced equally fine music. Their music may have been as finely observant, studied, graceful, complex, and beautiful as their cave paintings.

French anthropologist Stephane Breton lived briefly by himself in a remote village in Papua, New Guinea in 2001 and 2003, and he filmed intimate documentaries titled *Them and Me* and *Heaven in a Garden*. In one segment, he filmed the men of the village who would get together to walk single file on the narrow jungle pathways in the reverberant hillsides. In their mission that seemed mainly about camaraderie, the men would stop on the trail, and the man in the front of the line would turn toward the others and assign a rhythm and melodic motif to each one. As they walked, they sang their parts and produced a lively and layered music of melody, harmony, and counterrhythms.[5]

Famous jazz and classical vocalist and conductor Bobby McFerrin does the same with audiences, instructing them in groups to sing and produce rhythms, resulting in rich and varied music. Music is an art of collaboration. For early human beings, music was not necessarily simple and "primitive" but complex and diverse.

Why would we assume that the history of music evolved from basic, simplistic, one-dimensional beginnings? The above examples point to the joys and complexities of musical collaboration. The truth gives a boost to our perspective of humanity. We have not evolved from plodding, dim-witted beginnings. Nature is not like that. For our ancestors, survival and learning involved being alert, aware, thoughtful, creative, compassionate, empathetic, and many more competent capabilities. The evolution of all animals was not necessarily from dumb to smarter. The dinosaurs that evolved into birds could not have been passive slouches. They earned their wings! Why do we portray our own ancestors as grunting and ignorant? Perhaps it is our self-hatred and wanting to feel superior to those who went before. Disparaging those who came before us is self-hatred.

Music did not dawn on human beings out of a vacuum. There was music all around: birdsong, wolves and coyotes, owls, cricket rhythms, herds of bison, perhaps the roar of a saber-toothed tiger. There were human cries, whispers, and exclamations. Art is learning from Nature and our own human nature through exploration and interaction. It is a gift of discovery as well as a way of communing with oneself.

The depths of the universe offer infinite exploration, the same as the depths of the imagination. As musicians, when experimentation and exploration are our goal, we can lift away our dullness and inspire others to lift theirs. Nature and our own natural insight, being our teachers and our practice, are our means to break through to new realms.

Education Institution

If one is master of one thing and understands one thing well, one has at the same time, insight into and understanding of many things.
—Vincent Van Gogh

Music and all the arts offer a vibrant and healthy way to learn. Through music, many other fields of learning become open, but our current culture in the United States negates the pursuit of the arts in the public school system.

A friend told me a personal account (a story typical these days) of how schools cheat students. Her high school-aged son became interested in theater and acting and excitedly looked forward to taking drama classes. Just when he was old enough to register for his first class, the drama department was cut from the curriculum. It was a great disappointment. He took up saxophone and was happily anticipating taking classes in music, but before he could begin, the music department was eliminated. A young person with a real enthusiasm for learning can be turned down by an institution that professes to be a center of learning! The message is that our society does not regard the arts as worthy pursuits or even legitimate ways to learn. The message is that in an education, the arts are peripheral and dispensable.

To regard the arts as having little worth in education is far from the truth. The arts engage a person in learning in a profound way. In his article "U.S. Public Schools Should Revive Stagnant Humanities and Arts Education," John Ogden writes:

> *While practicing piano, drawing, executing the moves of a galliard or rehearsing a role for the stage, we are always engaged in one or more phases of a cycle: curiosity, experimentation, inquiry, reflection. These steps are analogous to working out a problem in geometry or conducting an experiment in biology. [Schools should recognize] the connection between the teaching of process in the arts and cognition…recognize the importance of teaching the arts,…and don't sequester them from other disciplines.* [6]
>
> —John Ogden

Many schools have dropped arts in favor of science, technology, engineering, and math (STEM).[7] Schools are obligated to focus on core STEM subjects and are denied federal funding unless they comply, which is essentially a bribe. With the threat of having money withdrawn, schools are shackled. Standardized testing has taken over as the purpose of school in the United States under the threat of being denied funding. When a school fails in testing, it falls prey to corporate privatization. Is locking down the lives of individual human beings normal? Without choice for individuals, culture is unenlightened. In that kind of world, people become cogs in the corporate wheels, and because the profits they generate are stolen off their backs by CEOs and shareholders, they struggle to support themselves and their families. In that kind of tyranny, there is no room for art in public education.

In Finland, the curriculum for students supports them in pursuing their interests, including the arts. In his film *Where to Invade Next*, Michael Moore interviews public school teachers in Finland. He asks a group of teachers and administrators what they think the purpose of education is. The answer comes back, "School is about finding your happiness, about finding a way to learn what makes you happy." With this healthy outlook based on the well-being of the individual, they produce some of the smartest, best educated, most winningly competitive, and happiest people on the planet in all fields. When Moore asked Finnish high school students how many languages they could speak, each student casually listed three to five languages as if it were natural. They were, of course, speaking to him in excellent English. Finland is rated number one in the world in education; the United States is currently ranked at twenty-nine.[8]

Encouraging imagination and creative thinking not only brings profound personal fulfillment but also generates advances and innovation. Art is research. Art is ideas—a fountain of human creativity from which we can learn a great deal. Instead of being merely awestruck by Leonardo da Vinci, we should *be like him*. Van Gogh worked extremely hard to teach himself to draw and paint. As he persevered in experimentation, developing keen observations of nature and of people, his process was spiritual and philosophical. In his letters to his brother Theo, which in collection (edited by Irving Stone) comprise a superlative literary accomplishment, he spoke of his dedication and daily practice, his love for what he saw in life, and with existential poignancy, he wrote of the land and people of his era such that a reader is transported and sees with his eyes. His elation in speaking of his art, what he was discovering and innovating, is down to earth and profoundly inspiring. He accomplished the enormity of his masterful development in art in ten years. In drawing, painting, literature, music, his knowledge is revealed to be broad as he wrote in Dutch, French, and English.

The value art brings to others is inestimable. In terms of money, it's no surprise that in the visual realms, works of art can bring about monetary transactions of astronomical sums. Van Gogh paintings are now valued at more than $100 million. Leonardo da Vinci's *Mona Lisa* in the Louvre Museum in Paris has an insurance value of approximately $790 million. In terms of monetary wealth, these accomplished paintings are more valuable than almost anything. How backward are schools that consider the pursuit of art worthless. Some of these priceless works of art are kept on permanent display in museums where the *real* value of their presence is in their power to enrich the life of each individual public visitor who has the very great fortune of seeing them. Experience is a greater wealth than ownership, and the experiences of appreciating and creating art are priceless.

The Art, Science, and Sport of Music

ACTIVELY PLAYING MUSIC FOSTERS DISCIPLINE AND dedication. A music student must be responsible, show up on time, work with other musicians, practice his or her part, and function on a developing perceptive and artistic level. Substantial challenges lead to building a student's courage.

Performing can present major challenges and is not for the faint of heart. Perhaps it is akin to public speaking, regarded as an activity that produces one of the highest levels of anxiety. How much better is it for a teen to dare to step on stage and perform a concert than to dare to drag race a car or ingest a damaging toxic chemical. The challenges of being involved in music add joy and satisfaction to the student's life. When I hear of a teen getting into trouble, I wish that individual had been offered more creative challenges. Art can be a "window on the world." For young people, that window is a good place from which to view themselves and all life. Playing music can be a pathway to a healthier worldview.

To play music requires attentiveness and physicality in countless ways over a long span of time. No wonder brain imaging techniques have revealed that playing music is not just a "right brain" activity but involves a range of areas of the brain: the prefrontal cortex, motor cortex, cerebellum, hippocampus, amygdala, sensory cortex, nucleus accumbens, auditory cortex, and visual cortex.[9]

> *It's one of the most complicated tasks that we have. Take a symphony orchestra. What you have is 80 or 100 of the most highly trained members of our society—more highly trained than astronauts or surgeons in terms of the numbers of hours and years of preparation—and they are performing the works of some of the greatest minds that ever lived. It's really extraordinary.*[10]
> —DANIEL LEVITIN

Sports are valued much more than music in the US school system. The fine physical coordination needed to play an instrument and the exacting teamwork required to play in orchestras or ensembles is far more demanding, educational, and enlightening than playing sports.

The visual arts are undervalued in our schools, yet as Leonardo da Vinci wrote, the practice of drawing brings greater knowledge and insight, innovative ideas, and deep observation of how Nature works. The practice of the arts brings enormous value to our appreciation for and communication with fellow human travelers on this Earth. Isn't this the learning, healing, and progress we all desire?

The gift of music is something we all have inside ourselves to give and be given. It can be what keeps us lifted to the best in humanity where we can serve each other well in spite of all the institutions of greed and cruelty that beat us down: poverty, violence, war. *El Sistema*, conceived by Jose Antonio Abreu, is a program of establishing free music schools for children in areas of poverty, raising people's dignity, hope, camaraderie, and sense of community. The music training program begun in 1975 in Venezuela, and now spread globally, is poignantly and compellingly shown in the documentary movie, *El Sistema: Music to Change Life.*

> *Children who are materially poor gain spiritual wealth through music. And once music has brought them such riches, their minds, souls and spirits can carry them onward and upward.*[11]
>
> —JOSE ANTONIO ABREU

The documentary reveals insights about the meaning of music not only in our lives but for generations to come and shows possibility for a future of peace that is palpable. I have seen the movie multiple times and each time see and realize something further and shed tears of love for the true human spirit.

Looking Back, Looking Forward

AS MUSICIANS, IF WE LOOK BACK AT OUR EXPERIence of learning, discovery, and accomplishments and forward to our artistic eagerness and performance possibilities, we can feel overwhelmed—with joy. We find ourselves to be capable human beings on an exciting ride of learning from ourselves and others. Available to us now is more shared information via the Internet. We can hear recordings and see video footage of musicians from around the world as well as performances of master musicians from the past. Master classes and detailed lessons are accessible online.

In looking back, we might berate ourselves. *You couldn't earn a living doing music. You didn't accomplish this or that in performance opportunities. You didn't win a Grammy. You didn't. You didn't. You didn't.* Those unreasonable and punishing thoughts get very wearing. There's got to be some way to hold and savor the gifts that we *did* receive. We can look at our hands and realize how smart they are and appreciate our heart and lungs and the whole dancing system of cells and nervous system that swims with us. In addition, we can realize that we are in good company.

> *Well, you may know that you are not going to be Rembrandt or Ingres, but not everybody has to be Rembrandt or Ingres. And the fact that you might know more about yourself at the end if you do this (act on your inspiration) means that you have added yourself to Rembrandt and Ingres. And that makes it worthwhile. That's what it's all about.*[12]
>
> —DAVID HOCKNEY

My First Lessons

THE LARGE, BRICK SCHOOL BUILDING WAS SO FULL of sound that it could not contain it all. Waves of musical fragments floated past the windows and danced in the autumn air outside. Musicians from the New York City Ballet Orchestra commuted by train each Saturday to our small Connecticut town to occupy the classrooms in the old high school where they gave music lessons to young students throughout the day. Students received discounts on the rental of their instruments by participating in the program.

At age ten, arriving for my first flute lessons, I was thrilled and nervous. I ran up the steps, opened the large front door, and stepped inside. The halls of the school were alive, transformed into pathways of learning in sound. There were the noble misty sounds of a French horn, a hesitant bow drawn across a violin string, a flute belting out an arpeggio, a trombone outlining an orchestral bass line, a dreamy cello humming peacefully, and a sparky piccolo putting on the polish. While passing each classroom, I heard the voices of instruction and encouragement accompanying each musical effort. I sensed that behind each door, teachers and students were engaged in focus and hard work, perhaps forging lifetimes of revelations. I fell in love with that cacophony of musical process, of continual seeking, testing, and trying things out in sound.

Writing from the vantage point of age allows me to look back at my years of music and pick out lessons learned that could be of interest to someone who is working on similar artistic and life issues. What did playing the flute mean to me throughout my life? It meant being in the company of a friend: the practice of music. This practice brought about more tuned-in and creative listening, physical health in breathing, a degree of mental health in pondering expression, and an appreciation of humanity and life.

I know well that my era of life had different sets of challenges, horrors, and beauties than those of the present era (and the future). The dire state of the planet—overpopulation, greed, and aggression continue to threaten our survival. It is a struggle for human beings and many other species to stay healthy, to stay alive. It is vital that we actively work to find new and better ways.

Whatever other positive actions we take to help save and heal the planet, we can consider our art an important contribution. Playing music is an effective action. Whether playing in a practice room or with other musicians, whether playing for small or large audiences, we are offering to the universe our understanding and life experience. Our being, our presence, and our fine insight spoken through the musical lines and phrases awaken understanding and enlightenment in ourselves and others.

The Art of "Jump Steady"

JUMP STEADY WAS THE HOT SPRING MY HUSBAND and I visited in the mountains of Colorado. What a funny name, Jump Steady. When I heard it, I was delighted and thought it could be my motto for music. It could mean bringing together stability and expression. *Jump* might indicate pushing off, jumping over, transcending, making a leap, reaching for the heights of inspiration, leaving the ground for realms of imagination, shaking things up, moving on, daring. *Steady* as a principle could mean a steady foundation, a steady direction, a steady flow of energy, a steady overview, a steady kind of excitement.

Freedom to fly with feet firm on the ground, Jump Steady can describe my aim in writing this collection of ideas on being an artist in music. I hope that this collection will generate further ideas to add to the enjoyment of the art of life, the art of music, the art of playing flute. This wish brings me happiness, as I hope it will others. The meaning of Butto's statement will become clear:

"Musicians are the happiest people, don't you think so?"

Epilogue

What happens to music practice as we age? Aging is not a popular topic, especially in our culture. The issues of age and continuing to play music are highly individual. Every person will be different, yet it is valuable to hear the stories of how others have sailed and to navigate our own ship as best we can.

On his first US concert tour, Pablo Casals was in San Francisco and invited by friends to hike the trails of nearby Mount Tamalpais. He was a young man and loved hiking. When the group stopped to rest, a rockslide occurred above them, and a sizable stone fell and smashed his left hand, causing serious injury.

> *When I looked at my mangled bloody fingers, I had a strange reaction. "Thank God I will never have to play again," I said. The fact is that dedication to one's art does involve a sort of enslavement.*[1]
>
> —Pablo Casals

After several months of medical treatment, his hand healed, and he went on to play throughout his life. He was still playing when he died at age ninety-six.

Upon facing his injured hand and a possible end to his ability to play, Casals reacted in an understandable yet unusual way. A more common reaction for most musicians would be trauma. The prospect of needing to stop playing because of physical difficulties would be hard to bear. I used to wonder what I would do if I were prevented from playing. I advised myself to cultivate other arts and interests to fall back on, but music stays in our whole system, nerves and cells. To be forced to stop at a younger age could bring great frustration and grief.

Performing can be halted for other reasons. Finding performance events and engagements can be tough. There can be too much "down time." The quality of musicality that we achieved can no longer be met. The spark can be compromised by too much pressure, perhaps by having to play back-to-back performances on tour. With too much pressure or not enough, a time of not playing at our best can be temporary, or the artistic edge might not return. Performing itself can become less significant. What can an individual do to pursue music in a way that still has meaning? Every individual must find his or her answers. Perhaps a life dedicated to teaching would be more fulfilling than a life of performing.

Violinist Kató Havas was a child prodigy and at age eighteen was giving concerts with a rigorous international touring schedule. With the pressure of constantly performing, she realized that her spark and flair in playing had worn down. Much of her built-in inspiration had come from the natural style of gypsy violinists she heard as a child. She decided to teach, based on this inspiration. She founded a music school in England, which produced miraculous musical accomplishment in young students and professionals who came from all over the world to learn her New Approach.[2]

There seemed no reason I would not go forward—ever learning, always improving, and feeling a more stable connection with what I wanted to say musically. I was at a satisfying place, and when playing, I felt I had a positive influence in the world whether people were listening or not. Age began to set in. My sixties were giving way to age seventy. The decade of the seventies is different for every individual, and I won't complain. The time is rich with wonders.

However, there is some sadness that I am no longer as strong and as able as I was even five years ago. Heart problems make breathing less expansive. Problematic eyesight makes reading printed music a challenge. Standing long hours to practice as I once did would take too much of the energy I budget to gracefully get through the day. Playing the flute takes a great deal of energy at any age. I will always remember a violist friend who observed that after a rehearsal, the wind players were always ravenously hungry. Breathing burns calories.

There is something about aging that is fair even though it is difficult. There are blessings to count yet a tiredness. There is the growing importance of making choices as to how best to use the time left. I never wanted to be like *The Old Guitarist*, Picasso's painting from his Blue Period.[3] The old, dying, emaciated guitarist, a blind beggar with ragged clothes, is sitting on the ground, dignified and introspective, still eking out a few notes from his guitar, perhaps holding onto the life of his art as he lets go of his own life. There are many interpretations of this painting. When he painted it, Picasso had been living in poverty and had recently lost a friend and colleague to suicide. We need not interpret the dying guitarist as losing life, nor should we disparage our own countdown. Perhaps it is a countdown for the takeoff, maybe a lucky turn of events. We are part of the universe in this particular form, this human form. There are many other forms. Perhaps because of our transient nature, we embody form and formlessness, being and emptiness.

Speaking the language of music continues to inform my joy and appreciation of the playing of others. My ears are more receptive than ever. Creativity has by no means ended. There are other creative pursuits that bring joy. In writing, drawing, and painting, my experiences in music continue to inform me. Music is present.

Ignoring our cultural taboo on the subject of aging can, at any age, open ways to contemplate the finite nature of our lifetimes. Psychologically and spiritually, it can be a relief, clarifying our purpose in music. It is helpful to recognize the deeper truth that we can never possess any art form but only be part of it for the moment. Paradoxically, our music is strengthened by knowing we will one day let it go. This realization brings added courage.

Truth is our artistic, moral, and lifelong goal. The practice of truth in music, in any art, in life, will make all the big changes we face more natural and bearable. The practice of music makes sense of life.

Life without music would be an error, a hardship, an exile.[5]
—FRIEDRICH NIETZSCHE (1844–1900)

ACKNOWLEDGMENTS

My long journey in writing this book evolved into wonderful connections with generous people who offered their time, energy and expertise. Their consideration and kindness has lifted the quality of the book as well as my life.

I am indebted to Kay Loa Knifer, artist, librarian, and longtime friend, who read the book as it progressed, offered her cheerful support, and helped me stare down my demons.

I thank Lorelle VanFossen, author, speaker, and trainer, for her professional enthusiasm and for setting me on a better course early on with her astute editorial feedback on the first chapters. Author and editor Susan K. Field read the entire final draft and provided edits and notes with detailed insights about the art of writing. It was supremely bighearted that while working on her own book, she took time to edit mine!

Ellen Hansen, musician, writer and international tour manager read an earlier draft and later proofread many chapters offering energetic and encouraging comments—even playing my CD on her European tours! Musician, photographer, translator, writer, and editor Jeanna Burrup thoughtfully read chapters and gave many poignant comments and lively discussions with her gift of diving into the deeper questions. I am grateful to poet Ann Farley for her keen-eyed proofreading and her considerate and honest feedback. A large thank you goes to Bob Abbey, musician, composer, professor and librarian, for reading the manuscript and for his uplifting encouragement. Talking with Bob makes you feel ten feet tall.

I warmly thank pianist and Alexander Technique practitioner Carol Toensing for her friendship of many years, her shared passion for music, and her encouragement.

Writers in the Grove is a writing group that attracts a diversity of writers of poetry, fiction and nonfiction in the Portland, Oregon region. I am indebted to these writers for their bountiful support. Author and poet MaryJane Nordgren leads the group and sustains a foundation of inspiration with her inclusive approach. I deeply appreciate that she has taken the time, in the midst of her own productive writing, to proofread many chapters of my book.

I thank Patricia Marshall, Owner-Editor of *Luminare Press*, for her professionalism and her assistance with a confident array of services to guide the work to publication. With gratitude I applaud the *Luminare* staff for their upbeat, personable, and detailed attention—and attention to detail. Lori Stephens, Editor, scrutinized the manuscript with sensitive and meticulous care that elevated and dignified meaning. Claire Flint Last, Graphic Designer, brought forth her professional eye and artistic considerations in designing the cover and interior formatting. Jamie Passaro, Mangaging Editor, added final touches in the editing process. Kim Harper-Kennedy, Projects and Operations Manager, kept communications clear in guiding the project to completion and publication.

Thank you to the staff of the Forest Grove City Library of the Washington County Cooperative Library Services, Oregon. Their help with research is always ready to go the extra mile with mercurial and professional poise.

With gratitude and love I thank Raven, Ahsha, Hebe, Caleb, Cheryl, Sylvia, Cherree, and Dillon. You are the lights of my life. Thank you for cheering me onward and for your positive outlooks in your busy lives.

Special thank you to my husband Ralph M. Cuellar, guitarist, for sharing your love of music as well as your love. Thank you for being a supportive sounding board and for rescuing me many times through the mazes of computer navigation. Your peacefulness, patience, and infinite support made the long journey a joy.

And I thank Romi, our "classical longhair" black cat who plays piano, holding down the keys until the tones fade out—all the while looking at us as if to say, "Listen to this!"

I would like to reach back in time to acknowledge in gratitude the flutists-teachers who lighted my pathway in the 1950s to the 1970s: M. Bové, Thomas Wilt, Lawrence Duckles, Jean Louis Kashy, Gary Gray, Paul Renzi, M. Pierre Cazaux, and Ransom Wilson.

NOTES

Chapter 1: Why Musicians Work to Play

1. Annada Pattanaik. For additional biographical information, see Lezima Gomes, "Annada Pattanaik, Unforgettablwe Tunes on Flute," *Qatar Tribune,* May 24, 2017, http://www.qatar-tribune.com/news-details/id/66671.

2. Albert E. Kahn, *Joys and Sorrows: Reflections by Pablo Casals* (New York: Simon & Schuster, 1970). Pablo Casals (1876–1973), world-renowned master cellist.

3. Frank Scheffer, *A Year with John Cage—How to Get Ot of the Cage*, 2012, EuroArtsChannel, https://www.youtube.com/watch?v=UaNGeuDuXl4. John Cage (1912–1992), American composer, innovator of modern techniques and philosophy of music, and a leader in the development of avant-garde music of the twentieth century.

4. Nat Shapiro and Nat Hentoff, eds., *Hear Me Talkin' to Ya: The Story of Jazz as Told by the Man Who Made It* (New York: Dover Publications, 1966). Charlie Parker (1920–1955).

5. Marc Ribot, *Rootless Cosmopolitan.* (New York: Island Records, 1990).

Chapter 2: Body and Sound

1. Wikimedia 6/2018, https://en.wikipedia.org/wiki/Ch%C3%B6gyam_Trungpa. Chogyam Trungpa Rinpoche (1939–1987), Tibetan Buddhist meditation master, teacher, author, poet, and founder of Naropa University.

2. 99arts.org, 4/2016, https://www.youtube.com/watch?v=a0GSNQSdO9Q. Pablo Casals, master class, early 1960s.

3. Carol Toensing, pianist, Alexander Technique practitioner and therapist, based in the Boulder-Denver area of Colorado, wife of composer Richard Toensing.

4. *Philadelphia Inquirer,* April 15, 1989, Daniel Webster, Montana Flute Association 2018, https://www.montanafluteassociation.org/2016-murray-panitz-yac.html. Murray Panitz (1925–1989), principal flutist with the Philadelphia Orchestra, taught at the Curtis Institute and Temple University.

5. Tchaikovsky *Violin Concerto in D Major* (Conductor Gennady Rozhdestvensky, who passed away 2018), David Oistrakh, https://www.youtube.com/watch?v=KP0a7aq_NyE.

6. Carlos Castaneda, *The Teachings of Don Juan: A Yaqui Way of Knowledge* (Berkeley: University of California Press, 1968). Carlos Castaneda (1925–1998) wrote twelve books; some were international bestsellers, translated in seventeen languages.

7. Naropa University, http://www.naropa.edu. Located in Boulder, Colorado, Naropa University is a nonprofit liberal arts college offering degree programs in art, music, literature, education, environmental studies, psychology, and religious studies. It is the "first and only accredited university in North America that is completely based on Contemplative Education."

Chapter 3: Breathe to Sing

1. William J. Broad, "Ancient Instruments Yielding Secrets of Their Music: Complex Eddies, Lovely Tones," *New York Times*, January 19, 1999.

2. Shunryū Suzuki Roshi, *Zen Mind, Beginner's Mind: Informal Talks on Zen Meditation and Practice* (Trumble, CT: Weatherhill, 1970). Shunryū Suzuki (1904–1971), master, teacher, author, founded the first Zen Buddhist monastery in the United States and the first Zen Buddhist center, both in California.

3. Copyright assigned to Arnold Jacobs, http:optimists-alumni.org/downloads/acrobat_downloads/Arnold_Jacobs_1990_Notes_Charles_Lipp.pdf. Books, dissertations, thesis about Arnold Jacobs and his teachings, 2018: Lyratheme http://www.windsongpress.com/writings-about-arnold-jacobs. Arnold Jacobs (1915–1998). Notes from classes for brass and woodwind players given by Arnold Jacobs in 1990, written by Charles Lipp, bassoonist-composer.

4. "Almost Live," Brian Frederikson, Nov. 2009, https://www.youtube.com/watch?v=KrNmbaRql0Y. Arnold Jacobs, series of classes.

5. Hariprashad Chaurasia, "Pandit Hariprasad Chaurasia plays Raga Miya Malhar, Sangeetveda," Aug 2016, https://www.youtube.com/watch?v=N0ZwlIA0Q6Q.

6. *wikiHow*, 2018, https://www.wikihow.com/Circular-Breathe. Circular-breathing: the ability to breathe in through nose while blowing out through mouth, thus continuing to play without the interruption of taking a breath.

7. Atmic Vision, 2010, http://www.atmicvision.com. Atmic Vision trio: bansuri, tabla, and double bass, Indo-American fusion.

Chapter 4: Brilliant Practice

1. http://www.ArtLande.com. Art Lande, jazz pianist, composer, drummer, teacher, recording artist.

Chapter 5: Avoiding Practice Pitfalls

1. *Le Carnaval des Animaux*, "Les Pianistes," Camille Saint-Saëns, https://www.youtube.com/watch?v=Hiz4j9P0PJ0.
2. Roger S. Stevens (1921–999), *Artistic Flute: Technique and Study* (Hollywood, CA: Highland Music Company, 1967). Flutist with the Los Angeles Philharmonic Symphony Orchestra, professor, University of Southern California.
3. Thom Hartmann, *Walking Your Blues Away: How to Heal the Mind and Create Emotional Well-Being* (Rochester, VT; Park Street Press, 2006).

Chapter 6: Aware Care

1. Monty H. Levenson, *The Japanese Shakuhachi Flute, A Guide to the Traditional Music and Notation* (Mendocino, CA: Monty Levenson, 1974).
2. International Shakuhachi Society, 2018, https://www.komuso.com/people/people.pl?person=1033. Monty H. Levenson has been making shakuhachi flutes since 1970 and has in more recent years developed new techniques using laser measurements.

Chapter 7: Approach and Perspective

1. Pilar Estevan, *Talking with Flutists*, vol. 1 (New York: Edutainment Publishing Company, 1976).
2. Ohshu Sashi, 2016, https://www.youtube.com/watch?v=52jncoWu4zs.
3. Muzio Clementi (1752–1832) was an Italian-born British pianist, composer, and pedagogue. He also became a music publisher and piano manufacturer. Clementi toured Europe often, and on one of his tours, the emperor in

Vienna challenged him to engage in a competition with W. A. Mozart.

4. Friedrich Kerst, comp, and Henry E. Krehbiel, trans., *Mozart: The Man and the Artist Revealed in His Own Words* (New York: Dover Publications, 1965). Republished from the Geoffrey Bles edition (London, 1926). W. A. Mozart, letter to his father, January 12, 1782.

5. Pilar Estevan, *Talking with Flutists,* vol. 1 (New York: Edutainment Publishing Company, 1976).

6. Aram Khachaturian (1903–1978), Virtual Museum of Aram Khachaturian, Aram Khachaturian International Enlightenment-Cultural Association (n.d.), http://www.khachaturian.am/eng/works/koncert.htm.

7. David Oistrakh writing about Khachaturian, Virtual Museum of Aram Khachaturian, http://www.khachaturian.am/eng/works/koncert.htm. David Oistrakh, Khachaturian *Violin Concerto in D Major*, Moscow Radio Symphony Orchestra, 1965, https://www.youtube.com/watch?v=TeKZAbFj83I.

8. Luis Alberto Aldama 8/2011, https://www.youtube.com/watch?v=lhHN69S5lgQ. In 1968, flutist Jean-Pierre Rampal, encouraged by Khachaturian, transcribed the violin concerto for flute, staying true to the original except for a different cadenza in the first movement.

9. W. A. Mozart, *Concertos 21 and 20*, Andras Schiff, Camerata Academica des Mozarteum Salzburg, Sándor Végh, conductor (London and New York: Decca Records, 1991).

10. http://www.RansomWilson.com. Ransom Wilson, flutist, conductor, educator.

11. Montserrat Caballé, Marlium Jamir, 11/2013, https://www.youtube.com/watch?v=WOY1bKOYOo&nohtml5=False.

12. https://www.youtube.com/watch?v=TtnCBK1CVgQ. Shlomo Carlebach (1925–1994) was a Jewish rabbi, religious teacher, composer, and singer who was popularly known as "The Singing Rabbi." He composed thousands of melodies and recorded more than twenty-five albums that continue to have widespread popularity and appeal.

13. "Si Dolce" Claudio Monteverdi, Christina Pluhar and L'Arpeggiata, Warner Classics, 12/2008, https://www.youtube.com/watch?v=woh1d7QxIKA. Philippe Jaroussky, countertenor, French musician who began as a violinist and pianist and is now a singer. He is known for his exquisite artistic interpretations of Baroque music.

14. Frank Scheffer, 2012, *A Year with John Cage—How to Get Out of the Cage*, EuroArtsChannel, https://www.youtube.com/watch?v=UaNGeuDuXl4.

15. Maurice Bourg, violinist (1902–1982).

16. Pilar Estevan, *Talking with Flutists*, vol. 1 (New York: Edutainment Publishing Company, 1976).

17. Ralph Stackpole (1885–1973), sculptor and painter, prominent West Coast artist of the 1930s and 1940s. Noted in the United States for his sculptures at the entrance to the San Francisco Stock Exchange building, his mural among the historic WPA murals in San Francisco's Coit Tower, his towering sculpture, *Pacifica*, at the 1939–1940 world's fair, and his friendship with noted artists and musicians including Frida and Diego Rivera. In France, his sculptures were recognized in prestigious salons such as the Salon des Artistes Francais.

18. Paul Strathern, *The Artist, the Philosopher, and the Warrior: The Intersecting Lives of da Vinci, Machiavelli, and Borgia and the World They Shaped* (New York: Bantam Books, 2009), 180.

19. Daniel Kish, PopTech, 11/2011, https://www.youtube.com/watch?v=xATIyq3uZM4.

20. Elliot McCaffrey, producer and director, *The Boy Who Sees without Eyes*, Firefly production for Five in association with TLC, 2007, https://www.youtube.com/watch?v=Ybvg_ay6T50.

Chapter 8: Experimentation and Discovery

1. "Stern, Isaac," Contemporary Musicians, Encyclopedia.com, (January 9, 2019), https://www.encyclopedia.com/education/news-wires-white-papers-and-books/stern-isaac.

2. Sun Valley Music Camp, founded 1963. Jacques Bourman, director, 1965. Flute instructor, Jean-Louis Kashy.

3. www.youtube.com/watch?v=YuBeBjqKSGQ, Diana Damrau, The Royal Opera.

4. John Holt, *Never Too Late: My Musical Life Story* (New York: Addison-Wesley, 1978, 1991).

Chapter 9: Character and Mood

1. Jane Glover, *Mozart's Women: His Family, His Friends, His Music* (London: Macmillan Publishers Ltd, 2005). From Mozart's letters.

2. Kristian Bezuidenhout, KristianBezuidenhout.com.

3. Kristian Bezuidenhout, *Sonatas,* vol. 4, Harmonia Mundi, 9/2012, https://www.youtube.com/watch?v=TWADEJ2YGtA.

4. John Holt, *Never Too Late: My Musical Life Story* (New York: Addison-Wesley, 1978, 1991).

5. https://billdouglas.cc, Bill Douglas, composer, pianist, educator, and recording artist.

6. Pilar Estevan, *Talking with Flutists*, (New York: Edutainment Publishing Company, 1976). Marcel Moyse (1889–1984), French flutist who played principal in orchestras of Paris, taught internationally and made many recordings.

7. http://www.russellbrand.com, Russel Brand, comedian, activist, author, advocate helping people to overcome addictions.

8. http://www.rsmits.com/eBIO.htm, Raphaella Smits, guitarist.

9. Bruce Bower, "A Mind for Music, Birth of the Beat," *Science News* (Aug. 2010), 18.

10. Bruce Bower, *Science News*, "A Mind for Music, Birth of the Beat," *Science News* (Dec. 2009), 14.

11. NPR "Morning Edition," September 10, 2002, 12:00 AM ET, https://www.npr.org/templates/story/story.php?storyId=1149739. Rolling Requiem was a succession of worldwide performances of Mozart's *Requiem* in response to the tragedy of the attack on September 11.

12. Jane Glover, *Mozart's Women: His Family, His Friends, His Music* (London: Macmillan Publishers Ltd, 2005).

Chapter 10: Creativity—Nakedness

1. https://clermont-ferrand.fr/presentation-du-conservatoire-emmanuel-chabrier, Pierre Cazaux, professor of flute, Conservatoire National de Clermont-Ferrand, France.

2. The Beatles, "Hey Jude," on *Revolution* (London, Apple, Capitol Records SWBO-101, 1968).

3. Philip Kapleau, *The Three Pillars of Zen* (New York: Harper & Row, 1966). One of the first English-language books to present Zen Buddhism not as a religion as much as a beneficial life practice.

4. Bob Seigetsu Avstreih, shakuhachi player and teacher of the Sui-Zen shakuhachi in Denver, Colorado.

5. Monty H. Levenson, *The Japanese Shakuhachi Flute: A Guide to the Traditional Music and Notation* (Mendocino, CA: Monty Levenson, 1974).

6. *Amadeus,* 1984 Academy Award-winning movie, directed by Miloš Forman, adapted from the stage play by Peter Shaffer, fictional drama of the life of W. A. Mozart.

7. Blaisdell, William, "Leo Eloesser: The Remarkable Story of a Medical Volunteer in Spain," http://www.albavolunteer.org/2016/12/leo-eloesser-the-remarkable-story-of-a-medical-volunteer-in-spain. excerpt from: *The History of the Surgical Service at San Francisco General Hospital* (2007, https://sfgh.surgery.ucsf.edu/media/234872/history%20of%20sfgh.pdf.

"He owned a flat on Leavenworth Street. Every Wednesday evening, a small group from the San Francisco Symphony would join him in his flat to play chamber music together. From time to time, this group was joined by distinguished visitors such as Pierre Monteux, Fritz Kreisler, and Yehudi Menuhin. He had a gift for languages—mastering German, Greek, Russian, French, Polish, Hungarian, Spanish, Italian, and Chinese—and once spent seven months teaching at the University of Tokyo Medical School in Japanese, having picked up the language from a dictionary and conversations with passengers on the ship going over."

8. Hephzibah Menuhin (1920–1981), Yaltah Menuhin (1921–2001), sisters of violinist, Yehudi Menuhin. Hephzabah was a concert pianist and human rights activist. Yaltah was a pianist, painter, and poet. My mother knew them in the1930s.

9. Yehudi Menuhin (1916–1999), considered one of the greatest violinists of the twentieth century.

10. The Humboldt Chamber Music Workshop, http://www2.humboldt.edu/cmw.

11. Leonardo da Vinci, *Virgin of the Rocks,* Louvre Museum in Paris (estimated to have been painted c. 1483–1486), National Gallery in London (estimated to have been painted prior to 1508). Two large paintings of Madonna Mary, Jesus child, John the Baptist child, and an angel in a rocky cave with distant landscape.

Chapter 11: Performance Delight

1. Caroline Duffner, "Havas New Approach," article from "A Tutto Arco," *ESTA Italia* 1 (April 2008), https://www.carolineduffner.com/english/pedagogue/havas-new-approach.

2. Claude Kenneson, *Musical Prodigies: Perilous Journeys, Remarkable Lives* (Portland, OR: Amadeus Press, 1998), 302.

3. Goody Cable, Rimsky-Korsakoffee House, Portland, Oregon, 2017, https://en.wikipedia.org/wiki/Rimsky-Korsakoffee_House.

4. Bourées have been composed as musical pieces since the middle of the sixteenth century. The bourée clog dance was popular since around 1665 in the Auvergne region of France.

5. Bill Douglas, Hearts of Space, Valley Entertainment, 2018, https://www.valley-entertainment.com/collections/bill-douglas.
6. William J. Broad, "Ancient Instruments Yielding Secrets of Their Music: Complex Eddies, Lovely Tones," *New York Times*, January 19, 1999.
7. *Saturday Night Live*, 2013, https://www.youtube.com/watch?v=Ls5UyVbbF1Y.
8. Johann Joachim Quantz, *On Playing the Flute, The Classic of Baroque Music Instruction*, Edward R. Reilly, trans. (London: Faber and Faber, Ltd., and New York, G. Schirmer, 1975). Originally published in 1752 as *Essay of a Method for Playing the Transverse Flute accompanied by several Remarks of service for the Improvement of Good Taste in Practical Music, and illustrated with examples*. Johann Joachim Quantz (1697-1773), German flutist, flute maker, and composer.
9. Claude Kenneson, *Musical Prodigies: Perilous Journeys, Remarkable Lives* (Portland, OR: Amadeus Press, 1998), 302.
10. *Amadeus*, 1984 Academy Award-winning movie, directed by Miloš Forman, adapted from the stage play by Peter Shaffer, fictional drama of the life of W. A. Mozart.

Chapter 12: Performance Anxiety

1. Albert E. Kahn, *Joys and Sorrows: Reflections by Pablo Casals* (New York: Simon & Schuster, 1970).
2. Pepe Romero, master class, Portland Classic Guitar Concert Series, Marylhurst University Portland, OR, 2015, https://www.youtube.com/watch?v=MaBzeWQpiGI.
3. Paul McCandless, 2018, http://paulmccandless.com.

4. Art Lande, 2018, www.ArtLande.com.

5. Seymour Bernstein, 2011, http://seymourbernstein.com.

6. http://rileylee.net. Riley Lee, the first shakuhachi player of non-Japanese descent to become a dai shihan or Grand Master. He famously played shakuhachi atop one of the roofs of the Sydney Opera House in Australia in honor of the worldwide New Year millennium celebrations in 2000.

7. Irina Kulikova, *Classical Guitar*, September 2010, interview with Guy Traviss, 2017, http://classicalguitarmagazine.com/irina-kulikova-injury-led-to-health-awareness-injuries-recovery-guitar.

Chapter 13: Plays Well with Others

1. Friedrich Kerst, comp., and Henry Krehbiel, trans., *Mozart: The Man and the Artist Revealed in His Own Words* (New York: Dover Publications, 1965).

2. Art Lande, 2018, http://www.ArtLande.com.

Chapter 14: Speaking Clearly

1. "Dolby effect," https://en.wikipedia.org/wiki/Dolby_Laboratories.

2. Maurice Bourg, violinist (1902–1982).

3. Friedrich Kerst, comp., and Henry Krehbiel, trans., *Mozart: The Man and the Artist Revealed in His Own Words* (New York: Dover Publications, 1965).

4. Aram Khachaturian, *Violin Concerto in D Major* Transcribed for flute by Jean-Pierre Rampal, (London: Boosey & Hawkes, 1968).

5. Les Weil, *Odd Meter Studies*, (Rogue River, OR: Evans Valley Music, 1973)

6. Bill Douglas, *Vocal Rhythm Etudes*, sold by ReallyGoodMusic.com, https://billdouglas.cc/printed-music.

7. Umm Kulthum sings "Enta Omri" (You Are My Life) at the Olympia Théâtre in Paris, Umm Kulthum November 1967, https://www.youtube.com/watch?v=XPGHpBOt5sE.

Chapter 15: Don't Let Them Tell You

1. *Seymour: An Introduction*, Ethan Hawke (New York: Room 5 Films, 2014). Documentary about pianist Seymour Bernstein (Kimball Gallagher, pianist).

2. Kenny Werner, *Effortless Mastery: Liberating the Master Musician Within* (New Albany, IN: Jamey Abersold Jazz, 1996).

3. Sergei Prokofiev, *Sonata for Flute and Piano, Op 94*. (New York, Boosey Hawkes, 2011) The sonata was transcribed for violin and piano by the composer and David Oistrakh.

4. Raphaella Smits, 2018, http://www.rsmits.com/eBIO.htm.

5. Jeremy Grimshaw, Artist Biography (article on website): AllMusic, https://www.allmusic.com/artist/paul-odette-mn0000044193/biography. Paul Odette, lutenist and conductor who specializes in Renaissance and Baroque music. He also plays archlute, theorbo, and Baroque guitar.

6. Ali Akbar Khan (1922–2009), virtuoso sarod player, who founded music schools in Calcutta, India, San Rafael, California, and Basel, Switzerland.

7. Claude Kenneson, *Musical Prodigies: Perilous Journeys, Remarkable Lives* (Portland, OR: Amadeus Press, 1998).

8. Paul Simon, "Diamonds on the Soles of Her Shoes," on *Graceland* (Burbank, CA: Warner Bros. Records, 1-25447, 1986). Recorded with Ladysmith Black Mambazo.

9. Boys of the Lough, 2018, http://boysofthelough.info.

10. Seymour Bernstein *With Your Own Two Hands: Self-Discovery through Music* (New York: G. Schirmer, 1981).

11. Isaac Stern (1920–2001), interview with James Day, *Day at Night*, 1973. Digital reproduction Cuny TV Foundation New York, 2009, https://www.youtube.com/watch?v=qTItYYew5UY.

12. Christopher Berg, "The Re-Imagination of Performance," *Soundboard: The Journal of the Guitar Foundation of America* 35, (2009).

13. Vincent Van Gogh, *Dear Theo: the Autobiography of Vincent Van Gogh* edited by Irving Stone, Boston Houghton Mifflin Co., (Cambridge, MA: The Riverside Press, 1937).

Chapter 16: Capable and Legitimate

1. Helen Lanfer, *Music Within Us: An Exploration in Creative Music Education* (New York: Tara Publications, 2013).

2. John Holt, *Never Too Late: My Musical Life Story* (New York: Addison-Wesley, 1978, 1991).

3. Sam Bush, 2018, https://www.sambush.com.

4. Arthur Rubinstein, *My Young Years* (New York: Alfred A. Knopf, 1973), 255.

5. Michael Pollan, *The Botany of Desire: A Plant's-Eye View of the World* (New York: Random House, 2001).

6. "Andras Schiff explains Bach," https://www.youtube.com/watch?v=0SclAUqaj2Q. George Malcolm (1917–1997), harpsichordist, organist, composer, and conductor. Andras Schiff studied with George Malcolm and later performed solo with orchestras with Malcolm conducting. They recorded Mozart's complete works for piano duet on Mozart's own piano.

7. Jane Glover, *Mozart's Women: His Family, His Friends, His Music* (London: Macmillan Publishers Ltd, 2005). Under Lector Carl Theodor, Mannheim became one of the intellectual centers of Europe. The Mannheim orchestra was highly praised throughout Europe.

8. Kathleen Krull, *Lives of the Musicians* (San Diego: Harcourt, Brace & Company, 1993).

9. "Coffee Cantata." Coffeehouses were introduced in Germany in the late 1600s. In the early 1730s, Johann Sebastian Bach composed the "Coffee Cantata" performed at Cafe Zimmermann in Leipzig. It may have been with his daughter, Elisabeth Friederica, in mind. "Leischen" is a nickname for Elisabeth. http://www.bach-cantatas.com/Texts/BWV211-Eng3.htm.

10. Irving Stone, ed., *Dear Theo: The Autobiography of Vincent van Gogh* (Boston: Houghton Mifflin, 1937).

Chapter 17: One Half of Humanity

1. Albert E. Kahn, *Joys and Sorrows: Reflections by Pablo Casals* (New York: Simon & Schuster, 1970).

2. Jane Glover, *Mozart's Women: His Family, His Friends, His Music* (London: Macmillan Publishers Ltd, 2005).

3. Donald J. Grout, *A History of Western Music* (New York: W. W. Norton, 1960).

4. Arnold Toynbee, *A Study of History* 1935–1939 from *A History of Western Music* (New York: WW Norton, 2014).

5. Leonard Bernstein, *The Harmonic Series/Norton Lectures: Musical Phonology*, Originally Produced by Amberson Video in cooperation with WGBH-TV Boston, 1973. (New York: Video Music Education, Inc., 2016), https://www.youtube.com/watch?v=9HjEAtJXssc.

6. Terpander, kithara player, singer, poet, who lived in the first half of the seventh century BCE.

7. Lucy Lamy, *Egyptian Mysteries: New Light on Ancient Spiritual Knowledge* (New York: Crossroad, 1981).

8. Merlin Stone, *When God Was a Woman* (New York: Harcourt, Brace, Jovanovich, 1976).

9. https://infidels.org/kiosk/article/the-koran-unveiled-761.html.

10. James Mellaart (1925–2012), British archaeologist noted for his discovery of the Çatal Hüyük site in Turkey.

11. http://www.catalhoyuk.com/content/review-consciousness-and-creativity, 2017. Çatal Hüyük, Çatalhöyük, large Neolithic city, 7500–5700 BC, near present-day Konya, Turkey.

12. Nazli Gürlek, 2018, http://www.nazligurlek.com.

13. Professor H. W. F. Saggs (1920–2005), inscriptions expert who worked on the excavations at Nimrud, Assyrian capital in present-day Iraq. He published 243 letters translated from cuneiform in *The Nimrud Letters*, 1952.

14. Halaf, 6100–5100 BCE, prehistoric culture in present-day Turkey, Syria, Iraq. Uruk 4000–3200 BCE, ancient city of Sumer.

15. There are earlier forms of writing using symbolic images, but cuneiform is the first writing discovered that uses syllables and letters to represent sounds made in speech.

16. Merlin Stone, *When God Was a Woman* (New York: Harcourt, Brace, Jovanovich, 1976).

17. Carlo Neuls-Bates, *Women in Music: An Anthology of Source Readings from the Middle Ages to the Present* (New York: Harper & Row, 1982).

18. Philo Judaeus (c. 20 BCE–c. 50 CE), Greek-Jewish philosopher who lived in Alexandria, the Roman province of Egypt.

19. Viki Leon, *Outrageous Women of Ancient Times* (New York: John Wiley & Sons, 1998).

20. Tetrachord—a series of four notes with the interval between the first note and the last note being a perfect fourth.

21. Peter Burkholder, Donald Grout, and Claude Palisca, *A History of Western Music*, 7th ed., (New York: W. W. Norton, 2006).

22. Andrew Barker, ed., *Greek Musical Writings* (Cambridge: Cambridge University Press, 1984, 1989).

23. Ragas are musical motifs of at least five notes that are the basis for improvisation. They are often associated with seasons and time of day. The word comes from the Sanskrit *raga*, meaning "color, dye, tint, shade." Indian ragas are said to create (color) and emotional states.

24. http://lyravlos.gr/ancient-music-sources-en.asp. Seikilos Pillar on which a short but complete musical composition is carved, dating 200 BCE–CE 100, found in Turkey near Ephesus.

25. St. Augustine (354–430), Christian theologian from the Patristic Era.
26. Stephen Greenblatt, *The Rise and Fall of Adam and Eve* (New York: W. W. Norton, 2017). Holy Bible, King James Version, Timothy 2:14, Ephesians 5:23.
27. Stephen Greenblatt, *The Rise and Fall of Adam and Eve* (New York: W. W. Norton, 2017). Holy Bible, King James Version, Timothy 2:14.
28. John Calvin (1509–1564), French pastor, theologian, and part of the Protestant Reformation.
29. Pilar Estevan, *Talking with Flutists,* vol. 1 (New York Edutainment Publishing Company, 1976). Doriot Anthony Dwyer, flute. The current principal chair flutist, Elizabeth Rowe, recently settled a lawsuit she brought against the Boston Symphony for pay inequity. She had been earning 75 percent of what male first chair players were getting, while working as much or more than they were. https://www.nytimes.com/2019/02/21/arts/music/boston-symphony-elizabeth-rowe-settlement.html.
30. https://csoarchives.wordpress.com/tag/helen-kotas, Helen Kotas, French horn, from the Archives, Chicago Symphony Orchestra.
31. http://cello.org/cnc/hilger.htm, Elsa Hilger, cello, "Groundbreaking Female Cellist," Internet Cello Society.
32. http://wrti.org/post/harpist-edna-phillips-and-philadelphia-orchestra-one-woman-hundred, Edna Phillips, harp, "Harpist Edna Phillips and the Philadelphia Orchestra: One Woman in a Hundred," Meridee Duddleston.
33. https://case.edu/ech/articles/c/chalifoux-alice, Alice Chalifoux, harp, Case Western Reserve University.

34. https://www.cmuse.org/contribution-of-women-musicians-to-symphony-orchestras. Cynthia Collins, harp, March 2015.
35. https://en.wikipedia.org/wiki/List_of_female_composers_by_birth_date. List of female composers by birth date.
36. Kathleen Krull, *Lives of the Musicians* (San Diego: Harcourt, Brace & Company, 1993). Nadia Boulanger (1887–1979).
37. https://www.france24.com/en/20180824-video-revisited-iceland-economic-crisis-europe-gender-equality, Sara Þórdardóttir Oskarsson, *France 24*.

Chapter 18: Art, Life, and the Dark Side

1. Jean Paul Richter, ed., *The Notebooks of Leonardo da Vinci, Vol. 1* (New York: Dover Publications, 1970).
2. Andrew Hultkrans, "The Wrong Note: How Western Pop Music Is Being Used as 'Touchless Torture' by the American Military," *Frieze: Contemporary Art and Culture* 119, Nov/Dec 2008, 35–41.
3. Eugene Debs (1855–1926), trade unionist, political activist, and democratic socialist who ran for president of the United States five times; Founding member of Industrial Workers of the World.
4. The Beatles, "Happiness Is a Warm Gun" on *White Album*, (London: Apple, PCS 7067/8, 1968).
5. https://www.ncbi.nlm.nih.gov/pubmed/21269927, C. M. Tanner, F. Kamel, G. W. Ross, J. A. Hoppin, et al. Environ Health Perspect. 2011, Rotenone, Paraquat, and Parkinson's Disease.

6. The Dead Milkmen, "Death's Alright with Me" on *Smokin' Banana Peels,* 1988, http://www.metrolyrics.com/deaths-alright-with-me-lyrics-dead-milkmen.html.

7. Attributed to Jesus Christ, Luke 23:34, Deuteronomy, *English Standard Version Bible* (Wheaton: Crossway Bibles, 2001).

8. Wilfred Owen, "The pity of war," https://owenstudy.wordpress.com/about.

9. Dwight D. Eisenhower, https://www.eisenhowerlibrary.gov/eisenhowers/quotes. "The hope of the world is that wisdom can arrest conflict between brothers. I believe that war is the deadly harvest of arrogant and unreasoning minds." Dwight D. Eisenhower, Address, National Education Association, Washington, DC, 4/4/57.

10. Mark Haefeli, producer and director, *Paul McCartney in Red Square,* 2005. Concerts as well as interviews about the black market of banned The Beatles' music in the 1960s and prevalent observation that Beatles music changed consciousness and led to the fall of Communism in Russia.

11. Paul Strathern, *The Artist, the Philosopher, and the Warrior: The Intersecting Lives of da Vinci, Machiavelli, and Borgia and the World They Shaped* (New York: Bantam Books, 2009) 180.

12. Earth Guardians, 2018, https://www.earthguardians.org.

13. https://www.rawstory.com/2014/07/sinead-oconnor-i-deserve-to-be-a-priest-music-is-a-priesthood, Tim Jonze, "The Raw Story," *The Guardian,* July 27, 2014. "Sinéad O'Connor, "Sinéad O'Connor interview: 'I deserve to be a priest. Music is a priesthood,'"

Chapter 19: Looking Back, Looking Forward

1. "Angry Birds, Crows Never Forget Your Face: Mess with a Crow, and It Will Remember Your Face for Over Five Years, Research Shows," Jen Viegas, Seeker.com 6/2011 https://www.seeker.com/angry-birds-crows-never-forget-your-face-1765286502.html.

2. Michael Pollan, "The Intelligent Plant: Scientists debate a new way of understanding flora," A Reporter at Large, *The New Yorker* (Dec.23& 30, 2013).

3. "Are Musicians Better Language Learners?" Liisa Henriksson-Macaulay, *The Guardian*, Feb. 27, 2014, https://www.theguardian.com/education/2014/feb/27/musicians-better-language-learners.

4. Werner Hertzog, *Cave of Forgotten Dreams*, 2010. Pasadena: Creative Differences, History Films, Ministère de la Culture et de la Communication, Arte France, Werner Herzog, Filmproduktion, More4. The oldest paintings discovered are found in Chauvet Cave in France.

5. *Them and Me*, 2001, *Heaven in a Garden*, 2003, Stephane Breton, Les Films d'Ici, https://www.youtube.com/watch?v=pSJBvQ94a44.

6. "U.S. Public Schools Should Revive Stagnant Humanities and Arts Education" July 13, 2016, John Ogden, https://www.truthdig.com/articles/u-s-public-schools-should-revive-stagnant-humanities-and-arts-education/page/2/#. John Ogden, retired school teacher, New York and Los Angeles.

7. STEM, 12/2012, https://www.stemschool.com/articles/what-is-stem-education.

8. Michael Moore, *Where to Invade Next*, 2015, Dog Eat Dog Films, IMG Films: wheretoinvadenext.com.

9. Susan Gaidos, "A Mind for Music, More than a Feeling," *Science News* (Aug. 14, 2010), 24.

10. "Music of the hemispheres: Playing instruments gives brains a boost," Rachel Ehrenberg, "A Mind for Music," *Science News* (August 14, 2010), 31. Daniel Levitin, director of the music perception, cognition, and expertise laboratory at McGill University in Montreal.

11. *El Sistema: Music to Change Life*, Paul Smaczny, Maria Stodtmeier, (Berlin, EuroArts 2009). Documentary

12. David Hockney, 2018, http://www.davidhockney.co. David Hockney, artist, wrote the foreword to Jeffery Camp's *Draw: How to Master the Art* (London: DK Press Adult, 1994). "I've come to the conclusion that drawing should be taught very seriously everywhere, in all schools, not just in art schools, because if you can draw, even a little bit, you can express all kinds of ideas that might otherwise be lost—delights, frustrations, whatever torments you or pleases you. Drawing helps you to put your thoughts in order. It can make you think in different ways. It naturally gives you a sense of harmony, of order. The longer a visual education is not treated seriously, the bigger the effect will finally be." *Draw: How to Master the Art*, Jeffrey Camp.

Epilogue

1. Albert E. Kahn, *Joys and Sorrows: Reflections by Pablo Casals* (New York: Simon & Schuster, 1970).

2. Kató Havas, *A New Approach to Violin Playing,* foreword by Yehudi Menuhin (London: Bosworth, 1961).

3. Pablo Picasso, *The Old Guitarist,* 1904. Currently at the Art Institute of Chicago.

4. Friedrich Nietzsche, Letter to Heinrich Koselitz 1/15 1888. *Twilight of the Idols, Or How to Philosophize with a Hammer*, Tracy Strong, Introduction: "Hammers, Idleness and Music," vii, Richard Polt, trans., (Indianapolis/Cambridge: Hackett Publishing Company, Inc., 1997).

SELECTED BIBLIOGRAPHY

Listing of books, movies, works of art, and music albums

Adams, Noah. *Piano Lessons: Music, Love and True Adventure.* New York: Delacorte Press, 1996.

Barker, Andrew, ed. *Greek Musical Writings.* Cambridge & New York: Cambridge University Press, 1984, 1989.

The Beatles. *White Album.* London: EMI Studios, Trident Studios, 1968.

Bekoff, Marc. *The Emotional Lives of Animals, A Leading Scientist Explores Animal Joy, Sorrow, and Empathy—and Why They Matter.* Foreword by Jane Goodall. Novato, CA: New World Library, 2007.

Bernstein, Seymour. *With Your Own Two Hands: Self-Discovery through Music.* New York: G. Schirmer, 1981.

Bezuidenhout, Kristian. *Mozart Sonatas,* vol. 4. Arles, France: Harmonia Mundi, 2012.

Bramly, Serge. *Discovering the Life of Leonardo da Vinci.* New York: HarperCollins, 1991.

Breton, Stephane. *Them and Me (Eux et Moi).* 2001. *Heaven in a Garden (Le Ciel dans un Jardin).* 2003. Paris: Les Films d'Ici.

Burkholder, J. Peter, Donald J. Grout, and Claude V. Palisca. *A History of Western Music,* 7th ed. New York: W. W. Norton, 2006.

Camp, Jeffery. *Draw: How to Master the Art.* London: DK Press Adult, 1994.

Castaneda, Carlos. *The Teachings of Don Juan: A Yaqui Way of Knowledge.* Oakland, CA: University of California Press, 1968.

de Lorenzo, Leonardo. *The Flute: The Instrument, the Performer, the Music.* New York: Citadel Press, 1951.

da Vinci, Leonardo. *Virgin of the Rocks:* Louvre Museum in Paris (estimated to have been painted c. 1483–1486) and *Virgin of the Rocks*, National Gallery in London (estimated to have been painted prior to 1508).

Davis, Kenneth C. *Don't Know Much about Mythology.* New York: Harper, 2005.

The Dead Milkmen. "Death's Alright with Me" on *Smokin' Banana Peels.* Culver City, CA: Enigma Records, 1988.

Douglas, Bill. *Vocal Rhythm Etudes.* Sold by ReallyGoodMusic.com, https://billdouglas.cc/printed-music.

Douglas, Bill. Fourteen albums, multiple titles. San Francisco, Hearts of Space (Valley Entertainment). https://billdouglas.cc/recordings.

Estevan, Pilar. *Talking with Flutists,* vol. 1. New York: Edu-Tainment, 1976.

Estevan, Pilar. *Talking with Flutists,* vol. 2. New York: Envolve Music, 1978.

Galway, James. *Flute.* New York: G. Schirmer, 1982.

Glover, Jane. *Mozart's Women: His Family, His Friends, His Music.* New York: Harper Perennial, 2007.

Greenberg, Blu. *On Women and Judaism: A View from Tradition*. Philadelphia: The Jewish Publication Society of America, 1981.

Greenblatt, Stephen. *The Rise and Fall of Adam and Eve*. New York: W. W. Norton, 2017.

Grout, Donald J. *A History of Western Music*. New York: W. W. Norton, 1960.

Haefeli, Mark, *Paul McCartney in Red Square*. New York: A&E Home Video, 2005.

Hartmann, Thom. *Walking Your Blues Away, How to Heal the Mind and Create Emotional Well-Being,* Park City, UT: Park Street Press, 2006.

Havas, Kató. *A New Approach to Violin Playing*. Foreword by Yehudi Menuhin. London: Bosworth, 1961.

Hawke, Ethan. *Seymour: An Introduction*. New York: Room 5 Films, 2014.

Heiligman, Deborah. *Vincent and Theo: The Van Gogh Brothers*. New York: Henry Holt and Co., 2017.

Hertzog, Werner. *Cave of Forgotten Dreams*. Pasadena: Creative Differences, History Films, Ministère de la Culture et de la Communication, Arte France, Werner Herzog, Filmproduktion, More4., 2010.

Holt, John. *Never Too Late: My Musical Life Story*. New York: Addison-Wesley, 1978.

Jacobs, Arnold. From notes from classes for brass and woodwind players given by Arnold Jacobs in 1990. Notes made by Charles Lipp, bassoonist-composer. Copyright assigned to Arnold Jacobs, https://www.optimists-alumni.org/downloads/acrobat_downloads/Arnold_Jacobs_1990_Notes_Charles_Lipp.pdf. See also: a list of books about Arnold Jacobs and his teachings: http://www.windsongpress.com/writings-about-arnold-jacobs.

Kahn, Albert E. *Joys and Sorrows, Reflections by Pablo Casals*. New York: Simon & Schuster, 1970.

Kapleau, Philip. *The Three Pillars of Zen*. New York: Harper & Row, 1966.

Kenneson, Claude. *Musical Prodigies: Perilous Journeys, Remarkable Lives*. Portland, OR: Amadeus Press, 1998, 2002.

Kerst, Friedrich, comp., and Henry Krehbiel, trans. *Mozart: The Man and the Artist Revealed in His Own Words* (New York: Dover Publications, 1965). Republished from the Geoffrey Bles edition (London: 1926).

Khachaturian, Aram. *Violin Concerto in D Minor*. Moscow Radio Symphony Orchestra, conducted by Aram Khachaturian; David Oistrakh, violin, 1965. Reissue Columbia Odyssey Y 34608 Melodiya. Also on YouTube (2013), https://www.youtube.com/watch?v=TeKZAbFj83I.

Khachaturian, Aram. *Flute Concerto in D Major* (*Violin Concerto in D Major*, 1940), transcribed for flute by Jean-Pierre Rampal. London: Boosey & Hawkes, 1968.

Krull, Kathleen. *Lives of the Musicians*. Illustrations by Kathryn Hewitt. San Diego: Harcourt, Brace, 1993.

Lamy, Lucy. *Egyptian Mysteries: New Light on Ancient Spiritual Knowledge.* New York: Crossroad, 1981.

Lanfer, Helen. *Music Within Us: An Exploration in Creative Music Education.* New York: Tara Publications, 1979, 2013.

Levenson, Monty H. *The Japanese Shakuhachi Flute: A Guide to the Traditional Music and Notation.* Willits, CA: Monty H. Levenson, 1974.

MacCurdy, Edward, ed. *The Notebooks of Leonardo da Vinci, Definitive Edition in One Volume.* New York: Dover Publications, 1970.

Mathiesen, Thomas J. *The New Grove Dictionary of Music and Musicians,* 2nd ed., Stanley Sadie, John Tyrrell, eds. London: Macmillan Publishers Ltd, 2001.

McCaffrey, Elliot. *The Boy Who Sees without Eyes.* Firefly production, 2007, https://www.youtube.com/watch?v=Ybvg_ay6T50.

Moore, Michael. *Where to Invade Next.* New York: Dog Eat Dog Films, IMG Films, 2015.

Mozart, W. A. *Piano Concertos 21 and 20,* András Schiff, Camerata Academica des Mozarteum Salzburg, Sándor Végh, conductor. London: Decca Records, 1991.

Neuls-Bates, Carlo. *Women in Music: An Anthology of Source Readings from the Middle Ages to the Present.* New York: Harper & Row, 1982.

Nicholl, Charles. *Leonardo da Vinci, Flights of the Mind, a Biography.* New York: Viking Press, 2004.

Nierenberg, Roger. *Maestro: A Surprising Story about Leading by Listening.* New York: Penguin/Portfolio, 2009.

Nietzsche, Friedrich. Letter to Heinrich Koselitz 1/15/ 1888. *Twilight of the Idols, Or How to Philosophize with a Hammer*, Tracy Strong, Introduction: "Hammers, Idleness and Music," vii, Richard Polt, trans. (Indianapolis/Cambridge: Hackett Publishing Company, Inc., 1997).

Owen, Wilfred. *The Collected Poems of Wilfred Owen*. C. Day Lewis, ed. New York: New Directions, 1965.

Parker, Charlie. *Hear Me Talkin' to Ya: The Story of Jazz as Told by the Man Who Made It*. Nat Shapiro and Nat Hentoff, eds. New York: Dover Publications, 1966.

Picasso, Pablo. *The Old Guitarist*. Barcelona, 1904. Painting currently at the Art Institute of Chicago.

Pollan, Michael. *The Botany of Desire: A Plant's-Eye View of the World*. New York: Random House, 2001.

Quantz, Johann Joachim. *On Playing the Flute: The Classic of Baroque Music Instruction*. Edward R. Reilly, trans. New York: G. Schirmer, 1975.

Rank, Otto. *Beyond Psychology*. New York: Dover Publications, 1941.

Ribot, Marc. *Rootless Cosmopolitans*. London: Island Records, 1990.

Richter, Jean Paul, ed. *The Notebooks of Leonardo da Vinci*, vol. I. New York: Dover, 1970.

Rozhdestvensky, conductor, David Oistrakh, violin. LIVE film, YouTube, Andy Granko 8/2017, https://www.youtube.com/watch?v=KP0a7aq_NyE.

Rubinstein, Arthur. *My Young Years*. New York: Alfred A. Knopf. 1973.

Saggs, H. W F. *The Nimrud Letters, 1952*. London: British Institute for the Study of Iraq, 2001.

Saint-Saëns, Camille. *Le Carnaval des Animaux*. "Les Pianistes," https://www.youtube.com/watch?v=Hiz4j9P0PJ0.

Savage, Candace. *Bird Brains: The Intelligence of Crows, Ravens, Magpies, and Jays*. Vancouver, BC: Greystone, 1997.

Scheffer, Frank. *A Year with John Cage—How to Get Out of the Cage*. Berlin: EuroArts/Silk Road, 2012. Also YouTube (7/2017), https://www.youtube.com/watch?v=UaNGeuDuXl4.

Seay, Albert. *Music and the Medieval World*. New Jersey: Prentice-Hall, Inc. 1965.

Shaffer, Peter. *Amadeus*. Berkeley, CA: Saul Zaentz Media Center, 1984.

Shorter, Alan W. *The Egyptian Gods: A Handbook*. Norfolk, England: Low and Brydone, 1978.

Simon, Paul. *Graceland*. Burbank, CA: Warner Bros. Records, 1986.

Stevens, Roger S. *Artistic Flute: Technique and Study*, Hollywood, CA: Highland Music Company. 1967.

Stodtmeier, Maria and Smaczny, Paul, *El Sistema: Music to Change Life*. Berlin, EuroArts 2009. Documentary.

Stone, Irving, ed. *Dear Theo: The Autobiography of Vincent van Gogh*. Boston: Houghton Mifflin, 1937.

Stone, Merlin. *When God Was a Woman*. New York: Dial Press, 1976. Previously published as *The Paradise Papers: The Suppression of Women's Rites*. London: Virago Press, 1976.

Strathern, Paul. *The Medici: Power, Money, and Ambition in the Italian Renaissance*. New York: Pegasus Books, 2016.

Strathern, Paul. *The Artist, the Philosopher, and the Warrior: The Intersecting Lives of da Vinci, Machiavelli, and Borgia and the World They Shaped*. New York: Bantam Books, 2009.

Suzuki Roshi, Shunryū. *Zen Mind, Beginner's Mind: Informal Talks on Zen Meditation and Practice*. Boston: Weatherhill (Shambala), 1970.

Tchaikovsky, Pyotr Ilyich. *Violin Concerto in D Major*. Gennady.

Toynbee, Arnold. *A Study of History,* vol. 3: *The Growths of Civilizations*. Oxford: Oxford University Press, 1934.

Weil, Les. *Odd Meter Studies*. Rogue River, OR: Evans Valley Music, 1973.

Werner, Kenny. *Effortless Mastery: Liberating the Master Musician Within*. New Albany, IN: Jamey Aebersold Jazz, 1996.

ABOUT THE AUTHOR

ANNE STACKPOLE-CUELLAR studied music in the San Francisco Bay Area, in France, and at the Naropa University in Boulder, Colorado. She has performed in various chamber music groups in southern Oregon and in Boulder and played on many of the albums of composer and pianist Bill Douglas. She taught flute for over thirty years. Anne independently recorded three albums, *On the Wing*, *Branching Out*, and *Gifts and Celebrations*, available on CD Baby.

For more information:

WWW.KEENEARARTS.COM

Made in the USA
San Bernardino, CA
28 January 2020

63612210R00215